FINDING
ANNIE FARRELL

ALSO BY BETH J. HARPAZ

The Girls in the Van

FINDING
ANNIE FARRELL

A FAMILY MEMOIR

Beth J. Harpaz

THOMAS DUNNE BOOKS

St. Martin's Press

New York

THOMAS DUNNE BOOKS.
An imprint of St. Martin's Press.

www.stmartins.com

Photographs, except where noted, are courtesy of the author.

Library of Congress Cataloging-in-Publication Data

Harpaz, Beth J.
    Finding Annie Farrell : a family memoir / Beth J. Harpaz.—1st ed.
        p.   cm.
    ISBN 0-312-30151-0
    1. Farrell, Anne, 1922–1983.   2. Harpaz, Beth J.—Family.
3. Harpaz, Beth J.—Diaries.   4. Farrell family.   5. Women
biographers—New York (State)—New York—Diaries.   6. Women
journalists—New York (State)—New York—Diaries.   7. Maine—
Social life and customs.   8. New York (N.Y.)—Social life and customs.
9. Maine—Biography.   10. New York (N.Y.)—Biography.   I. Title.

CT275.F4253H37 2004
974.7'1043'0922—dc22
[B]   2003058539

First Edition: February 2004

10   9   8   7   6   5   4   3   2   1

To my mother's four sisters—
Thank you for helping me find my mother.

CONTENTS

FINDING
ANNIE FARRELL

1

STRAWBERRIES

The day after my mother died in June of 1983, my sister, Nancy, and I cleaned out the little bedroom where she had slept for many years, a room separate from our father's. There, in a mildewy closet, stained with water from a leaking pipe, we found an envelope of papers she had saved. In it were her pilot's license and résumé, certificates showing she could type and take shorthand at so many words per minute, and a forty-year-old receipt for the purchase of a manual typewriter. There were a couple of old marbled notebooks filled with faded, penciled entries that turned out to be the diaries of our grandfather, a blacksmith up in Maine who had died many years before. There was her marriage certificate, which revealed, to our amused surprise, that she had lied to us about the year of her wedding. She was only married seven months before my sister was born, not a year and seven months as she'd led us to believe. She'd even celebrated her tenth and twenty-fifth anniversaries a year too early to preserve the myth.

And finally, there was a birth certificate for a woman who had everything in common with our mother except her name. Lena Farrell had been born on the fourth of December in 1922, in Athens, Maine, to Lizzie Noyes and William Farrell. That was our mother's birth date and birthplace; those were her parents.

But that wasn't her name.

Our mother wasn't Lena Farrell. Our mother was Anne Farrell.

We showed it to our father. He was seventy-two years old. He'd found out twenty-four hours earlier that his wife was about to die. And then he'd stayed up all night waiting for it to happen. Now his daughters were telling him that the woman he used to call "Annie Farrell" in a jaunty, singsong voice wasn't Annie Farrell after all, but someone else, with a name he'd never even heard of in the thirty-five years he'd been married.

He seemed dazed and old and exhausted. He had no idea what this birth certificate business meant. And he didn't really care. His mind was too full already.

So we asked our aunts, our mother's sisters. There are four of them, and two still live in Maine. They all knew about the name change, of course, but for forty years, they never let on, never slipped up once, always called her Anne and never reverted to Lena.

"It wasn't up to me to tell you," said Aunt Lee. "It never occurred to me! Why would I tattle on your mother?"

Aunt Peanut, the youngest of the four, said it happened so long ago that she couldn't even remember being told her sister's name had been changed. It was almost as if she had always known that the sister once called Lena was forever known as Anne. "We must have just started calling her Anne because she would write us a letter every week, and she would always send us birthday cards and gifts, and at Christmastime, she would send us something, and she would always sign it Anne," she said.

But why? Why had she changed her name?

The most practical explanation came from my Aunt Achsah, whose own unusual name I loved to look up in my little Bible dictionary when I was a child ("Daughter of Caleb; given in marriage to her uncle Othniel, Joshua 15:15–18, Judges 1:12–15"). Achsah said her sister told her she changed her name because there was a comic strip called "Leapin' Lena" and she was sometimes teased with that nickname.

But Aunt Deen had a different take. "Sometimes when you have a traumatic childhood, you just want to leave it all behind," she said. "Changing her name was a step toward making a new life for herself so she wouldn't have to think about any of that awful stuff from when we were little."

I didn't have to ask what that "awful stuff" was. I'd heard the stories. Their mother—my grandmother—had died in childbirth in the depths of the Depression, in a house on a river in Mechanic Falls, Maine. Their father, my grandfather, couldn't feed the brood of kids he was left to raise by himself, didn't send them to school, and disappeared for long stretches—sometimes to work, sometimes to drink. The state of Maine finally took the children away, sending them to live with strangers and to work for their keep. When their father couldn't reimburse the state for the cost of caring for his children, he went to jail.

But somehow, from this "awful stuff," my mother had managed to create what seemed like a glamorous life. She went skiing, flew a Piper Cub, left Maine for New York City, worked briefly as a model, and quoted bits of poetry to make her points the way other people quoted pop songs and the Bible. When I was small she kept pots of creamy, glittery eye shadow—blue and green flecked with silver—on the top shelf of the bathroom cabinet, and she decorated food like paintings on velvet, drizzling bright green crème de menthe on vanilla ice cream and studding her baked ziti with jumbo black olives, straight from the can. I don't remember her reading me children's books, but I do remember her reciting from memory poems by Edna St. Vincent Millay, Edwin Arlington Robinson, and Henry Wadsworth Longfellow, all of them from Maine. She particularly loved a sentimental epic by Longfellow called *Evangeline,* about two lovers who were separated when the British deported French settlers from Canada in the eighteenth century. The opening two lines always conjured up the Maine woods I knew from my childhood summers: "This is the forest primeval, the murmuring pines and the hemlocks."

But my mother had made a choice, to leave the forest primeval and everything else behind. And compared to her sisters, she had it made. They worked in factories, couldn't make ends meet; one had seven children, one had five, one lost a son to cancer. The two who stayed in Maine didn't get indoor plumbing till the 1960s. My mother, in contrast, had just my sister and me, lived in Manhattan with all the modern conveniences of apartment living, and never worked again after marrying my father.

Yet the fun-loving Annie Farrell my dad had once fallen in love with had taken to her bed years before she died—so depressed she went for days without changing her clothes, so fearful of the world she went for weeks without going outside, so sick she got drunk to block it all out. All of my mother's sisters, with all of their hardscrabble lives, outlived her, celebrating, in the two decades after her death, birthdays and milestones of old age that she never got near. I couldn't understand what became of the woman my mother once was—the skier, the pilot, the model, the bon vivant, the woman who was so determined to reinvent her fate as a poor, motherless country girl that she changed her name and moved to New York City. And I couldn't help but wonder if there were other secrets besides her name that might explain why she gave up the fight, and how everyone in the family, myself included, had allowed her life to end the way it did.

I arrived at the door to her hospital room on the night she died carrying strawberries in a brown paper bag. A doctor stopped me before I crossed the threshold, literally blocking my way.

"Your mother is very sick," the doctor said, looking me straight in the eye. "She will not make it through the night." She spoke slowly and emphatically, the way a grown-up tries to impress upon a child too young to understand: *Don't play with matches, you might start a fire.*

The doctor peered at me to see if what she said had registered. I felt myself slowing down, the rush I'd been in to get here from work instantly evaporating. This was not going to be the obligatory cheerful

visit to my invalid mother before I got back to my busy life. This was
the last visit ever, the only visit left. Much later I marveled at how
bluntly the news that my mother was about to die had been delivered.
There were none of the niceties or euphemisms I had always heard used
when I saw this scene played out in movies and on TV; no comforting
hug, no arm around my shoulder. Perhaps the doctor thought she was
doing me a favor by being so straightforward. After all, I had but a few
minutes to take care of whatever unfinished business my mother and I
had left. If I was to say good-bye, make my peace, or say I love you,
it had to be done now.

But if words like that were spoken, I don't remember. I only remember the strawberries I had brought, strawberries that I suddenly
realized she was too sick to eat. They were her favorite fruit, and I had
bought them at a fruit market on my way to see her, having been told
in a phone call from my father that she was in the hospital, but having
no idea that she was dying. In my mind, strawberries were connected
to my mother's childhood; they were a powerful food, a mythical food,
a healing food. My Aunt Deen had once told me when I was small and
wouldn't eat my dinner that when they were kids in Maine, sometimes
strawberries were all they had for supper. "That sounds very good," I
had said, at five or six years old not understanding that the point of the
story was not how lucky they were, but how *unlucky*. Ever since then,
I'd thought of strawberries as having life-giving powers. They had not
only sustained these poor, starving girls when there was nothing else to
eat, but they had also magically remained succulent and desirable, unlike
salt pork and boiled potatoes and other things poor people live on when
there is nothing else. Strawberries could only disappoint if the sweet-
and-sour juiciness was bred out of them, if they were so large and red
and unbruisable that they no longer tasted good. I wondered that day
if the strawberries I'd bought for my mother, unblemished and ripe-
red, would be okay, or if they would be dry and tasteless despite their
perfect appearance.

But of course it was too late to feed my mother strawberries. Shortly
after I arrived, they gave her morphine to ease her pain. The morphine
made her sleep. The sleep flowed into death. I ate the berries myself,

that night, as I paced the hospital hallways, waiting for it to end, and I have no recollection of how they tasted. By morning she was gone. The cause of death was cancer, all over. There was nothing to be done.

A few hours after we found the mysterious birth certificate for a woman named Lena Farrell, the phone rang in the apartment where my father now lived all by himself. I answered it. "Hi!" said a cheery voice, as if I was supposed to know who it was.

"Who is this?" I asked.

"This is Renée," said the woman on the other end. "Can I talk to your father?"

I didn't know anyone named Renée, but in the weeks and months that followed, it became clear that my father had known Renée for a very long time, and that they were more than very good friends.

When I'd dragged myself to see my mother a few weeks before she died, she'd seemed the same as always: miserable. I was twenty-two; I had a college degree, a job, a boyfriend, and my own place to live, and I was making plans to go to graduate school at Columbia the following year to become a journalist. I'd always wanted to be a writer with a capital W—someone who got paid to write as opposed to someone who did it as a hobby—and it had recently occurred to me that I'd be a lot happier making my living as a reporter than in the job I had at the time, which involved way too much Xeroxing and writing letters under my boss's signature for my tastes. I knew there was a straight line between the career I was headed for and something my mother had done for me when I was a child, but somehow I couldn't find the words to tell her this. Yet I thought about it all the time: When I was a very small girl, before I even knew how to read, she would write down stories and poems that I dictated to her, tie up the pages with a pretty ribbon, and call it a book. My poems were all about Maine—the call of the loons, the patterns of the waves—and my stories were always about fanciful creatures, grandmas who floated out of the colored rays of the sunset and tigers who could talk, and it seemed like my mother made the magic real by creating these books from my words. It was proof of her power: She'd wave her hand, and *poof*, I was an author!

But somehow I couldn't tell her, in her decrepit state, that I was still walking along this path she had put me on as a child. It felt almost cruel to remind her that outside of this apartment, with its swarms of roaches and peeling paint, people like me were fulfilling dreams, enjoying life, feeling optimistic about the future. Once I stepped over the threshold into her world, into the long, dark hallway with its flickering fluorescent light, forever buzzing and dim, the kitchen with its ancient cracked linoleum, and the bathroom with the old-fashioned claw-foot tub, it was almost hard to remember that outside, things were bright and clean and new and people were happy to be alive. She was so withdrawn by then that to be in her presence was to be consumed by her struggle just to summon the will to go on from one moment to the next.

I always brought her a few groceries when I visited, and I usually made her something simple to eat—an egg or toast. Then I would walk from front to back of the apartment I had lived in from the time I was born till the day I left for college. There were three small bedrooms off a hall, a kitchen so cramped there wasn't room for two people working side by side, and a living room covered with a blue carpet that had once been my mother's pride but that was now flat and faded down the middle where our footsteps had worn a path. Everything was old and clunky and seemed to belong to another era: a big, black phone with a steel dial so heavy you could get a blister on your forefinger if you made a lot of calls; a radio the size of a coffee table, with sparkly fabric where the sound came out and dark wood on the top and sides; and a couple of lumpy winged armchairs, the slipcovers my mother had sewn years before now as dingy as the upholstery they were supposed to conceal, dotted with my father's cigarette burns and stains from spilled drinks, the armrests gray from years of use. It was strangely comforting, all of this, comforting the way worn-out sneakers feel so good, but if I shook my head clear and looked again, I could see that it was also disgusting.

Outside, in the streets around our building, New York was changing. The old, decrepit tenements were being torn down to make way for buildings with doormen and skylights; two new words, *gentrification* and *yuppie,* had entered everyone's vocabulary; and the dark, cramped bodegas where you had to speak Spanish to buy a quart of milk were being replaced by brightly lit produce stands whose Korean owners handpicked every perfect tomato they sold and lined their storefronts with colorful bouquets. So what if just a few years earlier, the city had been on the verge of bankruptcy? Now we had Mayor Koch, so confident of his popularity that he walked around the city booming, "How'm I doin'?" without worrying someone would shout something obscene in return. The old men who used to play dominoes on the corner were gone, replaced by fashion-model handsome gay men and artsy young women dressed in black who favored Mouton Cadet. The store where I'd once bought a hand-knitted scarf for my mother from an old woman who sold her homemade wares was now a tanning salon. And the Puerto Rican salsa that used to blare out of open windows had disappeared; instead, we could feel the disco beat pulsing in our new upstairs neighbor's apartment as he cranked up Donna Summer.

But other than the rhythm of someone else's taste in music seeping into our living room through the spongy yellow ceiling tiles, our apartment seemed to have been sealed off to the changes outside. It was a rent-controlled pit in a neighborhood where everyone was happily "going co-op!" My mother had crawled in her bed long ago, and the house had decayed around her. I built a wall in my mind against feeling sorry for her, and I couldn't allow myself to be sucked into looking at it any other way. It was disgusting, not pitiful, that she never changed her clothes or bathed. It was disgusting, not pitiful, that she did nothing but lie in her small bed in a dark room. And it was disgusting, not pitiful, that she drank a fifth of vodka a day.

At one time, I'd poured her booze down the sink every time I came to see her, but eventually I gave up. There was no point. My father would just go out and buy her more at the corner liquor store, the store

I fantasized walking into with a machine gun to blast open every bottle on the shelves and blow away the man behind the counter, like a saloon shootout in a Western. In my mind I rationalized the morality of this. Surely if I murdered a heroin dealer whose drugs were killing someone in my family, the world would understand. So why would it be any different with the liquor store man?

But now that she was dead, my father said he thought she had known for a long time that she was dying, and that the vodka was her medicine. He said he was glad he had gotten it for her, and none of us really blamed him for thinking that way. For years she had refused to see a doctor. What could he do in the face of her adamant opposition that no, no, no, she would not go? And, we all reasoned, was a bottle of vodka a day really worse than chemo and radiation and being bald and throwing up? I guess with treatment, there is a chance of survival. But if survival just means more years of lying in a dark room waiting for death, maybe, I thought, she had made the right choice.

The only reason she ended up dying in a hospital instead of her bed was that her breathing turned suddenly, scarily, noisy. My father had called my Aunt Deen, who was once a nurse, for advice. Deen knew that a call from her brother-in-law (whose usual idea of palliative care was more vodka) was a serious sign that her older sister's long decline had taken a terrible turn. She didn't try to diagnose the case over the phone; she came right over to the apartment, took one look at Anne, and insisted that David take her in a taxi to the hospital. The doctors could feel the tumors all over her body, and they could see that she had only a few more hours to live. All they could do was drug her pain, and let her die.

It was hard for me to feel as sad as it seemed I was supposed to be. I was too young to see how much of what was good in my life had come from my mother, how much I would miss her in the years to come, and how much I would come to identify with the words from one of my favorite books about Maine's past, *The Country of the Pointed Firs*: "You never get over bein' a child long's you have a mother to go to."

Besides, it seemed like she had been dying for years. When people said, "So sorry about your mother," I told them maybe it was better this way, that death was her deliverance. The only alternative, it seemed to me, was more suffering for everyone.

My mother had been a stunningly beautiful young woman, with high cheekbones and auburn hair that cascaded onto her shoulders and across her face like a brunette Veronica Lake; she liked to wear bright-red lipstick and tailored clothes to show off the slender figure she was so proud of. But she looked so awful by the time she died—her skin almost as gray as her brittle hair, her stomach distended by tumors— that my sister and I were afraid of what we would see when we tiptoed over to the coffin for a last look. We hadn't realized that funeral homes are expert at making corpses look good, so it was a great surprise to see her beautiful again. Her hair was done, her lipstick perfect, the sallow skin made over with powder and blush, the wrinkles and the worry and the sorrow masked for eternity. I smiled when I saw her, and I can still remember the comments of people standing around me, gasping with amazement and murmuring about how lovely she was. It was as if all the years of depression and sickness had been wiped away; all it took to bring back our pretty mother was to be relieved of the life that weighed her down.

The day before, my sister and I had dug through her closet looking for the right outfit to bury her in. Most of her clothes hadn't been worn in a long time, and in the end, the choice was easy: her chocolate-brown knit suit, with a straight skirt and boxy Chanel-style jacket. It was at least twenty years old, but in good condition. That the suit had not been bought in a store was all the more reason to choose it; it was an artifact of one of the peculiarities of our family life. We almost never went shopping like other people. Instead, most of our clothes came from factories that had closed down. Our father liquidated bankrupt businesses for a living, so virtually everything we owned was a leftover from someone else's bad luck. The chairs we sat on had once graced corporate offices. The blankets on our beds bore the imprimatur of the once-elegant but now-defunct Vanderbilt Hotel. And the clothes on our backs were always in a style (fake fur for men, pleated skirts for ladies) that had led to some manufacturer's demise. Even the paintings on our walls—reproductions of famous works by Goya and Cézanne, framed prints of Audubon waterfowl—were not acquired by our parents because they had any interest in such art, but because Daddy found them hanging in the conference room for some long-gone board of directors, and figured if they were good enough for them, they were good enough for us.

Any clothes we needed that our father didn't bring home were sewn by our mother, back in the days before she took permanently to her bed, from the huge bolts of fabric he liberated while preparing bankrupt garment factories for auction. I was eleven years old before I realized that the comment, "I bet your mother made that dress for you!" was not a compliment or even an innocent observation but actually an insult. She was a fanatic about pockets, so everything she made had them—a nice improvement over most female attire, which rarely supplies space for keys and wallets, assuming that every girl and woman on the planet carries a pocketbook. But the pockets didn't compensate for the embarrassment of her other standard features—like elastic waistbands to cut down on troublesome zippers or any need for a perfect fit on a growing girl. Or her fondness for decorating every article of clothing with "notions" from the boxes full of pearl buttons, seahorse appliqués, and lace trim that also found their way from factories in Alabama and Pennsylvania to our small apartment in Manhattan. In photos from my childhood, I am always dressed in something sewn from the wrong fabric: a sagging, waterlogged bathing suit in a ribbed, mustard-yellow cloth never intended for swimwear, or pants made from a stiff material better suited for drapes or bedspreads, with a pattern of tall blue tree-trunks growing up each leg from my ankles to my thighs, the leaves and branches mismatched at the seams like wrapping paper carelessly taped around a gift.

At least the chocolate-brown suit that my sister and I picked out for our mother to wear to her funeral was respectable by comparison, understated and even a little bit classy in its simple straight lines and lack of adornments. Even so, she had not picked the suit out at Macy's or

Gimbel's the way other women did their clothes, choosing the fabric and style she liked best, an expression of her own personality and taste. Instead she had passively accepted it, without complaint and even happily, another addition to a wardrobe comprised of clothes that put designers out of business, another costume in which to masquerade as someone she was not.

My sister, Nancy, and I dropped the suit off at the funeral home, stopped at a printer to order death announcements to send to the many names in her address book we didn't recognize, and then went back to the apartment to sort through her things so our father wouldn't have to. Nancy wondered aloud if we should take her sewing patterns out of their envelopes in case she'd hidden things inside; it was just the sort of quirky thing she'd do. But I couldn't be bothered, so in the end we just packed them up with her other sewing supplies and brought them to a woman in Harlem whom we didn't even know but whose name had been given to us as someone who "still sewed" in an era when most people didn't. Years later, a woman who had once been my mother's best friend told me my mother used to keep all her grocery money in the pattern envelopes, a hiding place she figured would never be discovered if someone robbed the apartment. My sister and I laughed at the thought that this woman in Harlem might have ended up with my mother's secret store of petty cash.

When I was small, my mother turned a jumper dress that she had made for me inside out and snipped a scrap of fabric from the seam, which of course she had ironed perfectly flat. She'd left enough material on either side of the stitches that the small square she cut out did not threaten to damage the dress. Then she sat me down at the living room table, put the swatch of fabric in a metal ashtray, lit a match, and dropped it on the material. The fabric caught fire in a second and lit up with a *poof* like a balled-up newspaper in a fireplace. In another second the material was consumed by the flame and it went out, leaving nothing in the ashtray but a black residue. "Do you see how dangerous fire is?" she said to me. I nodded, wide-eyed. All the grown-ups we knew smoked, including her and my father. I thought this was a lesson to teach me to stay away from their matches and lighters, away from the cigarettes that dangled off-handedly from their mouths and fingers, away from the butts they sometimes forgot to tend, the butts that glowed in ashtrays growing long, perfectly round cylinders of ash until they burned themselves out. My mother never told me that the point of setting fire to a piece of my dress was actually a lesson about something else—about fires that consumed whole houses, fires that left families homeless.

But I knew about fires like that, too, because one had happened to a girl in my second-grade class. Her name was Anastasia, and she had lived in an apartment building not far from mine, an apartment building that was now a black shell, so gutted by the blaze that you could see the sky through the roof. Someone told my mother about the fire that destroyed Anastasia's building one winter night, and a few days later I saw Anastasia wearing a coat to school that looked exactly like one of mine. I had two coats that year, a green one my father had brought home from a bankrupt factory, and the other one, with big round black buttons and fuzzy brick-red fabric, that my mother had sewn. Anastasia was wearing the green coat, and I was wearing the one my mother had made. My mother told me not to ever tell anyone that Anastasia's coat had once been mine.

It was not the last time she tried to help a child I went to school with. She had no pity for the drunks we sometimes found lying in the doorways on our block or on the benches of the park where I played, and would sometimes call the cops to roust them. But if I came home from school complaining about the girl who sat next to me kicking my white tights till they were dirty, or about a boy in class tormenting me by stealing my hat or scribbling all over my work, she always withheld judgment until she did some investigating. Then she'd explain to me that the girl had been abandoned by her parents and was being raised by her grandmother, or that the boy was routinely beaten by a foul-mouthed mother the size of a house. These children were jealous of me, didn't I see? And I needed to feel sorry for them, because I had parents who loved me and took care of me, and they did not.

I was also supposed to feel sorry for American Indians, according to my mother's view of the world. Long before it became politically correct to call them Native Americans or to view them as victims of a great land robbery, at a time when the comical tribe featured on one of my favorite TV shows, *F Troop,* was considered an improvement over other depictions of bloodthirsty savages, my mother gave money religiously to a fund for the improvement of education for American Indians. Twice a year, she would send them a small check, and in return, we would receive in the mail bleak black-and-white pictures of reservation life somewhere and strange plastic artifacts, like snap-together napkin holders in the traditional colors of some tribe whose symbol of eagles' wings or a beaver's tail had been stamped on the object.

And unlike many other white parents in those racially divisive years, my mother also seemed to harbor no prejudices against the Puerto Rican and black kids who made up the majority of my classmates in the public schools I attended. My father would sometimes speak derisively of the black men he hired to help him with truckloads of heavy machinery, and my Jewish relatives would occasionally make remarks about "shvartzers," a derogatory Yiddish word for blacks. But my mother didn't seem to harbor those views. If I made friends with a Hispanic boy, she made friends with his mother and before long we were sitting in their living room looking at photographs of Puerto Rico. If I made friends with a black girl, my mother encouraged me to invite her home, and instructed me to ignore the nosy stares of certain neighbors. When this girl invited me for lunch in her apartment in a nearby housing project, my mother was happy to have me go there.

There was only one ethnic group my mother seemed to have an irrational dislike of, and that was a group I had never encountered: the Gypsies. I was forbidden to play outside without a grown-up watching, she said, because the Gypsies might steal me. I had never seen a Gypsy, but the image that the word conjured up in my mind was something out of a fairy tale—a band of colorfully dressed, dark-haired people with tambourines, kerchiefs, and horse-drawn caravans. It was hard to imagine anyone like that unobtrusively scooping up unescorted children on the sidewalks of New York. But my mother assured me that the

Gypsies were actually everywhere, even up in Maine. And after a while I simply accepted it as another one of her inexplicable quirks.

It always seemed to me that my mother's decay mirrored the deterioration of her adopted city, but that when New York began to turn around, she just kept going down. I was five in 1966 and just starting school when she began to spend more time in her bed, a time that coincided with rising crime, white flight, and a visible increase in vacant lots and burnt-out buildings. The news in the papers and on TV—race riots, radical bombings, cops on strike, Kitty Genovese stabbed to death on the street while neighbors watched from their windows without calling for help—terrified her to the point where she hated to go outside.

When the bell rang or someone knocked on our door, my mother often panicked. "Oh God," she would cry out, "who is that?" It was as if she was expecting the secret police to take us away, but most of the time it was just the mailman with a package or the meterman come to check our electric usage; we didn't really get many unexpected guests.

In art class in second grade, our teacher asked us to draw posters showing rats eating garbage. The posters were supposed to support an antilitter campaign, after municipal garbage collections were curtailed, and none of our parents questioned whether second-graders might be encouraged to focus on a more upbeat subject.

And no kid I grew up with was ever allowed to go trick-or-treating. The idea of knocking on a stranger's door, taking candy from someone you didn't know, or opening your own apartment door at night to someone with a mask on was so out of the question that it wasn't even discussed or debated.

The dirt and dangers of the city even found their way inside our home, infiltrating the very food we ate. I remember my mother moaning when she saw cockroaches crawling out of the toaster. And as the school year wore on, my mother got worse. It took her longer and longer to get up to answer the phone, so after a while I did it, then tiptoed down the hallway to see if she was awake enough to come talk to whoever had called. Some days she was late picking me up in the schoolyard, which panicked me the first time it happened, but which I accepted without complaint from then on after she explained how hard it was for her to leave the house. By the time we went to Maine at the beginning of July for our annual summer vacation, the city had sapped her energy dry, and she was like a zombie—no emotion, no speech, nothing but the lit-up end of a cigarette between her fingers to suggest that she was capable of rousing herself to act.

We always left to go to Maine in the evening, to avoid the traffic. But our departure after dark also made it feel like we were doing something clandestine, as if we were trying to escape from our urban nightmare without anyone seeing us. My father would drive all night long to get there by morning, swerving his truck along the roads at breakneck speed while my mother asked him to slow down. "I'm only keeping up with the traffic, Annie," he'd inevitably reply. Of course, there was no traffic at 4:00 A.M. And on the rare occasions when construction or an accident did bring us to a standstill on the road, my father never fumed or cursed, the way other drivers did. He just relaxed and shrugged and said, "Driving is like fishing. You have to be patient."

My mother, meanwhile, spent most of the trip rummaging through her black purse, a big leather satchel that looked like a doctor's kit or a magician's bag. She seemed to have everything in that purse that anyone would ever need to survive under any conditions: drinks, food, gum, Dramamine, Band-Aids, ice packs, aspirin, small toys, pens, paper, needle and thread, flashlights, maps, change for the tolls, washcloths, hand cream, hand towels, tissues, lip balm, and of course, plenty of cigarettes and matches. One year a bee flew into the car and stung me all over, waking me up screaming from a sound sleep while my father hurtled eighty miles an hour down the road. He didn't even have to pull over for my mother to attend to my needs. She simply whipped out her flashlight, the ice packs, the aspirin, and an antihistamine to reduce any possible allergic reactions, with a drink to wash the medicine down. In a few minutes, I was fine, and she had swatted the bee against the car window with some item from her purse. We had barely left New York, and already her energy and competence were returning.

I don't remember ever crossing the bridge that separates New Hampshire from Maine; it was still dark when we crossed the state line, and I'm sure I was always fast asleep amid the pillows and blankets and boxes piled in the back of the truck to form a makeshift bed. But when I finally began to wake up, sometime after dawn as we neared our destination, what always hit me first were the familiar smells of Maine: the evergreens, fir and balsam and pine, so sweet and spicy I started hyperventilating, my eyes still shut, just to get my lungs full of them. Then I'd turn around and look out the rear window at the road behind us. It always amazed me to see how inconsequential our truck had become in relation to the scenery. We were just a tiny moving dot on a narrow gray ribbon, the road a small incision in what appeared to be a massive dark-green forest surrounding us on all sides, beneath a bright-blue sky filled with big puffy clouds.

In New York, the view down any block was framed by the edges of buildings; if you could see the moon straight ahead between the rooftops, it wouldn't be there once you turned the corner. But here I had a panoramic view, so vast it made me dizzy, with nothing between me and the horizon but a border of triangle treetops, black-green where the raggedy points met the sky. Here and there we passed a lake or creek or river, little boats tied up along the shore, just like the little boat that we owned and that I would soon be riding in.

Then, as we turned off the road to our exit, we'd pass by the small towns whose residents were just waking up: the farmer already riding his grumbling tractor through a yellow hay field, the stink of crops freshly fertilized with cow manure, a chimney wafting friendly blue smoke from a woodstove fired up for breakfast, the nauseating odor of a skunk squashed by a previous driver. Finally we would leave the paved road for the bumpy dirt road to whatever house we were staying in that summer, and the truck would rattle and jump as we hit potholes and pebbles, leaving clouds of dust behind us.

Once we got near the lakeshore, where the dirt road turned into muddy driveways overgrown with wildflowers and saplings, there was always some last-minute confusion about exactly where we were supposed to go. But after some back and forth between my parents over whether we were in the green house on this side of the communal pump or the red house around the bend, we always managed to find the one we'd rented without barging in on strangers.

Once there, my parents would collapse on the unmade beds of the cabin, my father fatigued from the overnight drive, my mother in her usual funk from the previous ten months in Manhattan. And for the first few days of our vacation, I was on my own while they recovered. I would scout out the spider population in the outhouse, check the sleeping loft for bats, and survey the nearest trees for birds' nests. I wasn't allowed to swim without a grown-up supervising, so I'd sit on the dock and dangle my feet in the water, skip stones and try to guess how deep it might be—over my head and good for diving, or shallow enough to touch the muddy bottom? Each day I'd make two braids from my long, unruly hair as best I could, inevitably leaving tendrils escaping from every plait with a crooked part in the back where I couldn't see it, and I'd scavenge food from the supplies we brought from New York; it always took my mother a few days before she had the strength to go grocery shopping. I remember one day finding a can of sardines, which I loved, but not being able to turn the little metal key to open the can up. I knocked on a neighbor's door for help—in Maine we had no fear of strangers—and a child older than myself answered the door. She took one look at me with my unkempt hair, holding the can of sardines out, and said, "Are you retarded?"

"No," I shot back, "are you?"

But by the end of the summer, my mother was back to her old self—laughing and happy and cooking and taking care of me. She knew where things grew wild, and she let me in on the secrets: leaves of three, let them be; these red berries, clear and round like jewels, were poison, but these red berries, bumpy and mottled, were good to eat. She found mint by the water and rubbed the leaves to make them smell; she picked grass that tasted like pepper, teaberry leaves that tasted like the spicy gum, and fiddlehead ferns, coiled up like snakes. The dragonflies won't bite, she said; she taught my ears to hear the loon and the whippoorwill, and she taught my eyes to find the hummingbird. She took me to a farm to learn how to ride a horse and milk a cow; she didn't like big farm animals, but she didn't want me to fear them, and I didn't. I brought them tall stems of Queen Anne's lace to eat, I patted them like pets; and after we would pick string beans in the farmer's garden and strawberries from a field. If she was feeling very energetic and we had picked a lot of berries, sometimes she'd make jam, boiling the fruit with sugar and pectin, skimming the foam, and sealing each jar with a layer of hot wax. And I would always help her snap the beans, but sometimes I would get confused and throw the pointy ends in the cooking pot instead of the garbage bag, then make a little gasp and go looking in the pot for my mistake. "That's all right," she'd say. "I'll just put those stems on *your* plate when I serve them." But when supper was on the table, and I scrutinized my beans, the stems had disappeared.

She could cope with any problem up in Maine, or so it seemed. One summer I got lice, and she washed my hair every day for a month in kerosene. I couldn't open my eyes, didn't dare take a breath, until she was done; then she dropped a match to set the bugs on fire in the sink, where they'd landed after slipping off the stinking oil upon my head. I was amazed to learn as an adult that most parents treated their children's lice with a one-time medicated shampoo; my mother had seemed so certain that her way, however torturous, was the only way to rout the beasts.

Another summer up in Maine I got a sore throat so bad I couldn't speak, couldn't swallow. She put me in her bed, took my temperature, and hissed, "Don't tell your father! It's a hundred and five and if he finds out he'll take you to a hospital."

Clearly that was a fate we were to avoid. So I didn't tell my father, and he didn't ask; he just left every morning to go fishing and came home at night with a string of bass and perch that my mother would filet and bread and fry, and eventually I was well enough to eat them.

I didn't go in the lake the summer I was sick. I just sat in a rocking chair on the screened-in porch every day, wrapped up in blankets for the month of August. My mother never played games, not with children and not with grown-ups, so there were no cards and no Candy Land for me, but sometimes she would pick wildflowers—tiger lilies and black-eyed Susans and Queen Anne's lace—and arrange them in a jar and we would paint pictures of them. But most of the time, we just sat on the porch, her with a cigarette and a book, and me just watching the water change color with the light of the day.

One day a cheerful old woman with gray hair came to visit. She brought me a wide-mouthed gallon jar filled with tall striped peppermint sticks. "This is one of my oldest, dearest friends," my mother told me. "You can call her Aunt Boo. She brought these peppermint sticks for your throat." My mother didn't have very many friends that I knew of, and Aunt Boo seemed like an awfully strange name, but I spent the rest of the summer sucking on those sticks, and watching the lake from my view on the porch. The waves would always start out strong, I noticed, and get weaker and weaker with every break as they hit the shore with a slapping sound, and I tried to guess where they came from. A wind on the water that I couldn't feel? The wake of a motorboat I couldn't hear? The steady, silent paddling of a well-rowed canoe that I hadn't seen? A bass jumping for joy and then heading for the deep waters before he could be caught? Anything could churn the water up and send the ripples back to shore; they were echoes of some distant turbulence whose exact source I could never ascertain, but whose effects I could witness.

My sore throat was gone by the time we got back to New York, and at first when we walked down the street there, my mother's magic seemed intact. She would spot the morning glories in a windowbox three stories up, the dandelions growing up through a crack in the side-walk, the sparrow chirping from a nest in a crevice below a fire escape. We could see the Empire State Building from the apartment window, and sometimes we could see the moon there, too, so she taught me all its phases: full, half, crescent, new. She could forecast weather by look-ing at a scrawny city tree, planted in the sidewalk, its roots breaking up the concrete as it struggled to grow and its long branches seeking light between the buildings' shadows. "It's going to rain," she'd say. "See how the leaves are blowing backward on the tree?"

I could never tell the difference between the leaves blowing back-ward and the leaves blowing the way they were supposed to blow, but she could see things no one else could see, and she was always right.

Gradually, as our vacation receded and our time in the city wore on, her vision changed, and soon she couldn't see the rain coming or the birds nesting anymore. She withdrew, and spent more time in her bed, till the following summer, when she could go to Maine and begin the cycle anew. Over the years, the tonic was less and less effective; and by the time I was a teenager, it didn't work at all. We would get to Maine, but she never left her bed there either; there was no homemade jam, and if she knew the rain was coming, she didn't tell. Back in New York, she would just look out the window at all the tall buildings, sirens blaring from the firehouse located across the street, horns honking in the distance, and sigh. "I just wish I had a little house by the side of the road," she'd say.

Two years after my mother died, I started working as a reporter, and for the last two decades or so, I have spent much of my time chronicling other people's bad luck—political fiascos and trials by jury, plane crashes, fires and murders, and even, one sunny September day when I had expected to be writing about a mayoral primary, the attack on the World Trade Center, whose towers I had taught my kids to recognize in the skyline as soon as they were old enough to talk. It all seems so important, this writing down of things that happen in the world, and yet, when I am home, I am just another mother, trimming the fat off the chicken breasts, checking the fifth-grade math homework I can barely figure out myself, playing checkers and Go Fish with my younger child, and walking the dog that someone told us was the first mutt he'd seen in a neighborhood of purebred pugs and Labs and bichons frises.

Sometimes when I think about the differences between my life and my mother's, it's hard to begin to know where to start taking stock. If I ever saw a roach in the apartment where I live now, I'd probably scream so loud the neighbors would call the police; that's how long it's been since I smashed them dead on my mother's kitchen wall. I am ashamed of the comfy sofa in our living room because it is dirty and lumpy; of course I have no idea how to make a slipcover for it, nor have I any interest in learning how to sew, and so it must go out with the trash, to be replaced by another disposable sofa that, in five years, will meet the same fate. A stain on the ceiling is a sign of a leak, and I will not live in a place with leaks; so a plumber is called, the plaster is fixed, the painter comes next to make it all disappear. When my mother stopped vacuuming, the vacuuming didn't get done; but when I stopped vacuuming, I hired someone else to do it for me. And there is simply no equivalent for the heavy black phone with the metal dial and the colossal ancient radio that my parents owned for decades; we get new phones and music players every year or so, each one cheaper and smaller and lighter and chockful of more gizmos than the last, till they are so small and light and packed with digital information that I can no longer figure out how they work and have to rely on my ten-year-old to set them up for me.

It's easy to explain all of this. I am simply in a different social class than the one I grew up in, a class where convenience takes precedence over a bargain, where jeans with torn knees are discarded, not mended. Which is not to say I have no complaints; of course I do—it's part of human nature. But my biggest problem is a lack of time to do all the things I want to do, not a lack of will to get up in the morning and start doing them. And so I also count my blessings—my children, my marriage, my work, my health, my sanity, my comfortable life—every single day.

But some days I can't help but wonder: Why is it so easy for me, when it was so difficult for her? Was it chance, or choice? Something inside her, or something beyond her control? Something we witnessed or something we did?

Or did the explanation for her miserable life lie in something she kept hidden, the way she hid her own name for more than forty years?

When my mother buried her own father, my grandfather, in 1954, she picked out a plot for herself right next to his. It's a peaceful spot, under a pine tree, in a small town in Northern Maine where the black-flies are thick in the spring and the snow piles deep in the winter. We always go there in late summer, when hints of autumn are in the chilly early morning air and the maple leaves seem to turn color before our eyes, more golden and red the further north we drive.

Nearly thirty years after my grandfather died, my father buried my mother there, and more than a decade after my mother died, my sister and I buried my father there. Each year we find a new flag left on his grave by the men of the local VFW, who still march down Main Street every Memorial Day and pay tribute to the veterans; my father's World War II service is listed on his grave. But the only thing ever left on my mother's plot are the flowers my sister and I put there when we bring our children to scrape away the moss and sap that collect inside the engraved letters of her name. There was no question that "Anne" would appear on her tombstone; she would have been appalled to know that we'd found out about Lena, and she wouldn't have wanted that name on her tombstone any more than she would have wanted to be buried in the dirty rags she was wearing when she left her bed for the last time. We only ever stay a few minutes in the graveyard, and not being very religious, we don't pray or sing; it's just enough to see it, and think of her, and show it to the kids.

For many years I think that I was looking for a clue there, hoping that some revelation would take place as I stood above her grave. But now I see that what I needed was not to focus on her death, but on her life. At first she seemed invisible, an ordinary woman who left behind no exploits for the history books, no fortunes to be tracked. But once I started looking, I found her anyway, in the sisters who survived her, in the letters that she left behind, in the rural life she fled, in the generation she belonged to. I found her in the vanished world of a poor family in a small town in Maine in the 1930s, a world that was more like the nineteenth century than the twenty-first, a world that became real to me through the memories of my aunts. I found her in hand-written Census sheets, in typed-up reports about neglected children and the old-fashioned laws that shaped their destinies, and in newspaper clippings about fires and floods. I found her on the Internet, in the genealogies of ancestors she never knew she had, by talking to distant cousins I never knew I had, by visiting the places where she lived. And I found her in my own memories, by looking with a new point of view at the stories that I thought I understood. One day I asked an aunt, "Do you remember when you had nothing but strawberries for supper?"

"Sometimes," she answered, "we didn't even have that."

I can never go back to that hospital room to make my peace and say good-bye and say I love you, but twenty years later, I have found my mother and the stories that she never told me, stories many women never tell, about families and the ordinary struggles of day-to-day life, stories of love and despair. When I finally learned her secrets, they made sense the way the pieces of a tricky puzzle come together in a frenzy, at the end, all at once. And by the time I found out all the things she never told me, it seemed as if I was merely remembering something I'd known all along.

2

CHRISTMAS

Lizzie Noyes Farrell.

Lizzie Noyes Farrell was thirty-one years old when she died, shortly after giving birth to a healthy baby boy on the eighth of December in 1933. Her body was laid out in a casket in the bedroom for a few days, then taken down to a wooden house by the graveyard where the corpses were kept till spring, when the ground would be soft enough for burial.

In those first few weeks after her death, neighbors and relatives tried to be helpful. One family took the baby home, promising to feed and care for him for a few months until he was big enough to be entrusted to the care of his five older sisters. And on Christmas Eve, two complete dinners were delivered to the clapboard house that Bill Farrell, suddenly a widower, had built by the side of the road just three years earlier, on the banks of the Little Androscoggin River in Mechanic Falls, Maine.

Lizzie's sister Alice brought a box full of oranges and grapes and cookies as she did every Christmas. Some of the grapes were moldy, having been in storage since the end of the fall harvest, but it was still a treat to get fresh fruit in the winter. And there were presents, too: mittens and scarves and socks that Lizzie had knitted for the children throughout the year, then hid in a trunk in her closet. Some of the kids had discovered the trunk several Christmases earlier, but they always refrained from raiding it, so as not to spoil the holiday. There were even some old toys squirreled away among the hidden woolens: dolls and other castoffs, left for the kids by people who brought horses to Bill Farrell's blacksmith shop to be shod. If the toys were metal, Bill Farrell made new pieces for them on his anvil; if they were wooden, he carved new parts and painted them so they looked brand-new.

Lizzie had sewn little costumes for the dolls on her treadle sewing machine, using the same grain bags that she made her daughters' clothing from. The bags were cotton and came in different colors, depending on whether they contained flour or sugar or whatnot, but the store would let you swap them if you didn't have enough in one color to finish your pattern. The white bags were always saved to make bloomers and slips, and the salt bags, which had the finest, softest texture, went for handkerchiefs. All of these gifts from their dead mother awaited the children when they awoke Christmas morning, like a letter arriving from someone who died after mailing it.

All that was missing was the tree that Lizzie always had Bill cut down on Christmas Eve, the one she always stayed up half the night decorating with her delicate collection of a hundred glass ornaments. When the children beheld the sparkling tree in the gray light of a Maine December morning, it was as if their mother had conjured it whole with one wave of her hand in the dark of night.

But this Christmas, it seemed as if the spell had been reversed. Instead of having a decorated evergreen appear, seemingly in an instant, as a result of their mother's magic, their mother's life had instead, in the same instant, vanished forever, leaving only her cold body behind.

In between the day their mother died and the holiday, the older girls went back to school for a few days, with Lee and Achsah taking part, as scheduled, in the school Christmas program. Little Achsah, as the local newspaper dutifully reported, played the part of Mrs. Green in a playlet titled *Oh, That's Different!* performed by the subprimary class, while Lee, identified in the newspaper as Leona, her full name but not the name she was commonly called, took her turn with other fourth graders singing songs, hers called "Christmas Wishes."

Bill Farrell had made no secret of his own wishes. He cried and told the kids he wished it had been him that died instead of Lizzie. He was forty-seven years old, left to raise all those kids by himself, and he couldn't take the sight of that casket in the bedroom that he and his wife had shared. Christmas Day was no celebration for him; he and Lizzie had been married at Christmastime twelve years earlier, and for the rest of his life the holiday would be colored by thoughts of the anniversaries they never had.

As for the baby that Lizzie died having, well, he was just fine, the doctor said. It was the afterbirth that caused the trouble; it didn't come out, and the bleeding wouldn't stop. Bill Farrell had been out in his shop, starting up the coal-heated forge in the dark before dawn, when one of the kids ran out to get him, saying their mother was sure the baby was coming. He tried to start his truck to take her to the hospital, but no matter what he did, he couldn't get the engine going in the cold and the snow. Finally he sent one of the kids to the firehouse to get help. But by the time the ambulance arrived, the baby had come into the world and Lizzie had nearly left it. She'd lost so much blood that she barely had a pulse.

Bill had always assumed that those damn idiots in the medical profession didn't know what the hell they were doing, and this just proved it. He had taken Lizzie to the hospital two days earlier, and they had sent her home, saying the baby wasn't due for two weeks. She'd been warned against getting pregnant again when the last baby, Leathene, who was eventually called Peanut, was born the year before; Lizzie's womb was weak from too many pregnancies, and the doctors told her that the next time there might be trouble. Yet when she showed up at the hospital in Lewiston, pregnant with Frankie, saying her contractions had begun, they turned her away, insisting it was only false labor.

And now she was dead. Which is not to say that Bill held himself blameless for the fact that Lizzie had gotten pregnant again. But certainly Bill had never imagined for a moment that it would end this way. And now that it had, he couldn't imagine how he was going to manage all those kids without Lizzie.

Lizzie had found out she was pregnant with Frankie shortly after FDR's "nothing to fear but fear itself" speech was broadcast by radio all across the country in the spring of 1933. She agreed with her husband that if it was a girl, they would name her Eleanor, after the first lady, and if it was a boy, they would name him Franklin Delano Roosevelt Farrell. Bill Farrell had never been anywhere near Washington, D.C., but FDR had been to Maine, many times, traveling through the state on his way to his family's summer home on Campobello Island, off the southeast coast. That made FDR's faraway federal government seem less remote to a man like Bill. He had faith that the new president would somehow lighten the load of a blacksmith with too many mouths to feed in the middle of the Depression, and not enough horses to shoe in the burgeoning era of the automobile. Besides, the Roosevelts seemed to care about people like them, poor people, country people, regular people; surely that's who FDR had in mind when he talked about "the forgotten man at the bottom." The New Deal promised farm relief, old-age pensions, and even a hydroelectric dam for Maine that would bring cheap power and create hundreds of jobs. And with half the people in America already living hand to mouth, it was hard to believe that things could get any worse even if Roosevelt couldn't carry through on all his promises.

But for all kinds of reasons, many of Bill Farrell's neighbors disagreed with his political point of view. Maine was one of just five states to vote against FDR in 1932, and one of just two states, along with Vermont, to vote against him in 1936. Three generations after the Civil War, upright Yankee Republicans were still proud to belong to the party of Lincoln and abolition, the party that had kept the Union together; besides, they didn't see why someone in Washington ought to be telling them how many pigs to raise or what the price of potatoes ought to be. And they didn't like the alphabet soup of federal agencies—the CCC, the WPA—hiring unemployed vagrants to build trails in the woods for *recreation*, for God's sake, not logging, or to write a travel guide to Maine that would only be used by people from out of state anyway.

But it wasn't just Bill Farrell's vote that made him different. Like the majority of Maine's Democrats, he was a Catholic with Irish-French roots, and by Maine's standards, he was practically a newcomer—even though his family had lived in the state since the early 1800s. His wife's family, proper Protestant Yankees who looked none too kindly on Lizzie's marriage to Bill, could trace their genealogy back to colonial settlements in Massachusetts in the 1600s; they were immensely proud of their old English surname, Noyes. Bill was an outsider in comparison: a Catholic with an Irish surname, born into a French-speaking family in Aroostook County, in the northeastern corner of Maine on the Canadian border. Bill's children picked up quickly on the notion that there was no advantage in having a father who could speak French, as Aunt Achsah once put it, "a million miles an hour."

"Our father spoke beautiful French," Aunt Deen agreed. "And I remember us telling him, 'Go away, we don't want people to think we're foreigners!' We used to think people would think we were from the outside of the world if we spoke French."

Given FDR's popularity among Catholics and immigrant families, Bill's support for him was not all that surprising. But there was an additional reason that Bill Farrell liked FDR. He'd promised to repeal Prohibition. Lizzie disapproved of smoking and drinking, and when she caught her husband with liquor, she'd poured the bottles out. But Bill had always been fond of his homemade elderberry wine, and in 1933 it became legal again for him to drink it—along with many other alcoholic beverages that he could suddenly buy, ready-made and bottled. Maine was the very first state to pass a law banning alcohol, back in 1851, a time when—in stark contrast to its votes in the 1930s—Maine was not only setting trends for the rest of the country, but was also supplying the lumber for booming industries, Western expansion and shipbuilding. The man who'd led Maine's temperance movement, Neal Dow, saw the dark side of Maine's logging and fishing trades, which fueled the state's economy but kept so many men away from home and family. Dow preached that the "excitement of drink took the place of the comforts of life." And sad to say, those words prophesied Bill Farrell's fate after drink was made legal the year Lizzie died.

Of course, you could always get some kind of booze in Maine, even before Prohibition was repealed. "Who's got a settin' hen?" was the question asked to suss out local moonshine makers. "It's about time for her to come off," went the reply, if affirmative. Making it legal just made it easier, and without Lizzie there to scold him, Bill had no reason to curb his hankering. "Before my mother died, people used to see my parents and say, 'There goes Bill Farrell with his wife,'" said Aunt Achsah. "But after she died, they'd say, 'There goes Bill Farrell with his bottle of beer.'"

In some respects, Lizzie and Bill had been a quirky pair. Even in appearance, they were different as could be: He was long-boned and skinny, from his narrow face to his nimble fingers to the long legs inside his pants, held up on his wiry frame by suspenders; she was round-faced and matronly, every part of her body, from her wristbones to her dumpling cheeks to her ample bosom, pleasantly plump.

Bill was sixteen years older, as rough and undisciplined in his ways as Lizzie was particular about hers. Bill's mother had died of consumption when he was twelve years old, shortly after his family had left Northern Maine for the city of Waterville, where new textile and pulp mills were creating more dependable sources of income than the dying lumber industry in the dwindling forests of their native Aroostook County. But city living had its downside. Bill's mother, Lena, for whom his eldest daughter was named, was arrested for public drunkenness in 1895; she pleaded innocent, but was jailed and sentenced to thirty days' hard labor notwithstanding. Lena died three years later, and Bill, at age fourteen, was placed in the state reformatory in South Portland, along with three dozen other boys sent there for behavior that ranged from using profanity and breaking the Sabbath to vagrancy and petty thievery. The home for wayward boys was one of scores of institutions opened around the country by righteous reformers who believed that boys like Bill were better off growing up under the strict watch of authorities who were paid to straighten them out than at home with their families. Just as Bill Farrell still had his father and grandmother to care for him, most of the children sent to these institutions weren't actually orphans; they were simply kids whose families did not measure up to the era's Victorian moral codes. And most of them weren't criminals; they had simply engaged in behavior deemed unacceptable under the prevailing social morés. The director of the South Portland reformatory even acknowledged, in a report around the time that Bill was there, that most of his charges hadn't yet broken any laws; they were merely nascent criminals and "children of misfortune" who'd been neglected, often having lost a parent to drunkenness, prison, and/or death. The director went on to note that the boys' outlook would be greatly improved if their living quarters could be "relieved of the general appearance of a jail."

Bill never went back to live with his family. His father eventually remarried, to a woman named Delphine whom Bill despised, and for that reason he swore he'd never force his own children, after Lizzie died, to endure life under the thumb of an evil stepmother.

The first house Bill and Lizzie lived in after marrying was in Athens, a small town in Central Maine where Lizzie's grandfather, Thomas, had a farm that her parents still ran. Thomas Noyes was a proud Civil War veteran descended from seven generations of Americans, beginning with an English colonist named Nicholas Noyes who arrived in Massachusetts in 1633. Like many other early settlers, the descendants of Nicholas Noyes over the next hundred and fifty years migrated northeast, first to New Hampshire and then to Maine, which became a frontier territory long before the West opened up to later generations of restless opportunity seekers. Land in Maine before it became a state was cheap, timber was plentiful, and farmers had far more to fear from Maine's harsh winters than its dwindling native tribes, the Penobscots, Micmacs, and

Passamaquoddies, who had been so decimated by disease and war that only several hundred remained by the mid-1800s.

But the Indians left their mark in the place-names that many of Maine's towns and waterways and mountains retained, names like Androscoggin, Skowhegan, and Mattawamkeag. Unique in the world, these names translated into descriptions of the natural attributes of Maine's dramatic landscapes, the mountains and valleys and rivers and lakes and forests and beaches that the Indians had inhabited for ten thousand years before whites arrived in the 1600s. Yet for every wild-sounding Cobbosseecontee Lake or Mount Katahdin, the map of Maine shows just as many locales named for famous, faraway places where civilization had existed for centuries, places like Madrid, Calais, Naples, Moscow, and Poland that were not even remotely reminiscent of the quiet Maine towns named after them. Even the pronunciation of the towns' names sometimes bore little resemblance to their namesakes. Madrid, Maine, was called MAD-rid, the emphasis on the first syllable. And only an out-of-stater or a Quebecois would pronounce Calais the way it's done in France, Ca-LAY. In Maine, it was pronounced the same way you refer to extra skin on work-hardened hands: Callous.

There's not much you could do to change the pronunciation of Athens, of course, where Bill and Lizzie first set up housekeeping, but its name was about the only thing it had in common with the ancient Greek metropolis. Athens, Maine, was a typical rural village, sparsely populated, with silos, barns, and farmhouses—some prettily painted, some tumbledown shacks—occasionally dotting the fields that had been carved from the woods and given over to tall rows of corn and grazing sheep and cows. Great stands of trees and rolling hills framed the horizon, and the downtown's handful of buildings—a row of stores and a simple white church—were so unassuming that visitors could easily pass right by them and continue on the crossroads without ever being sure when they had actually arrived in Athens and when they were on their way to somewhere else. The Kennebec River was ten miles away; like Maine's other mighty rivers, it served as a highway from the state's interior to the Atlantic Ocean, and it bled into a blue network of ponds and small lakes throughout the countryside. The wet earth created a fertile valley, drawing farmers like Lizzie's grandfather and generating enough work for a blacksmith like Bill Farrell to get by on.

Bill and Lizzie had a little shop on Athens's main street, and they lived there in a small house, not far from her family's farm. The oldest girl, Lena, was born in Athens in 1922; Leona was born two years later. Then, shortly after Achsah's birth in 1928, progress came to Athens in the form of electric wiring. There was much excitement and anticipation about the replacement of kerosene with clean light available at the touch of a switch, and one winter's day Lizzie got a ride to a store in Skowhegan, some twenty miles away, to buy lighting fixtures. She planned to spend the night with her sister Alice, who lived in Skowhegan and worked there in a sawmill. But when Lizzie arrived back in Athens the next day, her house was gone—burned to the ground. A spark from the woodstove had ignited clothes hung to dry nearby, and although Lee was too little to remember it herself, she would always recall the dramatic story that her father told of their escape: the family dog barking to alert them to the smoke, Bill Farrell piling the three little girls, six, four, and one, on a sled to drag them to a neighbor's house, only to have them tumble off, one by one, into the snow. He turned around, picked them up, and continued on his way. Hearing her father tell the story so many times, Lee never knew the part Bill Farrell left out: that after the sled was out of sight, a man who assisted him in the blacksmith shop ran to the house, knocked the door down, and retrieved something Bill Farrell had left behind. Just what it was remained a secret for three-quarters of a century.

After being burned out in Athens, Bill moved his growing family to an apartment in Lewiston, a bustling manufacturing city on the Androscoggin River whose six-story, turn-of-the-century buildings were among the tallest in Maine. Lewiston was essentially a company town, largely developed in the mid-1800s by Boston industrialists. In the decades that followed, thousands of French-Canadians migrated to Lewiston to work in the mills; they lived in tenements in neighborhoods called Frenchville and Little Canada, attended the local Catholic church, and kept their language alive, a world apart from the Yankee factory owners who lived in gracious homes on the outskirts of town, up on hills to escape the polluted river and its destructive floods.

Bill must have felt right at home here, back among French-speaking Catholics like those he grew up with in Aroostook. But Lizzie was unhappy. The awe she probably felt when she first laid eyes on the city's tall, block-long stone buildings with their arches and columns quickly wore off; she must have yearned for the peaceful, green, open spaces of Athens. In the country, in the summer, the Big Dipper hung so low in the sky that it looked like you could stand on a haystack and touch it; there was nothing to block the view but the occasional spike of a tall evergreen. But here, in Maine's largest industrial city, even the river, whose powerful falls provided the energy for the factories, was no scenic respite from urban life. It was called the Stinkin' Andy, and for good reason: It was used as a sewer, a garbage dump and a sink for the chemical wastes from the factories. Later generations would quantify the levels of mercury, dioxin, and other pollutants that killed all the fish and made it so undesirable to live near the riverbank. But in the 1920s, the locals only needed to know what their senses told them: The Androscoggin's putrid water ran into manmade canals all around town in oily colors that no river should ever be.

The Farrells also arrived just after Lewiston's fortunes had peaked; the city had already entered an economic decline brought on in part by a general downturn in New England's textile industries that would never be reversed. Already the city's once-grand music hall was largely unused, and the windows of the grand banks and massive factories had begun to crack and discolor. For Lizzie, the last straw was the silverfish she found skittering under the sink. She didn't mind mice and spiders and the usual creatures found in a house in the country; she could put up with blackflies in the spring and mosquitos at dusk in the summer, but she couldn't bear those bugs in her kitchen.

So Bill found work as the blacksmith at a dairy not too far from the outskirts of Lewiston. The place was called the Morey Farm, and they lived there in the hired man's house. It was the nicest home they ever had, with electricity and running water and an indoor bathroom. Sometimes the cows would come plodding right up to the back of the house, where the pasture ended, and even though the children had grown up around farm animals, they were all frightened of them. Lee dreaded her nightly chore of retrieving a gallon of milk from the barn. Lena hated crossing the field on her way to school each day; she'd been told that wearing red might incite the bull who grazed there to charge. And Achsah had to be rescued by a grown-up after climbing atop the wood-pile, where she was immediately marooned by a group of curious cows who lumbered over, surrounded her, and then just stood there, staring at her dreamily, blinking their massive, fly-infested eyes. The girls were even afraid of horses. Too many times their father had warned them to stay out of his shop if he was shoeing a nasty horse; they'd seen the awful bruises where he sometimes got kicked, and that was enough to scare them from ever having any interest in riding.

On Saturday nights sometimes, the whole family would go up the road to a neighbor's place. Bill Farrell would bring his violin, and some-one else played the piano, and people would come to dance. Bill played magnificently, and could perform, by ear, a few well-known classical melodies, like the tune to *Moonlight Sonata,* but on these nights, he played country music—folk songs and Acadian tunes that sent his fingers and bow flying, square dances and waltzes that got his neighbors up and dancing. The kids would just sit and watch and listen, and eventually fall asleep.

At home, to music on a radio, their mother would sometimes en-tertain them by dancing the Charleston, her dark hair nearly coming out of its bun as she shuffled, her long skirts gathered in her hands so she could turn her ankles daintily, first one foot forward and back, and then the other, in time to the words: "Charleston, Charleston, made in Carolina, some dance, some prance, I'll say, there's nothing finer than the Charleston." At night, she'd tell the kids stories, and checked on their progress in school by making the older girls read aloud from the newspaper. Lizzie was raised Protestant and did not want her children brought up Catholic like their father, but she never seemed quite at home in any one particular religious group, instead taking the kids each Sunday to a different church, sometimes to the Seventh-Day Adventists, sometimes to the Baptists. They'd attend whatever Sunday school was being held, and afterward there would be picnics and games, and they'd all get their father to join in the fun, even though it wasn't his church. For his part, he taught the kids to count in French, and say *"bonjour"* and *"bonsoir"*; it was something they remembered all their lives. Life was good at the Morey Farm, and they knew it.

The stock market crashed in 1929, but the economic troubles that followed were not immediately felt by people like the Farrells in places like the Morey Farm. For Christmas that year, Lee and Lena both got new sleds. But by the time Nadeen was born, in April of 1931, things were different. Financial panics around the world were hurting trade, and that meant factories at home were firing workers. Farm surpluses around the country drove down prices; farmers couldn't sell a pig or a potato for what it cost to raise them. The Morey Farm could no longer afford a hired man, and the Farrells had to leave.

They moved—the fourth time in a decade—to a small, clapboard house, one and a half stories high, that Bill Farrell built in Mechanic Falls, a small town that was much bigger than Athens but much smaller and more peaceful than Lewiston. The Farrells lived just outside of town, between a train trestle and a bridge; the back of their house faced the side of the road, and the waters of the Little Androscoggin River—a tributary of its bigger namesake—surrounded the house on the other three sides.

The house had one distinguishing feature that was literally its claim to fame: a wooden chimney that Bill constructed using two barrels and a trough. "Ripley's Believe It or Not," a syndicated newspaper column, actually mentioned it shortly after they moved there, describing it as the only wooden chimney in America. But the house was a big step down from the relatively modern comforts of the Morey Farm. There was no electricity; it was back to the kerosene lamps, with their soot and stink. And there was no water inside the house; it had to be lugged in by the pail, drawn from a pump with a heavy metal handle that went up and down with a rhythmic two-toned creaking—hard work on a hot day, or for a pregnant woman or a child, or on a morning so cold that a layer of ice would form on the top of the bucket before the water could be brought back to the house. There was an outhouse and a slop jar, and a hand-cranked washing machine with a wringer; wet clothes were hung on a line. In winter, the clothes would freeze into sheets of ice, then gradually dry as the ice evaporated. For bathing, there was a galvanized tub and a basic rule: The smallest child would always get the first bath, using water heated in a large pot on the woodstove. Another dipper of hot water went into the tub as the next-largest child took a turn, ending up with the tallest washing up in the dirtiest water.

Although they lived on the banks of the Little Androscoggin, the children never played in the water. It was dirty, and uninviting, more a menace as it went up and down with the spring floods than a place to play. But they did watch, wide-eyed, on the coldest winter days, as huge blocks of ice were chiseled from the waters and hauled up a chute by teams of oxen to a wooden icehouse on the riverbank. The blocks were so solid, and the icehouse so cool, that the ice would stay frozen for months.

To her children, Lizzie seemed almighty, almost awesome, a powerful but potentially explosive whirlwind whose benevolence was not to be taken for granted. She could make a winter's meal out of a dried-up cheese rind, macaroni, and a jar of tomatoes from the previous summer. She could turn a long summer day into a carnival by making popcorn or fudge or homemade ice cream. She'd conjure fake honey from wild roses, clover blossoms, sugar, and water. And she'd boil molasses, then transform it into candy before their very eyes, stretching and twisting the sticky clump back and forth with Bill till it turned into a ribbon as smooth and shiny as the river in the moonlight.

Lizzie loved flowers, too, and not just the Queen Anne's lace, purple pickerel flowers, and black-eyed Susans that grew wild. She also culti-vated tall stalks of colorful gladiolas and dahlias with their fat, showy blossoms in the big garden that ran from the edge of their house all the way down to the water. She grew them right along with the cukes, tomatoes, corn, spinach, green beans, shell beans, peas, Swiss chard, and radishes that everybody else grew, but the children knew that only their mother raised these exotic, brightly colored blooms.

Of course, some people wondered if a family with as many mouths to feed as theirs had a right to indulge their mother's gardening fancies. "Look at all those flowers!" one man sneered to another as they passed by on the road behind the house one day, speaking loudly enough that Lizzie was sure to hear. "You can't eat flowers."

Lizzie brooded over the remark, rightly sensing the judgment being made on how she and Bill were providing for their family. But when she told Bill, he knew just what to say to take all the poison out of it. "Oh well, never mind, Lizzie," he said, seeing how hard his wife was taking it. "When those two die, I'll just throw an onion on their grave."

The kids all had to help picking and weeding the vegetables, and every day during the growing season, Lizzie would cook some up to preserve for the winter. Bill made a wooden contraption for the top of the stove that held two quart glass jars for boiling; Lizzie would fill them halfway with raw vegetables, then add water almost up to the lid, and boil them down. Once they were sealed tight, they were stored in the cellar, where it was cooler and dark, on shelves Bill had built. There were gallons and gallons of pickled cucumbers, and as each berry came into season, the older children would go to pick them, taking along two big buckets—one filled with sandwiches and one filled with water, to be eaten before they began working and then refilled with berries to bring home. That night there would be all you could eat of the berries, plus shortcake or ice cream, and the next day Lizzie would make jam with what was left.

Bill had a root garden where he grew potatoes and carrots and turnips, things that stayed edible well into the winter and did not need to be preserved like the more perishable greens, tomatoes, and corn. He also had a smokehouse where pigs were prepared for slaughter and bacon and hams were cured. But it was hard work, living this way and taking care of all those kids, and when it got to be too much for Bill, sometimes he'd disappear for a few days with his drink and then sleep it off. That wasn't Lizzie's way, of course; she was more tightly wound, and perhaps more weighted down by all she had to do. Yes, she was the type of mother who hid presents and made fudge and grew pretty flowers in the yard, but she also wanted things done her way. And when the order she strove to maintain amid the poverty and chaos of all those children underfoot was challenged, her cheerful competence gave way to a dark despair and rage.

"She used to say, 'I'll set my hair on fire and jump out the window,' " Aunt Achsah said, adding, confidentially, and with a little smile, "Any crazy streak we have, we come by natural."

Other times Lizzie took whatever was tormenting her out on the children. She'd line them up and hit them, one by one, with a stick. Once, when Achsah refused her mother's order to pick up some handkerchiefs that one of the other kids had left lying on the floor, her mother grabbed her by the hair of her head and swung her around like a chicken. Achsah, four or five at the time, lived in terrified awe of her mother after that. If Lizzie so much as allowed her to sit in the kitchen and watch her cook, or hold one of the babies that just seemed to keep on being born, Achsah thought, "Boy, am I lucky!"

Once, as a little girl, Achsah thought to herself, as children often do, "If my mother was dead, she wouldn't be able to do anything to me." Achsah was a grown woman with children of her own before she told anyone else about that childhood wish. A wish that came horribly true.

Lena's recollections of Lizzie, the ones she talked about all her life, began with a noise, as early memories often do. It was the echo of a click-clack, click-clack, click-clack that she would never forget, the sound of Lizzie's shoes on a hard floor as she marched down the hallway of a hospital to visit Lena, who'd had appendicitis.

Another time when she was small, Lena was sitting in front of a fireplace in a rocking chair, rocking, rocking, back and forth, hypnotized by the motion and the flames, when she rocked so hard that she pitched over into the hearth, landing on her hands. Her mother packed the burns in butter to relieve the blisters and the pain, and for the rest of her life Lena would proudly show her unscarred fingers, proof of a mother's magic.

. . .

After Lizzie died, the industry and resourcefulness with which she'd managed everything died as well; there was no way Bill Farrell could measure up. "Take care of all those kids? He couldn't do it!" Aunt Lee said. "He would take jobs. He was a guard in a mill. He'd go down and punch a clock and he would contract to paint a bridge or paint somebody's house. But when our mother was alive, he would work more. After she died, he went out drinking."

Deen remembered it differently. "As I got older, I said, 'How did that man ever handle taking care of us with no mother in the house?' " she said. "He worked two shifts in the mill to feed us. And the third shift, he had a bellows, and we used to push the bellows so he could shoe horses. I can remember him getting kicked by the horses and getting thrown out on his back, but I guess he felt he had to go back to it to keep the money coming into the house."

Sometimes their father was gone for days at a time. The kids would send their dog, Pal, out to find him, but if the dog knew where his master was, he never let on. And when Lizzie's flowers bloomed, six months after her death, the kids picked them all and sold them, twenty-five cents for a large bouquet and ten cents for a small one. The icehouse was still across the street, but there was no reason for the Farrell kids to go there; there was no food in the house to keep cold. Bedbugs turned up, too, despite Bill's best efforts to get rid of them by taking the metal-framed beds out in the yard and setting them on fire; and one day Achsah even found maggots in Frankie's wooden crib. She took him out, washed him off, and put clean clothes on him, but she'd never forget the sight of those slimy white worms crawling all over that baby. A couple of times, Bill went so far as to hire a housekeeper, but once they realized they weren't likely to be paid, they all left—even the one whom the children had observed rolling around with their father in a tent in the yard that had apparently been erected expressly for that purpose.

"A lot of times after my mother died, we'd have fried potato and salt pork for supper," Aunt Achsah said. "And salt pork is so salty you'd do well to eat one piece. In the thirties, there were so many pigs that they wouldn't sell for anything. There was no demand for them. A lot of these pigs that were killed and were supposed to be buried, people just ate them. If somebody had raised a pig, they took the ham and the bacon and the roast pork and the pork chops, but they didn't want the salt pork, so they just gave it away. They weren't worried about fat in the arteries. You'd fry it out so hopefully it would be crisp, but it would be so Goddamn salty, you couldn't handle it."

Their father also used to mix up something he called Lazy Man's Bread, which was basically just flour and fat baked in dollops like biscuits. "It was so gross," Aunt Achsah said. "It might be one reason I've never been a biscuit fan. I can eat biscuits, but you know how some people are crazy about biscuits? Not me. I don't care if I never saw one again."

Sometimes their father allowed strangers to stay in the house. Whether they were friends of his or paying for the privilege or just bums who'd shared a bottle with him, the kids never knew. But many of them were unsavory. One used to taunt Achsah about her name, calling her "Axe-handle! Double-sided axe!" So one day, all of five or six years old, she turned around and said to him, "I'll kill you, I'll kill you with an axe!" The next thing she knew, he was holding an axe, a real one, chasing her around the house. She sought the protection of one of the housekeepers who happened to be in the house that day, bursting in on the poor woman as she tried to lace up her corset. Her tormentor—who probably didn't mean to hurt her, but just wanted to scare her—slinked away, and Bill Farrell kicked him out when he heard what had happened. But Achsah couldn't help but think to herself, "My mother would never have let that man into the house."

By the time Christmas rolled around again, a Dickensian grimness had descended upon the wooden house surrounded on three sides by the Little Androscoggin River.

"The first Christmas after our mother died, we had two complete Christmas dinners brought to us in big glass jars by some rich people in town," Aunt Lee said. "The next Christmas, we had nothing. There was nothing to eat in the house whatsoever. Not even a crust of bread."

There was no wood for the fire, and no kerosene for the lamps. Bill Farrell was nowhere to be found. And certainly, with no mother staying up late to sew dolly clothes and decorate a tree, there were no presents.

As darkness fell that Christmas Eve, a year and sixteen days after their mother's death, the little ones moped and whimpered. They were cold and hungry and miserable. Lee and Lena, age ten and twelve, put their younger siblings in their beds, and covered them up with as many blankets as they could find, save one. Then the two big girls curled up in a chair together in the dark and wrapped themselves in the last blanket, singing Christmas carols till they'd gone through every song they could remember.

Bill Farrell, wherever he was, must have made himself a miserable toast: Happy thirteenth wedding anniversary, Bill. And a merry second Christmas without Lizzie.

As adults, my younger aunts don't remember how nice Christmas was when Lizzie was alive, and my mother never said a word. But Lee, being the second-oldest, remembered everything about it, and one hot summer evening, I sat with her as she conjured up for me a cold Maine winter morning and that magical scene of the sparkling tree that her mother created.

Funny thing was, I knew what she was describing almost before she said it. My mother had also waited, each Christmas Eve, until I was asleep to decorate the tree, so that when I woke up Christmas morning, it was there in all its glory, having miraculously appeared sometime in the night, an evergreen tree just like the trees from Maine, with blinking lights and silvery tinsel and twinkling ornaments so beautiful I had to touch them to make sure it wasn't just a dream. She studded oranges with cloves, and rolled out mincemeat tarts, and showered me with presents, large and small, all wrapped in colored tissue paper, that she had squirreled away throughout the year. One Christmas there were even mittens, knitted by Aunt Peanut, just as my mother and her sisters had gotten mittens from their Aunt Alice. Before the winter was over, I lost one of those mittens, knitted from a white yarn flecked with every color in the rainbow; I cried and cried and thought that I would never have mittens so nice again, as long as I lived.

And then, just as Aunt Lee explained how Christmas disappeared after Lizzie's death, at some point my mother gave it up, too. She said she didn't have the strength or the desire; it was too much work and too much mess, and maybe—though I didn't know it when I was young— too much sorrow, because it brought back Lizzie.

I still love mincemeat, but hardly anyone else in this day and age even knows what it is. It's one of those desserts that's fallen out of fashion, its very name a handicap in an era when people eat ice cream made from tofu. But sometimes my sister makes some for us to share, and I like to eat my portion for breakfast, warmed up till the filling bubbles out of the crust, so gooey and sweet that it sticks to the plate. My children and husband have no interest in even tasting it, but I like to pretend that I am hiding it from them. I curl up on the sofa in my nightgown, before anyone else wakes up, a greedy little girl with her mincemeat mess, raisins and apples in a thick, black brandy sauce, mine all mine, like the tarts my mother made me, back when she made Christmas.

One day after Lizzie died, someone brought a Victrola to the clapboard house on the Little Androscoggin River. The children were fascinated by the glass cylinders and the mechanisms. "They left it there for the longest time," Aunt Lee told me. "I don't know why they never came to get it. It might have been stolen and they ditched it till it cooled off."

"Was there any music for it?" I asked her.

"It only played one song," she said. The song told the story of a hobo who steps in front of a train to prevent it from going over a burning bridge. My aunt closed her eyes and pulled what she could remember of it from her memory, singing the chorus in a soft voice:

"Though he's only a bum, only a bum,
He saved the lives of us all,
Last night he slept in some farmer's barn,
Tonight he sleeps in heaven.

"I don't sing worth a damn," Aunt Lee said.
I smiled. "That sounded pretty good to me."
"Well," she said, "that's all I can remember."

3

JUNIOR

Bill Jr. and Nadeen, with her poodle.

When the phone rang, my mother was doing the laundry in the portable Hoover that hooked up to the sink and made more noise than the subway. I was in my room, watching a *Patty Duke Show* rerun on a little black-and-white TV. It was the early '70s, when color TVs were still a very big deal and most people I knew didn't have them, and because I wasn't quite yet a teenager myself, Patty Duke's 1950s dating rituals were endlessly fascinating to me.

But after the phone rang a second time, I figured my mother couldn't hear it, so I pulled myself away from the TV and ran out to the living room to answer it.

I knew it was long-distance before I said hello. I could hear the static on the line. Probably one of the aunts from Maine, I thought, without wondering why they'd be calling in the middle of the day, before the rates went down.

"I'm calling from Pineland about Mr. Farrell," said the lady on the other end.

Farrell was my mother's maiden name, I knew, but I didn't know of any "Mr. Farrells" in the family; all my mother's sisters had married and changed their last names. And I'd never heard of a place called Pineland.

"I think you might have the wrong number," I said politely, as I'd been trained to do when people called up speaking Spanish or asking for a name I didn't know.

"Is this AL5-5341, in the 212 area code?" the woman asked.

"Yes," I said. "But there's nobody here named Mr. Farrell."

"I know there's no one there named Mr. Farrell," she said, sounding angry and impatient now, perhaps having realized, finally, that she was dealing with a child. "I'm not calling to speak with him. I'm calling *about* him. It's his sister Anne that I need; Bill Farrell is her brother."

Now I was certain she had the wrong number. "You mean my mother Anne? She doesn't have a brother," I said.

She paused and sighed. "Is your mother home? May I speak to her?"

"Hold on." I laid the heavy black receiver down carefully on the glass top of the small bureau that we called the telephone table, and went into the kitchen where the Hoover was burping *glub-glub, glub-glub* and spitting dirty sudsy water through a black rubber hose into the sink. My mother was standing there in a beige bra and a flowered nylon skirt, a Pall Mall cigarette dangling casually between two fingers on one hand while the other hand patted the lid of the washer, bent over as if to urge the machine on in its convulsions, the way you'd monitor a child throwing up in a pot to make sure he didn't choke or miss.

"Ma!" I yelled. "Ma!"

On the second call she turned around. Her hair was tied up in an old scarf and her face was wrinkled and chalky-pale. Still I could see why she'd been a model once—the prominent cheekbones, the long line of the lips, the sparkling brown eyes, the elegant arch of the eyebrows.

"What is it? What do you want?" She seemed irritated and exhausted, as usual.

"Someone's on the phone for you."

"Oh Jesus." She stuck the cigarette in her mouth and opened the lid, which brought the machine's spinning and spitting to a gradual stop. "Who is it?" she asked as she wiped her hands on her skirt and walked toward the phone.

"I don't know. Some lady asking for Mr. Farrell, Bill I think she said. I told her there's no one by that name and then she asked for you."

She took the cigarette out of her mouth and looked at me severely. "Go in your room." I started to turn, then hesitated as she picked up the receiver. She saw me slow down and hissed, "Get out of here," with one hand over the mouthpiece, waiting till I'd disappeared to speak into the phone.

I crouched in the hallway around the corner from the living room, trying to make sense of what I was hearing. It wasn't very revealing, just a lot of yesses and nos, and then a "Just a minute while I get a pen." I heard the drawer to the telephone table open; I assumed she was getting out her address book, a long, skinny thing so old and stuffed with cards and slips of paper and mailing labels peeled off of envelopes that it had long ago burst its binding and was held together now by a rubber band. A moment later she hung up and I darted back to my room so fast that I stubbed my big toe on my door. The television was still on; *Patty Duke* had given way to *Popeye*, which I hated, but my toe throbbed so much I didn't want to take the four steps to change the channel. I just flung myself on my bed and held the toe tightly with both hands, saying "Owwwww" softly to myself over and over, assuming that any minute my mother would come in and explain everything. Explain that it was a mistake, that Bill Farrell was some long-lost second cousin, or someone who happened to have the same last name. I was eleven years old, and I thought I knew a lot about my mother's family, and I knew there was no Farrell brother named Bill.

Just to be sure I wasn't overlooking anyone, in my mind I constructed the family tree: My mother Anne had four sisters—Peanut, the youngest and skinniest, whose real name was Leathene; Achsah, with the Old Testament name that I loved but had a hard time spelling; Leona, who went by Lee; and Nadeen, called Deen. I had fourteen first cousins on that side of the family, and I ticked off their names, too, just to be sure, but none of them were Farrells, and none of them was Bill.

Gradually as I sifted through my mind all that I knew about my mother's family, and whatever I'd been told about her childhood, there began to come into my head a story about a brother of hers who died as a child. But I was certain that his name wasn't Bill; he'd been born in the middle of the Depression in rural Maine and named, with hopefulness and faith in a faraway government, Franklin Delano Roosevelt Farrell. Their mother, my grandmother, had died in childbirth having him, and Frankie, as the aunts called him when they described his brief life, was run over by a truck at age four. He'd been sent, as they all had, to live with a stranger after their mother died and their father went to jail. The stranger, an old woman, sent Frankie across a busy road every day to fetch her mail, and he was struck and killed on one of those errands.

There was probably a story like that about this mysterious Bill Farrell, and any minute my mother would come in my room, sit on my bed, and tell it to me. But now *Popeye* was over and *The Dating Game* had begun, and I heard the Hoover start up again, slowly at first, chugging and churning like a train pulling out of the station, then working up to full speed, the *glub-glub* resuming just as before. I wanted to run in the kitchen and say, "Don't do the laundry! Tell me who Bill Farrell is!" but more than that I wanted her to tell me without my asking. Why didn't she come in? Didn't she know that I wanted to know?

"Bachelor number one," said a young woman in a halter top and matching polka-dot maxi skirt, "what would you say if I called you and said I was sick?"

A man with shoulder-length hair and a double-breasted bell-bottom suit rubbed his hands together and grinned. "I'd tell you to get right into bed," he said. The audience oohed and the bachelorette bounced up and down in her seat, giggling. But it wasn't funny. I felt like crying.

After *The Dating Game* I watched *The Mike Douglas Show* and then a

Lost in Space rerun and finally the news, but she never came in. Through my window I could see my father's white underwear, bleached to perfection, sailing by on the clothesline as she hung the wash out from the kitchen window, using a squeaky pulley to send it toward the bathroom window where the other end of the rope was attached. There it would dry overnight, hanging six stories above a grim alley. Occasionally specks of soot from a nearby incinerator would float over and land with a smudge on something she'd scrubbed snow-white with a bar of soap on an old-fashioned washboard that she kept to supplement the Hoover. And when she'd notice this airborne stain, she'd wail with fury, moaning, "Why do I bother?" But that didn't stop her from hanging it out there, and it never motivated her to get a dryer or use the dryer in the basement of our building. The clothesline was how you dried clothes, and it was a waste, according to her, to do it any other way.

When the clothesline stopped moving and the clatter of pots and pans announced that she'd moved on from hanging the wash to making dinner, I couldn't stand it any longer and marched into the kitchen.

Her back was to me; she'd put a blouse on over her bra and taken the scarf off her salt-and-pepper hair, which hung in brittle layers around her head, some ancient hairdo long grown in. Another Pall Mall sat in a silvery ashtray, stuck between the open beak of a little metal swan, the ashes falling in neat cylinders to the ribbed tray beneath the bird and the smoke curling in a blue column to the ceiling. I stood in the doorway for a moment as she rinsed lettuce in the sink.

"Ma," I finally said, unsure if she knew I was there and was intentionally ignoring me or if perhaps she hadn't heard me.

"What?" she said without turning around.

"Who's Bill Farrell?"

She put the lettuce down, picked up her cigarette, and thoughtfully took a long drag before facing me. "He's my brother, but he's dead," she said.

I'd kept the other brother's name on the tip of my tongue for just such a conversation. "I thought the dead brother's name was Franklin Delano Roosevelt Farrell," I said.

She considered this for a moment, as if surprised that I knew or remembered the story of Frank. "Well," she finally said. "Bill was my other brother."

"You had another brother?"

I waited for a response but there was none. "Why didn't you ever tell me?"

Again, no answer. I tried a different tack: "Why was that lady calling?"

"She just needed to tell me something," she finally responded without looking at me. "Nothing that matters. Nothing that's any of your business."

I stood my ground, looking at her, waiting for more.

"I'm not going to tell you anything else. Do you have to ask so many questions? That's it."

I went back to my room and switched from the news to *The Flintstones,* and we never discussed Bill Farrell again. Later I found the entry in her address book, right there under Farrell, with the address and phone number of this place called Pineland. But I never spoke to my mother about it again; there was no point.

I guess in some ways I had always known, from the time I was very small, that my mother had a lot of secrets. My dad always talked about his childhood, and the differences between then and now, or if we were going to visit one of his relatives, he would tell a story about the person. In fact, most grown-ups I knew started their conversations with me by saying, "When I was your age . . ." They shared something about themselves as a way of connecting with me.

But my mother wasn't like that. She did what she did without explanation, and if she made a certain dish—like mincemeat—or if she quoted a poem—like *Evangeline*—she never said who taught her to cook the dish or where she first read the poem. And if a brother of hers appeared out of nowhere, she wasn't going to talk about that, either. It was just her way of being. Her existence had no context, and she wanted it that way. I suppose I could have been hurt, or angry, at being shut out of whatever it was that only she knew. I suppose I could have felt sorry for her, that she had to be alone, in her mind, with everything in her life that had come before. But somehow I knew it had nothing to do with me.

Later in life, I looked back and saw that she had to keep those secrets in order to remain the person she had become. If everyone knew who she really was—not a sophisticated woman named Annie Farrell, a pilot and a skier and a model, but a dirt-poor country girl named Lena whose father was a drunk and whose brother Bill, as I would eventually discover, was retarded—she might not be able to keep up the charade.

But at the time, as an adolescent, I just saw it as a power play. She was the grown-up, she got to keep secrets; and I was a busybody of a girl, who wanted to know everything (a quality that has served me well in my work as a reporter). It was almost a game, and I was determined to win—mainly because I couldn't stand the fact that I had gotten so close to figuring out one of her walled-off mysteries only to be shut out at the last minute. I was going to get to the bottom of this. I *had* to know about Bill Farrell, and I knew just the person to ask: my Aunt Deen.

Aunt Deen was divorced and had no children of her own, but every now and then I got to sleep over at her house, and she always made me feel like I was a grown-up by talking to me about grown-up things: how to devein shrimp for shrimp cocktail, the relative merits of leg makeup versus stockings, what marvelous new renovations she was planning next in her endless series of home improvements. She always treated me like I was her friend and confidante, not her little niece. Besides, Aunt Deen wasn't like other grown-ups. She was too old and too proper to be a hippie and wear jeans, but she seemed much less careworn and more glamorous than my mother. Her hair was always colored peach and neatly coiffed in an upswept poof around her face, and she always seemed dressed up, even when she had no plans to go out. She wore elaborate necklaces and rings and pins, and fussy blouses—in pinks and peaches and creams and beiges—festooned with beads or bows or buttons, fancy collars or necklines, then matched with sweaters or jackets or vests and skirts or pants. She smelled like flowers, and her face was smooth and unlined—no creases, no blackheads, no moles or crevices. Her house was full of exotic things—teardrop chandeliers with electric candles and dimmer switches, bottles of Jean Naté and colored soaps that matched the hand towels in the bathroom, fringed pillows and embossed tablecloths, curtains and drapes with swags and ruffles, chairs that reclined and beds that vibrated, and lamps with stained-glass shades. She always had a small poodle that she would alternately scold and cajole; when one dog got old and died, she immediately got another one in a different color.

Deen was the only one of her sisters who was Catholic. After her mother died, her father had sent her and some of the younger kids to a Catholic school in Lewiston. For Deen, the school was a haven. "I remember the nuns loving me, taking me to the chapel and feeding me," she'd say dreamily. And when she was given the honor of reading aloud, in the school auditorium, a speech she had written, she told the teacher she couldn't do it because she didn't have a proper dress—just long hand-me-downs that fell to her ankles. The teacher brought her a suitable dress the next day, pinned it on her, and stitched it to fit so she would have something to wear.

Deen had also inherited her father's ear, and a music teacher who recognized her gift gave her free lessons on the violin, the piano, and the trumpet. Deen wanted desperately to practice, but she had no piano, so she asked the town clerk if she could play in the town hall. By then she was living with a foster family that gave her a dime-a-week allowance, and she offered to turn over the ten cents to the clerk as payment for access to the piano. When Christmas came around, the clerk had a surprise for her: She'd saved all those dimes, and she gave the money back to Deen in one lump sum. As an adult, Deen acquired an electric organ and loved to entertain us all by playing it. She knew songs like "Mona Lisa, Men Have Named You," and the theme from *Dr. Zhivago,* and I felt honored because she always let me play her precious instrument as much as I wanted. I had fun sounding out "Hot Cross Buns" and "Doe a Deer" on the white plastic keys, then flicking levers labeled *oboe* and *percussion* to change the timbre of each note, notes that never died away like a conventional piano, but that quavered on and on and on until you picked your finger up.

Deen also had a burglar alarm system that I once set off, inadvertently summoning the police, but since she didn't yell at me when that happened, and since she was so nice about letting me fool around with her organ, I figured it was probably safe to ask her about her brother Bill.

So one day, I told her the story of the phone call I had intercepted, and what my mother had said.

"Bill's not dead," Deen said emphatically, without appearing angry or surprised that my mother had told me that he was.

"He's not?" I said. "Why did she tell me that he was?"

"I guess she's just ashamed. Or maybe she thought she was trying to protect you."

She then explained that Bill was mentally retarded and that he lived in an institution in Maine called Pineland. "I go up to Maine to visit him a couple of times a year," she added. "He's a really sweet guy, but he just never had a chance in life, you know?"

I never mentioned my conversation with Aunt Deen to my mother. But from then on, I edited all the stories in my brain about her childhood to include Bill Jr. My mother didn't talk much about her growing up, but now when I recalled the few stories she did share, I'd always add a boy named Bill to the image conjured up by her description.

Her earliest memory, she always said, was being in a hospital and hearing the soles of her own mother's shoes clicking in the hallway, on her way to visit. But now I wondered: What was Bill's earliest memory?

If I burned myself on a hot pan, my mother always smeared the burn with butter, because that's what her mother did when she fell into the fireplace. And now I saw the story through Bill's eyes: Had he been old enough, or smart enough, to understand why his sister had her hands covered in something usually spread on bread?

Then there was the goat story: A little goat used to pull them around on a sled when they were young, but one day his horns got tangled in a chicken-wire fence, and he injured himself so badly that he died. I used to imagine all those little girls trying to fit together on that sled, with one or two of them always falling off, laughing, in the snow, and the goat struggling to pull the load, and how sad they all must have been, crying and crying, when they found the goat dead in his pen. Now I re-imagined it all, with Bill. Did the girls include their brother in the game, and was he just as sad when the little goat died? Or was he too small to remember, and only knew the story like I did—from being told?

And when their mother died, it dawned on me one day, their father was left not only with five girls and the newborn baby, but also with Bill, his namesake, and until the last birth, the only boy. I then rethought every aspect of the story. When the doctors told Lizzie to stop having babies, she had already borne not just the five girls, but also Bill. And the children, whom I had always mentally divided into the three older girls and the two little girls plus Frankie, I now realized included Bill, smack in the middle. The older girls were old enough to understand that their mother was gone forever and be traumatized by that, and the three younger children really had no memories of her and were too little to remember her death. But Bill, just a week shy of four years old when his mother died—did he know enough to be sad or frightened when her body was laid out in the casket? And did he remember what it was like to have two parents to share the burdens and joys of family life? Could he recall his mother's love, or her rage, or what she looked like, or was it just something the others talked about, something he could never understand?

It turned out that my sister Nancy knew about Bill, too. Once every summer, Nancy told me, while our parents were on vacation in Maine and before I was born, they would get a babysitter for her—a very rare event in their lives—and get dressed up and be gone for three hours. "I didn't know where they went," Nancy, who is twelve years older than I am, said. "It was all a big mystery." Then one year, Deen joined them, and as the grown-ups readied themselves to leave, she told Nancy, as if it were a perfectly normal and reasonable subject for discussion, "We're going to see our brother."

"Your brother?" Nancy said. "What brother?"

Deen calmly explained that Bill lived in a home for retarded people, and that they were going to take him out to lunch and buy him some presents.

Nancy, at age ten old enough to realize that this information had been purposely concealed from her, but too young to understand why, became hysterical.

"Why can't we take him home?" she screamed at her mother. "Why can't he live with us? It's your brother! So what if he's retarded? Why can't I go see him?"

Anne, in turn, began shouting at Deen. "Why did you tell her?" she said. "It wasn't your business to be the one to tell her!"

Nancy didn't get to go with them to visit Bill that day. But many years later, after Anne died, Deen took Nancy to see him.

"We took him out to eat in a nice restaurant and we went to the ten-cent store and bought him some things, and we went to the shoe store and bought him new boots," Nancy said. "We had a really nice time. And it was really very normal."

When he was little, they called him "Junior," not Bill. Bill was their father; Junior—pronounced "Jun-yah"—was the son. Why he wasn't all right in the head was a matter of some dispute.

"Your mother's claim was—and I don't believe it—she claimed that I pulled him off the bed onto the floor," said Achsah.

"The caseworkers told me that when my mom brought Bill home from the hospital, my two older sisters, Anne and Lee, were arguing over who was going to hold him, and then they both said, 'You take him,' and dropped him on his head," said Deen.

"He was a baby on a blanket and Achsah pulled him off the bed," said Lee. "And then his glands didn't develop right, and he was mildly retarded. But it happens in the best of families. Look at the Kennedys!"

Lee added that when Bill was little, he didn't seem all that different from the other kids. "His parents might have known it, but we didn't know it," she said.

"The story I heard was that he drank kerosene," Peanut said. "Our father used to keep a jar of kerosene by the stove and if the fire wasn't going strong enough, he'd throw a little kerosene on it. And one day Bill took a swig of it."

Peanut also maintained that Bill might have lived a nearly normal life if he'd had better care. "Now when kids are slow learners, they put them in special classes so it's no time at all before they catch up," she said. "But back then if you were a slow learner, they said, 'You can't learn him nothin'!' "

But Achsah remembered Bill being slow—"wicked slow, all around. I used to play school with the other kids. But I couldn't get across to Bill his colors. He couldn't learn them. I didn't have any problem teaching the other kids. I tried my best, but I just couldn't teach Bill. My father used to call him 'Blockhead.' "

When Achsah started third grade, she took him to school with her to start kindergarten. "I remember he took his shoes and stockings off and put them on top of his desk, and then he said: 'I got to shit,' " she said, imitating his low voice and slow way of stretching out his vowels. "I'm sure the teacher was horrified. She had me show him where the bathroom was. And at the end of the day, the teacher said, 'Take him home. And don't bring him back.' After that, Bill just got left home. In those days if you had a kid who was backward, there were no laws providing for their education. You either put them in an institution or you kept them in a corner."

But eventually Bill learned to tell time, and Achsah took that to mean that he could have been educated to some extent. "I think if they did then what they do now, he could have learned a lot," she said.

Still, Bill had a way of finding trouble, or, as Achsah put it, "He had ideas of imitating things he'd seen." One day he decided he was going to chop some wood. He got an axe, and he got some wood, and he asked his little brother Frankie to hold the wood up. Then he chopped Frankie's finger. Fortunately, a doctor was able to stitch it up.

Another day he and Frankie got hold of some matches and set a few patches of dry grass on fire outside their house. "I caught them, and I scolded them," said Achsah. "I'm sure I told my dad. But what good did it do?"

Bill, like my mother and all their siblings, was taken away from his father in 1938 by the state of Maine. Their mother had died in 1933; their father was neglecting them. Bill was first sent to a foster home with Achsah and Frankie, but the woman they were placed with soon realized there was something wrong with Bill, and eventually she asked that he be placed somewhere else.

A few years later Achsah went to visit him. She was a teenager, and it was all she could do to try to keep track of her siblings in various schools and homes around the state. But somehow she found out where Bill was living and figured out a way to get there. Turned out it wasn't worth the effort. "He just sat in the house," she told me. "And I thought, if he's just going to ignore me, there's no sense in my trying to see him."

It was many years, after her seven children were mostly grown, before Achsah involved herself in Bill Jr.'s life again. She asked the state to place him in a boarding home near her so she could visit him. The first time she went to see him, probably for the first time in twenty or twenty-five years, he didn't know who she was. She told him, "I'm your sister. My name is Achsah." And after that he always knew her: Achsah. And he was happy to go for a ride in her car or eat a box of crackers she had brought.

His placements and treatment over the years appeared to have made worse whatever was wrong with him to begin with. He was placed as a child with a deaf-mute couple; his speech slurred and his temper grew as his ability to communicate deteriorated. Later, he was medicated with a drug that caused a tongue thrust; his teeth were removed after he bit someone; his Social Security payments often disappeared without his social workers accounting for the lost money. And although he had not been violent or mean as a child, as an adult he developed a bad temper and could lose control. Achsah wondered if perhaps he'd been abused somewhere along the way but couldn't describe what had happened to him.

I asked Aunt Achsah why she thought my mother had kept it from me. "There used to be a certain stigma attached to a child who was retarded," she said. "Years ago, people had a child like that, they either put him in an institution or they kept him hidden at home somewhere, shut up in the bedroom. And people used to refer to them as idiots instead of saying mentally challenged or whatever they say now. If you had a retarded relative, they'd think you were retarded as well."

• • •

Bill was nine years old and Deen was six when they were split up. They saw each other a few months later at Frankie's funeral, but did not see each other again until Deen was an adult, living on her own in New York. She wrote to the Maine Department of Social Services and was given information about the home he was living in at the time. She visited him there the next time she was in Maine. "He cried when he saw me," she said. "He couldn't hardly remember me. But that guy was always in the back of my brain. Nobody would admit that they owned him. And since nobody would claim him, I made it my mission."

The older she got, the more involved she became in his life, eventually calling him every Sunday, sending him packages of clothing and small gifts, going up to see him, and even hiring a caretaker to bring him to New York to visit her a few times.

Peanut was five when she was taken away from her father in 1938, and over the years, with no one reminding her what her family had once been like, she forgot all about Bill. "I guess back then it was a terrible stigma to have someone in the family who wasn't quite right," she said. "As time went on, and I never saw him again, it escaped my brain. I didn't even know he existed till your mother told me in 1959. She thought I could get him and use him for a babysitter."

Peanut had three children by then and would have two more. She and her husband went to see Bill. "We sat around the benches and talked to him," she recalled. "But he wasn't talking like anyone else would. Achsah said all he did was mutter and mumble, and he couldn't carry on a conversation. Case closed." Bill, it was clear, was not a suitable caretaker for Peanut's children. But her husband, who worked in a mill, made a point of telling her that a lot of the men he worked with were in worse shape than Bill.

In 1994, a year or two before Bill Jr. died, I went with my sister and Aunt Achsah to see him. He was a tall man with a large, slack-jawed face and ears that stuck out. His breathing was labored because one lung had been removed, and it was difficult to understand his speech. Aunt Achsah explained to him that I was Anne's grown-up daughter, and reminded him that Anne was his sister, and that she was dead. At first he didn't understand. "Who are you?" he kept asking me, peering at me with suspicion. "That's Anne's daughter," Aunt Achsah kept saying patiently and slowly. "You remember Anne. She was the oldest one. And remember I told you she died a while back, so she's not here anymore. But this is her daughter."

When he finally made the connection, he began to cry and softly moan, "Anne, Anne." But we cheered him up with some little presents, a flashlight that he kept turning on and off, two pairs of white socks, and a new hammer for his collection of tools; he'd been trained in basic carpentry and gardening and was actually able to build simple things as part of his activities at the home. I had brought my oldest son, who was two years old at the time, and Bill grinned happily as he held Danny in his arms while we took their picture. We went to lunch at a diner, where he ate meat and potatoes very politely, using his knife and fork and napkin properly and attracting the attention of other diners only when he spoke in a voice that was loud, the words too slurred to make out. Then we all went to a small zoo where animals that had been injured in the wilds of Maine—eagles and raccoons and moose and such that had been hit by cars or shot or caught in traps—were being reha- bilitated. Bill loped from cage to cage with an awkward gait, grinning and pointing and as happy as my two-year-old to be there. My husband later observed that the animals at this place received better care than Bill had for most of his life.

I wondered what was so bad about this; why did my mother have to hide it? I wished I could go home at the end of the day and call her up and say, "I saw your brother Bill. What's the big deal? Daddy knew; Nancy knew." But as with so many other aspects of her life, by the time I had puzzled out the secrets, she was no longer here to explain them.

When I tell the story of my mother's secret brother to other people my age, I am amazed at how many of them have similar stories in their families. There are dead children whose existence was too painful to acknowledge, sisters and brothers who were removed from the family tree in anger or shame, and sometimes even parents—their absence hidden by phony stories or second marriages—whom children would prefer to forget.

It's hard to understand the morés that encouraged people to hide their own flesh and blood because we live now in a culture that has no secrets. Discretion went out with white gloves, and that's why most of the people who tell me their stories of hidden relatives are describing something from an earlier generation, something that was revealed to them—as Bill Jr. was revealed to me—accidentally, through a phone call or a surprise encounter or a reference inadvertently made in conversation by someone who didn't know they weren't allowed to tell. In today's world, we've deemed secrets to be bad—bad for our health, bad for our relationships, bad for our families. We don't want our government or our corporations or our churches or our movie stars or anybody else in America to keep secrets, and the revealing of private information—our addictions, our black sheep, our affairs, and our failures—has become one of the great spectacles of postmodern life.

But my mother didn't want to be a spectacle. She'd already been a spectacle, too many times, an object of pity and ridicule and everything else that you can be in a small town when your mother is dead and your father's a drunk who can't keep his kids clothed and fed. She changed her name and kept most of her bad memories to herself, and if there were certain other facts about her life that she could conveniently omit from any conversations—like her brother—then that's what she was going to do. And so, in a funny way, I eventually came to understand why she had hidden Bill Jr. and so many other things about herself. Because if we all knew who she really was, then she wouldn't be able to continue living as the person she'd tried so hard to become.

The irony of all this is that much of my professional life has been spent getting people to unburden their most private thoughts to me, and then turning those thoughts into news stories for all the world to read. Call important people out of the blue, knock on strangers' doors in the middle of the night, stand outside the church where some innocent victim is being mourned, and incredibly, more often than not, I could get the story. It has very little to do with me or my skills as a reporter; that's just how most people are. They want to tell their stories.

As it turns out, one of the few who refused to talk was the person whose story mattered more to me than any other—my mother.

4

NEW SHOES

Bill Farrell and his kids: Lena (holding Frankie),
Lee, Achsah, Bill Jr., Nadeen, and Peanut.

The way Aunt Deen remembered it, a car with New York plates pulled alongside of her and Peanut and Bill and Frankie as they walked along the road one day. The couple inside asked them where they could get some bait.

The kids offered to show them the little river that ran behind their house, and the couple offered, in return, to drive the kids there. But the kids knew their dad wouldn't like it if they got into a car with strangers, so they told the couple to follow them, slowly, along the road, as they walked the short distance back to their house on the Little Androscoggin River.

When they got there, the strangers asked them where their mother was.

Well, the kids told them, she's dead.

And their father?

Working at the mill.

"We'd like to take you downtown and buy you all new shoes," the woman said after a few moments.

The children huddled and decided that it was probably okay to get in the car after all. As little as they were, they figured they could beat these out-of-staters up if they tried to do anything wrong. So off they went to the shoe store, where each of them got a brand-new pair. The couple also gave them a box of candy, and brought them home.

When their father arrived, the strangers took him on the side. Deen said she never knew what the discussion was about until my mother told her, many years later. "They came back to tell my dad they wanted to adopt one of the children," she said. "They offered Dad ten thousand dollars for me. It was the Depression. And my dad said, 'Give me the night to think it over.' The next morning they came to collect me and pay the ten thousand, and my dad said, 'I wouldn't know how to part with one of them, but you can have all of them.' "

They decided to leave without taking any.

The way Aunt Lee remembered it, these rich folks had stopped at the house in search of a particular herb or plant. The husband was a botanist from New York or New Jersey, and their father thought he knew where the plant that they were seeking grew wild. Turned out, Lee recalled, the plant Bill Farrell showed them wasn't what they were looking for. "But it was something like ninety-nine percent the same," Lee said. "Only a true botanist would know the difference."

The couple was so taken with the family that they brought all the kids new shoes and socks and sweaters and rubber overshoes for rainy days, and even new toothbrushes and Dr. Lyon's tooth powder. "It was heavenly to get new shoes and stockings," Lee said. "And they wanted to adopt me. But my father said no, because at night, when he counted noses, they all had to be there."

By the time I asked Aunt Achsah about it, I was confused. Were these people after bait or an herb? Did they want Lee or Deen?

"They were looking for catnip for their cats, catnip growing wild," Achsah said without hesitation, a trace of annoyance in her voice that I had been led to believe it was any other way. "They'd come every summer and they'd take us downtown to buy shoes, two very rich couples with a chauffeur in a big limousine."

And what about adopting a child? Who was it that they wanted?

"Well," she said, considering this one for a moment before answering. "I don't think I was their particular favorite. But I think they would have been happy to have any one of us."

So this much we know: They were looking for bait, or catnip, or a child of their own. And they kept coming back, at the end of each summer, to see the poor kids by the riverbank. There are two or three photos of the kids from around that time, and sometimes I look at the pictures through the eyes of these do-gooders, trying to imagine the impressions they took away on their brief visits, and whether there was any way they could have realistically distinguished one kid from the other, or if they even tried. There was Lena, tall and skinny, with her daddy's long fingers and hardly enough flesh on her arms and legs to cushion the bones; Lee, who looked more like the picture of their dead mother hanging inside the house on a wall than the other kids, with a round face and a ready smile; Achsah, who had neither Lena's quiet intensity or Lee's talkative charm, but who exuded a grown-up seriousness from a face as sweet as a bunny's, framed by an apple chin and hair that hadn't been cut quite evenly on both sides; Bill Jr., his face a long box with a jaw that closed and opened ever so slowly; Nadeen, peach-skinned and bright-eyed and cheery, a curtsying attention-getting sort of a girl; Peanut, like a miniature Lena with fine bones and dark eyes on a tiny frame, but shy and preferring to stand behind the others; and finally Frankie, an adorable little boy who could stand on his head and run circles around his laconic older brother.

But what I've always wondered, knowing that something kept pulling these rich folks back to this poor family, was what happened the year they drove up in their fancy car and found everything was gone? Were they smiling as they drove up, in anticipation of their annual good deed?

And did they gasp, or cry, or clutch their faces, when that first glimpse through the windshield revealed no sign that a house had ever stood here? Did they argue about directions, wondering if they'd turned in the wrong yard, and did they go back along the road to see? It was this much past the train trestle, no doubt about it, and just before the bridge over the river, yes indeed; yet there's nothing there, how can it be? Did they drive on to the next house, knock on a neighbor's door, try to get the story straight? Did they drive away with a shudder, maybe try to find some other family to help? Or did they get out of their car, scratch around in the dirt where they thought the foundation would be, notice the charred wood left behind by the rain and the scavengers, and simply assume the worst? And did they wipe a tear or two away, or did it even matter?

There was a big drawback to living in a house surrounded by water on three sides, and that was the flooding, every spring, when the ice on the river cracked and the rains came and the ground turned to muck. Bill Farrell always seemed to know when it was coming. One time he put a plank up to the bedroom window and took the children out that way because they couldn't get to the door. Another time he had a wooden platform waiting, chained to the trees, so he could drive his car across the yard to the road. And once they had to escape in a boat. The heaviest flood, in 1936, left a watermark in the house halfway up the walls that never disappeared.

But it was fire, not water, that finally did in the house in Mechanic Falls. It was April Fool's Day of 1937, a spring day so warm it was like summer. Lee was home with the little kids, playing outside, when she noticed that the boys were missing. She went in to see what they were up to, and there she found the wall of the house ablaze. She got the kids out and ran down the road to a gas station, where she asked the workers to call the fire station, then ran back, thinking the fire truck would arrive any second. But minutes passed, long minutes, and no one came.

Finally a neighbor saw the smoke and called the firehouse. Three dozen firemen arrived, the Lewiston *Sun-Journal* reported the next day, and pumped water from the river to squelch the flames. But the house burned down anyway.

The story in the paper said the fire was of "unknown origin," but it mentioned the wooden chimney and the "Ripley's Believe It or Not" column. No doubt some readers wondered if perhaps the blaze had started in that very chimney, but the Farrells knew better. They were certain the little boys had set it, playing with matches.

Your mother was at the Connicks', a family she knew in town," Aunt Achsah said after I sent her the old newspaper clipping about the fire. "She stayed there a lot. Hey, I don't blame her! They had running water and electricity, and we didn't. And I had gone down there that day, too, to get my hair washed. It was about noontime, and the fire alarm sounded. And I remember thinking, I hope that's not our house."

We were all outside," Aunt Lee recalled when I asked her what happened. "We were playing on the swings. But then I realized I was missing the two boys. I went inside and there the side of the wall was going up in flames. I got the kids out, which was what I had been told to do if there was a fire, and I ran down the road to the gas station and told them the house was on fire and to call for the fire department. They might have thought it was an April Fool's joke. They didn't come for a long time. And when they came, they just let it burn. They never did put it out.

"We had pictures on the wall. We had them up on the wall in two elegant frames, oval wooden frames filled with photographs. If I'd known the house was going to burn, I'd have gotten those pictures down. But I didn't know the house was going to burn. I thought the firetruck was coming! And then we couldn't go in because it was engulfed in flames. We lost everything in that fire. We had absolutely nothing."

What I remember about that horrible day in my life was a big burly fireman, holding two children, one in each arm," Aunt Deen said. "That must have been Frankie and Peanut. He told me to stay with him and

I realized my snowsuit, left inside the house, was going to burn. I started to lurch away from the fireman to get it, and he tripped me, then placed his big foot across my back, keeping me belly down, with my legs and feet sprawled down in the ditch."

But regardless of how the fire came about, or who was to blame, or what wasn't done, the Farrells were now homeless, a fact that the newspaper didn't mention. Bill farmed the children out to whoever would take them—cousins, uncles, neighbors—while he tried to figure out where they were going to live.

"He put me to live with my Uncle Lee, my mother's brother, in another town," Aunt Achsah said. "I didn't go to school for the rest of the year. But when May came around, we made May baskets there. You'd take a cardboard matchbox that wooden matches came in, put a little crepe paper and penny candy inside, and that was a May basket. My father came and got me sometime around the last of May, and I remember thinking, 'Oh boy. I hate to see May go by, because there won't be any more May baskets.' "

Achsah and the other kids—except for Lena, who remained with the Connicks—eventually moved with their father to a town farm in Wellington. Town farms had originally been set up in the nineteenth century by communities all over Maine as a way to house destitute families and provide them with the means to grow their own food. But by the 1930s they were mostly abandoned shacks overgrown with weeds, occupied by squatters if at all. No one stopped the Farrells from moving in, but it had been so long since anyone lived there that there wasn't even an outhouse. Bill built one, but only bothered to put a front door and two sides on it; it was open in the back.

When school began again in the fall, Bill started keeping Achsah— then nine years old—home two or three days a week to help with the little ones. By October, she'd tired of scrubbing the clothes in the washtub and building the fires and being the mother, and she knew a family in Kingsbury that was willing to take her in, so, following the example of her big sister Lena, who'd all but moved in with another family, Achsah went to live with the people in Kingsbury. She had chores to do there—picking apples, leading their horses to water—but it was nothing compared to taking care of her little siblings. Besides, in Kingsbury, every Sunday morning, she woke up to a feast of candy, brought back by one of the grown-ups from a trip to town on Saturday night.

One day at school, Achsah was summoned outside. Someone from the state welfare office wanted to have a little chat with her. She was escorted over to the swings in the school yard, then questioned.

"They tried to get me to say that I had seen my father molest one of the girls," Aunt Achsah told me. "That's what they were getting at. I hadn't seen it, so naturally I wasn't going to say that I did. And I don't know if I had seen it, if I would have told them."

"But the fact is, you didn't see it," I said. "So there was nothing to tell."

"Well," she said after a moment, "you know, when you're a little kid, some things you keep to yourself. And some things, you tell."

I thought about that for a moment. What she'd said was, in itself, a puzzle, a syllogism that made my head spin. She revealed nothing because she'd seen nothing. But if she *had* seen something, she wouldn't have told anyway. Either way, the secret stayed hidden, and apparently always would. I turned the words over in my mind again: Some things you keep to yourself, some things you tell. In other words, no matter how many of Annie Farrell's secrets I might discover, there was always a chance that more remained hidden.

Achsah would have stayed in Kingsbury for as long as the family there would have her. But in December, Bill insisted that she come back to help him take care of the younger kids. He'd moved from the town farm to the home of an acquaintance in Harmony, living in one room of the man's house with all his kids—except for Lee and Lena. When Achsah returned to live with her father, her oldest sisters were gone. They'd been taken away by the authorities, and sent—just as their father had been, some thirty-seven years earlier—to a state reformatory.

"I was in seventh grade," Lee remembered. "I would have been thirteen. It was a school where they put you if you couldn't get along with your parents, or you were in trouble, or you couldn't be placed anywhere else. They just took us and grabbed us and broke us all up. I guess that was the only thing they could do in a hurry. This woman came and took us, because we weren't getting good care from our father, and they put us in there, because they had no family to put us with."

There might have been other reasons, too, and not just the suspicions that prompted the social worker's chat with Achsah by the swings in the school yard. There were rumors that Lena had been seen driving around with her blouse off in a car with some boys; Achsah wondered if Lena had been molested by her father. Or maybe during her stay at the Connicks', someone realized that whatever conditions had led Lena to leave home meant that her father was an unfit parent.

Either way, Maine's laws at the time clearly stated that any girl age nine to seventeen who was "leading an idle or vicious life . . . or in danger of falling into habits of vice or immorality . . . may be committed" to the state reformatory, known variously as the Stevens Institute or the Hallowell State School for Girls. As long as "any three respectable inhabitants of any city or town" were willing to sign a complaint about a girl deemed "in danger of falling" (today the phrase is "at risk"), the state had the legal authority to place her in the reformatory. No doubt three such respectable citizens lived in Mechanic Falls; no doubt three such citizens could be found just about anywhere to report on just about any kid whose behavior was, well, if not exactly illegal, then offensive. And once Lena arrived at the school, she was made to pay for whatever it was that got her sent there by scrubbing the floors and working in the kitchen.

The reformatory was founded more than a half-century earlier, in 1875, by John Stevens, an abolitionist and U.S. ambassador who established it as an institution for "homeless and vagrant girls." Over time, of course, that mission was modified. A report written a few years after Lee and Lena arrived in late 1937 described it as a "penal and corrective" facility for girls whose "crimes" consisted mostly of truancy, running away from home, disorderly conduct, and "wanton and lascivious" behavior.

The author of the report and school superintendent, Miss Nellie French Stevens, noted that only two or three girls were accused of anything as serious as assault or larceny, but she did catalogue the treatment of numerous cases of sexually transmitted diseases among the one hundred and fifty residents, in addition to the births of ten babies. Miss Stevens was also careful to point out that although the school tried hard to improve the girls, "the institution cannot work miracles such as changing the habits of fourteen and fifteen years."

Lee and Lena were separated when they arrived, lived in different parts of the dormitory, and barely saw each other again. Lee, diagnosed with a heart condition, was spared the rigorous work that her sister and most of the other girls were forced to perform. And the few times Achsah was brought to visit over the next few years by someone driving down that way, Lena was too busy in the kitchen or polishing the floors to see her. So Achsah spent her time with Lee, and took her meals in the dining hall, where the girls sat at card tables in complete silence. The only communication that was permitted was the occasional polite whisper: "Please pass the salt."

"The food was terrible," Lee said. "The house mothers, their food was sumptuous. But our food was barely edible. They had all this butter and cream on their plates, and they were all old fat ladies and didn't need it, while we were all skinny little girls. I cried a lot at night."

But the matrons, whom the girls were forced to address as Aunt So-and-So, weren't completely heartless. Enterprising Achsah, saving up money she earned picking beans and doing other odd jobs, once sent each of her sisters a comb, brush, and mirror set. To her astonishment, the ladies who ran the Hallowell State School for Girls decided to reward this sisterly act of devotion by mailing back to her, all wrapped up, a brand-new dress.

One day in the house in Harmony, Achsah was lying, feverish with the flu, on a cot in the single room she shared with her father, sisters, and brothers. Suddenly the man whose house it was appeared in the room, climbed in the cot with her, and said he was going to rape her.

Her father wasn't home, so she called on her only other alternative for help: the little kids. They were in the kitchen, hitting each other with long, brown socks that they'd filled up with other socks, a silly, harmless game they called, for some reason, "bongos."

"Come on, kids, bring your bongos over here!" their big sister Achsah hollered, and they came charging into the bedroom to help, smashing her attacker over and over again in the face with a barrage of lumpy socks. He backed off and didn't bother her after that, but she never told her father what happened.

"What would you tell him, you know?" she said matter-of-factly. "I never told anybody."

Turned out it wasn't just strangers the Farrell girls had to worry about. One night Bill Farrell got in bed with Achsah. At first she didn't know what was going on. Then she realized his intentions, and slapped him away. He left without saying a word, and it never happened again. Achsah never told, until years later, as an old woman, when she told me.

A month after Achsah moved back in with her father, state authorities paid another visit to the family. This time they took the rest of the children, just as they had already done to Lee and Lena. Justification could have been any number of things; the law clearly stated that any parent whose kids had been neglected, gone hungry, or kept home from school could lose custody of those children, and Bill Farrell was clearly guilty on all of those counts.

"They said the old man wasn't a decent parent," Peanut remembered. "He liked his women and he liked to not stay home and take care of us kids but just run wild and run free."

Deen, just six years old, remembered a sheriff in the house, his gun drawn, putting her weeping father up against a wall while someone else escorted the children out. But Achsah remembered it as much more routine than that. There was no screaming, no histrionics, no resistance by the children; they simply went unquestioningly with the people who'd come to take them away. "When you've been through as many things as I'd been through, it was just another page in the book," she said.

Bill Farrell had known the day was coming when his children would be taken away; he'd been notified by mail of the exact date and time. And while Deen remembers him being put up against a wall by an officer, Achsah says he was nowhere to be found. Maybe it was because he just couldn't bear to see his children taken away, or maybe it was because he feared the legal consequences to himself. Either way, he'd also been informed that while state law could "divest the parent of all legal rights" regarding custody of their children, such action did "not relieve the parent or parents of liability for the support of such child." In other words, the state took Bill Farrell's kids away because he couldn't support them. But he remained financially responsible for them; he was now supposed to reimburse the state for whatever it was costing strangers to take care of them. And if he couldn't come up with the money, he would go to jail. Needless to say, he didn't have the money. And when the authorities finally caught up with him, a few weeks after the kids were taken away, they put him, at age fifty-one, in the county jail in Skowhegan.

"This was one smart move on the state's part, putting him in jail because he couldn't pay," Peanut said sarcastically. "You put anybody in jail, they can't pay anyway. They kept him there till that fall, I believe, and then they let him go. So he said to them, 'Hmm. You can go to hell.' And after that, when he got money, he flaunted it, he drank it, he did everything he could with it."

After the workers from the state removed them that winter's day in 1938, Achsah, Junior, and Frankie were sent to live with an old woman named Ida in Hartland, a small town with a couple of factories and restaurants surrounded by miles of farmland, woods, and lakes. The only connection they had to this place was a few miles down the road in Athens, where their mother had grown up, where the Farrells' first house had burned down, and where Lizzie Noyes was buried.

Peanut and Deen were sent to live on a farm with a family that already had six foster boys. All the children were expected to help out with the chores, even five-year-old Peanut, who was supposed to keep the oxen that hauled the hay carts from wandering away. "But if I got fidgety and walked around, the oxen were just dumb enough that they would follow me," she recalled. "They'd just rumble along, happy as a bunch of clams," and one of the farmhands would have to go bring them back.

Deen's memories are different. "We were abused something terrible there," she said. She was molested and beaten, she says, and believes her sister Peanut was too little to remember.

Years later, when Deen was living in Manhattan, one of the boys who had been a foster kid on the same farm wrote to her. "I don't know how he got my address," she said. "But I took that letter and I ripped it into a million pieces and I never answered him. All I could think was how I got abused by those other kids, and they let them do it."

Achsah was happy to go to school every day once she was living with Ida, and she was smart enough to catch up on all she'd missed like it was nothing. But Junior became increasingly unmanageable, and Ida eventually decided she didn't want him there anymore; he was placed with another family. Frankie, at four and a half years old, was the one who caught Ida's fancy; he could stand on his head, he was adorable, and he was as smart as Junior was slow. Ida thought it was cute to send Frankie on a little chore every day, across the road to fetch her mail. One day, nearly a year after they had been living with Ida, and a few minutes after Frankie went out to get the mail, someone came pounding on the door. It was a man, holding Frankie, limp and unconscious in his arms and making an awful noise every time he took a breath. The man had backed his truck up, never realizing Frank was standing there, and run him over. A doctor was summoned; he sped Frankie away in his car, but called that night to say that the cute little boy was dead.

"I guess Ida probably felt bad, but she never said anything," Aunt Achsah told me. "I'm sure she didn't intend for that to happen." And it never occurred to Achsah to hate her for it. "What good would it do?" she asked. "You just accepted it."

Bill Farrell was brought from jail for Frankie's funeral, and the boy whose birth had caused his mother's death was buried in the same cemetery in Athens where she'd been laid to rest not five years earlier. There was no money to buy markers for either one of them, but many years later, Deen bought a stone for Lizzie; her grave was easy to find because she'd been buried in a Noyes family plot. But Frankie was interred in a lot for the poor, the location lost forever, his grave unmarked for eternity.

With Frankie dead and Junior sent away, Achsah was the only one who remained with Ida. It wasn't awful by any means; Achsah was fed and sent to school and didn't have to care for a bunch of little kids the way she had when she was living with her dad. Still, there were the small humiliations of being a "state kid" that every foster child endured. Ida had a daughter of her own, and that girl got real toothpaste, but Achsah had to use baking soda because the state wouldn't pay for toothpaste for her. And she never knew what she'd be wearing; she just accepted what the social workers brought. Once she ended up with a gorgeous blue coat that was twice her size; but Ida made them take it back, and they replaced it with a coat made from an ugly rough weave known as "shit brindle." Many years later, as an adult, Achsah noticed an appeal in the newspaper for donations to the Salvation Army. She sent in twenty-five dollars and a note, telling the story about the ugly coat she'd received from welfare as a child, and expressing her hope that her check might be used to buy a nice pair of boots or jacket for a poor child somewhere. The newspaper printed her letter.

One night, while still in Ida's care, Achsah dreamed that she'd buried Ida and her daughter in the woodpile. "I didn't have any really bad feelings about them, but I never dared tell anybody, till long after I was grown-up, about that dream," she said. "I thought they would lock me up, say, 'This kid's crazy, we better put her away somewhere.' So I kept my mouth shut."

Deen and Peanut, meanwhile, left the farm with the oxen and the six boys when the farmer's wife took ill, and were sent to live in Pittsfield, not far from where Achsah was. Peanut and Deen called their new foster parents Aunt Kate and Uncle Mac; they stayed there for five years, and it was the closest thing the girls—who were too little to remember their mother—ever had to a normal family.

"Aunt Kate said that when she got us, we were string beans and we didn't dare take a second portion because we were used to being hungry all the time," Deen recalled. "But we didn't know it was okay to take another portion. They didn't hug us or put their arms around us, and they were very strict, but they didn't beat us up or abuse us, and they fed us and we had clean clothes. They treated us pretty good, but I had to learn later to show my personal affection."

When the girls came down with scarlet fever, the farm was quarantined; Aunt Kate and Uncle Mac milked their cows and dumped the milk. And when Deen got rheumatic fever, Kate kept her home from school for a year till she was strong enough to go.

When Bill Farrell got out of jail at the end of 1938, he began to follow the state and county fairs around from one end of Maine to the other, working as an itinerant blacksmith for the pony ride attractions and harness racers. The fairs would winter in Presque Isle, in the northern part of Maine, then head down to Cumberland Springs in the southwest, and come back through Scarborough, Skowhegan, Gorham, and other large towns in Central Maine. When he got near to where his kids were, he'd hitchhike from the fair to see them.

On one visit to Achsah, perhaps feeling flush from a good run of work at the races, he told her, "Let me buy you a new pair of shoes."

"Never mind," Achsah shot back. "The state took me; let them buy 'em."

Peanut was so young when all of this was happening that she can only remember one visit from her dad, and the details are foggy in her mind. "I didn't even remember what he looked like," she said. "I don't remember any conversation. I just remember a man being there in the house."

But Deen remembers him coming once each year, even though his hosts didn't make him feel very welcome.

"The poor guy, he came hungry, he left hungry," Deen said. "If I was a foster parent, I would tell the man, 'Have a nice rest with us.'

But Aunt Kate didn't think like that. She never offered to put him up or feed him anything. We were paid for by the state, so if someone came as a guest to see us, I don't think she put out a glass of water for them."

But once Aunt Kate did give Bill Farrell a small photo of Deen. The little girl had recently cut her face on a jagged wooden post, but didn't know what she looked like because there was no mirror in the house. When Bill Farrell showed her the picture and she saw the scar, she grabbed it and tore it into shreds. Years later, he wrote her a letter asking for a new photo. "Maybe now that you're grown up you'll give me a picture," he said. "Yours is the only one of all the kids I don't have. Do you remember, you tore it up before my face?"

Sometimes Achsah would ride a bike or get a lift over to visit her little sisters in Pittsfield, or she'd send them a treat in the mail, paid for from money earned picking vegetables or collecting firewood or doing other odd jobs.

"Dear Achsah used to send us for our birthdays little gifts," Deen said. "She sent me a beautiful jump rope, and a gorgeous Pinocchio book, where you opened it up and the whale pops up. I'll never forget that book."

Peanut got her nickname while living with Kate and Mac. "Nobody could pronounce my name—Leathene—and nobody could spell it and everybody hated it," she said. "I've been called lunkhead and Lithuanian and everything under the sun. They'll even say 'Leatherene.' How you get Leatherene out of Leathene, I don't know. But I was always the smaller one, and the shyer one. So Nadeen would go marching into school saying, 'I'm Nadeen, this is Leathene.' This is how the story went all my life. Half the time I couldn't even pronounce it. But the teachers wouldn't call me Peanut. And eventually I wouldn't even look at them; I'd look under the chair."

When Aunt Kate developed high blood pressure, a life-threatening disease in those days, the girls were sent to a series of other homes for short periods, until one day, sometime in the mid-1940s, when she was a young teenager, a man showed up in a suit and Deen was told, "This is the judge from Skowhegan. He's going to put you away."

Shortly after that, she recalled, "They put me in a car, took me to court like I was a criminal, and hauled me away to the Hallowell State School for Girls. They just took kids who didn't have parents, and when they got to be twelve and thirteen, they decided they were headed straight to trouble and told them they were bad kids, and put them there." At least she—like her sister Lee—would be spared the floor polishing that Lena had endured; the rheumatic fever had left her with a heart condition. Her only chore was to read aloud the schedules for the other girls' work assignments.

Those girls did not include her older sisters. By the time Deen arrived at the Hallowell School as a young teenager, Lee and Lena, by then young women, were long gone.

I sat in Deen's home not long ago, with my tape recorder and my notebook, and listened to her stories. As an adult, she has lived in many different places, but they are always filled with pretty things, lace curtains and chandeliers, mirrors and cut-glass candy jars, candlesticks and a music box with figures that spin like a merry-go-round. She's retired now from the real estate business, but many of these items came from a gift shop she once owned "so I could have dolls and musical carousels and bathe myself in all these things I couldn't have as a kid." Her fridge is always full of yummy food—fruit and roast chicken and salad—and the phone rings constantly with calls about the many organizations she's involved in—an alcohol treatment center, a disability rights group, a hospital board of directors, a campaign to reduce noise from local airports. A knock on the door brings in a neighbor's daughter to report that she did well on a school assignment Deen helped her with; a priest from a Catholic church she attends drops in to say hello.

Sometimes Deen still thinks about those rich people who came from out of state, who bought them new shoes and offered to adopt her. She thinks about the opportunity her dad passed up to let her go, and his desire to keep the kids together, not knowing they'd be split up soon enough.

"I've always asked myself, did my dad do me a favor by making me stay with my family and suffer the hardship and some of the things I went through?" she mused. "Did I come out of it better, did I enjoy my life better? Or would I have been better off if he had let me go?"

"Well," I said, after a moment, "which is it?"

"The truth?" she asked as she petted the white fur of her toy poodle, Winston, named for Winston Churchill. "I learned a great lesson coming from poor people. If we don't look out for people who have less, who are we? I think from that I gained a great perspective in life. It was tough. I was abused along the way. But I think I used that abuse and turned that around."

She tells me a story I have heard before, that when she joined a group called the Toastmasters, which helps people become better public speakers, she was asked to give a talk about her life.

"I told them we started in a rural area, how we had outhouses, no flush toilets; we read by kerosene lamps and had to clean the black soot off the glass chimneys; I told them everything," she said. "And when the evaluator got up to discuss my presentation and how I'd done, she started to cry. I got up and put my arm around her and said, 'I didn't even tell you the worst! I didn't tell you this to make you cry.' "

"Why *did* you tell her?" I asked.

"I told her," my aunt replied, "so she could be happy for me that I got to where I got."

In later life, Aunt Deen changed her name to Nancy. It's hard for me to call her that; I'm not trying to be mean about it, but I forget, I stutter, I can hardly bring myself to do it, even though she's told me so many times that she hates the name she was born with because it brings her back to all the awful things she went through as a kid. But Nancy is my sister's name, after all; it's not the name I grew up calling my aunt, and it's not the name I have on the tip of my tongue when I think of her or see her. All this makes it even more amazing to me that my aunts always called my mother by her new name, even though in their childhood memories, she was always Lena.

5
BECOMING ANNE

LEFT: *Lena, in Maine.*
RIGHT: *Anne, in New York.*

Under state law, any girl sent to the Hallowell School could be "entrusted to the care of any suitable person and may be required to work for such person." In practice, this meant that many of the girls, once they turned fifteen or sixteen, were boarded out to families who used them as housekeepers, farmworkers, or babysitters. As with any such system, the conditions the girls experienced in these placements varied tremendously. Lee remembered being treated "like a slave in the attic" by the family that she went to live with; and with the country gearing up for World War II, she knew there were better opportunities

than cleaning someone else's house. She got training in electrical weld-
ing, and she was hired by Bath Ironworks to help build ships and sub-
marines. "Half the women my age did it; it was nothing," she said.

Lena, meanwhile, at age sixteen, was sent to live with the family of
a high school principal in a town on the southeast coast of Maine. She'd
lived all her life in the towns of Central Maine, with their vast lakes,
rocky rivers, and evergreen woods, the farmland dotted with cows and
divided into neat rows of tall corn, and the endless ribbons of country
road interrupted only by an occasional Main Street or Four Corners
with a tanning factory, church, or general store. So the scenery and
lifestyle of a coastal community must have seemed very different to
her, with scrubby pine trees jutting out from stark cliffs along an ocean
so cold and rough that only the hardiest souls dared swim in it, and bald
eagles and seals such common sights that the locals didn't even notice.
She loved to stop and smell the pink rose of Sharon that grew abun-
dantly wild near the ocean shore here, and she liked the sight of the
little lobster boats bobbing offshore each day as the fishermen baited
and checked the traps marked by colored buoys. Elsewhere, of course,
lobster was regarded as a luxury, but here it was so plentiful that according to local legend, indentured servants in colonial times organized
to demand that their employers feed them lobster no more than three
times a week. But Lena quickly learned to love lobster, and how to
cook it, and she gladly picked the shells clean. She even ate the parts
that others left on their plates, sucking the morsels from the spindly red
knuckles and eating the green tomalley, which most people—assuming
that the liver of a creature that fed on dead animals was toxic—wouldn't
touch.

Lena's duties in the principal's home included caring for a mentally
retarded youngster. Perhaps because she'd grown up with Bill Jr., Lena
had no qualms relating to the child. She socialized him, calmed him,
and taught him to feed himself; the family saw this as miraculous, akin
to Annie Sullivan's taming of Helen Keller. And Lena did well at the
local high school, joining the debating team and earning praise for her
writing. She even won a poetry prize, but the principal insisted the
award be taken away from her and given to someone else. He told her

it wouldn't look right if a student living in his house won a contest at the school.

At night the house was so cold and her bedding so threadbare that she used to light a candle and huddle with her head under the blanket in a feeble effort to feel warm. The candle burned a hole in the spread, and when it was discovered, her meager stipend was docked for weeks to come until the blanket had been deemed paid for. Whatever miracles she had wrought with the retarded child had not earned her any margin for error.

When the school year was over, she left, returning to Central Maine to take a position in Augusta, the state capital, not far from the Hallowell School. She moved into the grand State Street home of Judge Robert Cony, whose family had been serving as jurists and lawmakers in New England since colonial days. The governor's mansion was nearby, along with the domed state capitol building, state offices and courts, and the Conys knew all the players in Maine's political establishment through the judge's long career in public life.

A graduate of Bowdoin, Maine's finest college, Robert Cony started out as a reporter and linotype operator at the local paper, the *Kennebec Journal*. He got a law degree from Georgetown University and decided to stay on in Washington to work for the *Kennebec Journal*'s owner, Edwin Burleigh, a U.S. senator who had previously been governor of Maine. After years as Burleigh's assistant, Cony entered politics himself, and he was elected mayor of Augusta and later a state senator in Maine. He was also vice president of a local bank, and his attainment of a judgeship in Superior Court at age sixty-four, right around the time Lena came to live in his home, was considered a well-deserved honor by his admirers.

The judge looked like he'd walked right out of one of the dusty old town-father portraits that hang anonymously and indistinguishably on the walls of every City Hall in America: white-haired, pink-skinned, fleshy-faced, solemn gaze, dark suit. His distinguished ancestors included Nathanael Cony, who arrived in Massachusetts from England in the late 1600s; Daniel Cony, who served as a judge and one of the electors who chose George Washington for a second term; and Samuel Cony, elected

governor of Maine for three terms in the Civil War era. While living
with the judge and his wife, Louise, Lena attended nearby Cony High
School, a public institution that had been founded and originally en-
dowed in the early 1800s by Daniel Cony.

Louise Cony, who was nicknamed Boo, came from far humbler circumstances than her husband. Born in New Brunswick, Canada, she
worked in a bank and in the state library, near the courts and government offices, until she and Robert Cony met. They were married for
thirty years, until his death, but had no children.

Mrs. Cony, a tall, large-boned woman and one of the original blue-
haired ladies, was a combination of a pragmatic Yankee and a proper
New England lady of the upper class she'd married into. Oh, she'd put
on a nice wool dress or a skirt-suit with her pearls when the ladies came
for tea, but she also wore tennis shoes and slacks around the house.
They were neat, white slacks, with a crisp crease down the middle, but
they were slacks nonetheless.

In return for her room and board, Lena was expected to help Mrs.
Cony around the house. Mrs. Cony had a very busy social life, and she
was often called upon to entertain the fine ladies of Augusta society,
the wives of lawyers and businessmen and politicians who frequently
arrived at her home for lunch or tea or a late-afternoon game of bridge.
So before Lena left for Cony High each morning, she had a long list
of chores to do to get the three-story house with its stately columns
ready for whoever might drop by. She had to wash the sixty-odd windows, clean the floors, polish the silver, and make the finger sandwiches
if company was expected for lunch or tea.

Lena was also taught to play bridge, in case one of the ladies should
cancel and a fourth player was needed to fill in at the card table for a
late-afternoon game. But a funny thing happened when Lena joined
these games. The more she played (speaking only when required to, of
course), the more she realized something. These sophisticated women,
with their department-store dresses and impeccable manners and expensive taste and lovely hairdos and perfect grammar and fine New England
accents, were all cutthroats at cards, and they cheated whenever they
possibly could. Cheated at a silly game of cards, with nothing at stake,

in games with their supposed friends and fellow travelers in the state's highest social circles! Lena was appalled, even sickened, by this realization. And once Lena left the Cony house, she never, ever played cards, or any other game, again.

Despite the cheating at cards and the white-glove standards for housework that required her to rise at dawn, Lena grew to love and admire the judge and his wife. And the Conys saw in this rough country girl with no family to speak of the potential for a fine young woman. Under Mrs. Cony's tutelage, Lena learned that real Wedgwood was spelled without an *e,* and Limoges was pronounced with a silent *s;* that refined people didn't have a lot of children, or talk about bodily functions, or curse, except when they were so justifiably angry that a "damn" or a "hell" was warranted; that a proper Sunday dinner consisted of rare roast beef, with the juice served in a gravy boat as an accompaniment to baked potatoes; and that sherry was what ladies drank in the afternoon, while rosé wine went with a meal.

Living with the Conys transformed the way Lena saw herself, and the way she saw the world. When Lena thought about how her family had come apart—the kids hungry, their home destroyed by flood and fire, their reputations ruined by gossip about Bill's drinking and her own running around, their lack of basic necessities so evident that total strangers bought the children shoes and other families let them move in for months at a time, the negligence so pervasive that finally the state had to swoop in and break them up and put her father in jail—it made her head spin. And now that she had seen how genteel people lived, she realized even more clearly how utterly desperate and squalid her own family life had been. Because even when her mother Lizzie had been there to keep order in the household and maintain a veneer of respectability, they had still grown up as outsiders. No matter how well Lizzie managed to make do, they were poor, and there was always someone looking down on them—whether it was for their grain-bag dresses or the gladiolas in their yard or their French-speaking Catholic father with the Irish name, the one who named his son after a Democrat president most of Maine despised. Judge Cony was the opposite of all that: a Republican, an Episcopalian, and a Yankee with a pedigree that went back generations, and yet, a man who could also rightly claim that his many accomplishments were due not just to his birthright, but also to his hard work and intelligence. "Judge Cony did not rely on his prominent ancestors for his successes," one admirer said. "He created them rather than inherited them."

In the Conys' elegant home, as she polished the silver and wiped the many-paned windows, Lena saw firsthand the rewards of a work ethic. She never wanted her own life to be hand to mouth again. She wanted to live like the rest of America, with all the modern conveniences that the mid-twentieth century had to offer—flush toilets and nice clothes and water that came pouring out of the faucet and heat without chopping wood. Louise Cony had beautiful teacups and beautiful handwriting and even a kiln for making pottery—not for any practical purpose, but just to make something beautiful, for self-satisfaction, for fun. Lena wanted a life like that, with pretty things and vacations and hobbies; she wanted to become a different person, and shed the traces of her former self.

And even as Mrs. Cony demanded perfection from the girl who turned down the bed covers just so and trimmed the crusts off the sandwich bread, she must have detected a spark of something that made her want to play Pygmalion. Perhaps Mrs. Cony sensed that no matter how well Lena carried out the tasks she was assigned, she also resented her station in life and yearned for something more. Or perhaps she recognized that in this girl's appreciation for antiques and china, for flower arranging and poetry and paintings, she had an instinctive good taste that would surely grow if cultivated. Especially since she had no children, Mrs. Cony couldn't help but take the teenager under her wing. In the end, the judge's wife treated Lena not just as the latest in a series of student-houseworkers from the Hallowell School, but as a sort of protegé, and a potential friend.

Lena graduated from Cony High School, and with the Conys' support, she enrolled in business school, where she learned typing, shorthand, and dictation, skills that would enable her to support herself without slinging hash or working on the assembly lines where so many women were taking jobs to replace the men gone off to war. Judge Cony then hired his wife's former maid as his own secretary, and when she announced her desire to change her name, he was more than happy to make it legal for her. She hated with a passion the "Leapin' Lena" taunt that echoed in her head; originally, she told her sisters, it referred to a character from a comic strip, but with the advent of the war, it was also the nickname for an army Jeep. She knew, of course, that it was a family name, the name of Bill Farrell's mother, her paternal grandmother, Lena Michaud, but her grandmother died before she was born, and she had never even seen a picture of her, so it meant little to her. Besides, it was also true, though she never acknowledged it, that Lena was a common name among French Canadians, an identifying tattoo that was obvious to anyone in Maine who cared enough to have an opinion about family origins. Her middle name was Angie, printed just that way on her birth certificate, as a nickname for a full name she had never known. But now, at age eighteen, while still living under the Conys' roof, she traded them both in for one name: Anne, with an *e,* a proper-sounding Yankee name, a name the Pilgrims brought with them, a name of English royals. And once Judge Cony made it official, Anne Farrell wrote to her sisters and father, informing them that from now on, she was never to be called Lena again.

"Dumb kid that I was, I wrote back and put 'Lena Farrell' on the letter," Achsah recalled with a laugh. "She wrote me in no uncertain terms that her name was not Lena anymore. I didn't make that mistake again. It was hard at first but I got used to it."

Anne Farrell moved out of the small room she had lived in in the Conys' home and got an apartment of her own in Augusta. She worked for Judge Cony until 1942, then was hired by the Augusta Draft Board, no doubt with her patron's kind help. Occasionally the men who decided which Maine boys would go to war had meetings or appointments or correspondence, but many a day she was in the office by herself, answering the phone, taking care of the mail, and maintaining the files. The pay was decent and steady and it was not unpleasant work, and besides, she had someone to go home to now: a boyfriend named Ruel, pronounced, not in accordance with its unusual spelling, Roo-ell, or like the conventional name Raoul, but simply, in that obstinate way that Mainers have of coming up with their own variations on the English language, like the word *rule*. Ruel worked as a court reporter, transcribing the proceedings in the courthouse where Anne had worked for Judge Cony. He had thick glasses and was more than twenty years older than she; she called him "my poppa." But he was anything but a fuddy-dudd. In his spare time, he flew a yellow-and-black Piper Cub—a tiny, easy-to-fly plane that had become all the rage with the country-club set since its introduction in 1938. He liked fine wine and nice clothes, and he was an avid photographer, particular about arranging the backdrops and lighting and composition before he would snap a photo with his Brownie camera. He performed with an amateur acting troupe, the Augusta Players, and he liked to ski, a sport that was just becoming mainstream. Its popularity was fueled by the Civilian Conservation Corps' construction of ski trails in Maine and elsewhere, and the sudden arrival in America of European war refugees who had skied in the Alps all their lives and could easily teach the sport to make a living. Anne had used snowshoes as a child to get to school on bad winter days, but before long, she was skiing with Ruel. She took flying lessons, too, becoming the youngest woman in Maine to earn a pilot's license, and she joined the Civil Air Patrol, in which citizen volunteers scouted the coast for the enemy subs that at the start of the war were sinking American ships in devastating numbers. She even helped Ruel's acting troupe out as stage manager, and she developed a lifelong habit, learned from her photographer-boyfriend, of making sure the sun was shining over her shoulder and a tree was in the background any time she took a photograph.

Because the Conys were active in politics, Anne also became acquainted with an up-and-coming Republican congresswoman, Margaret Chase Smith, who had replaced her husband in Congress when he died in 1940, becoming one of just seven women in the House of Representatives at that time. Women had been allowed to vote only since 1920, but by 1940 they already made up nearly two-thirds of Maine's registered voters, fueling an interest among women in political affairs that in other states remained the domain of men for generations to come. Women's organizations in Maine, from auxiliary groups to the DAR, sponsored political forums and discussions, and Mrs. Smith never forgot her female volunteers. They staffed her campaigns on shoestring budgets and built the base that enabled her to become the first woman elected to the U.S. Senate in her own right when she ran in 1948.

Anne was very impressed by this slender, silver-haired woman, tough and smart but charming and genteel, with her pearls and ever-present rose in her lapel. "I guess she is about the very nicest person we know and certainly the most prominent," Mrs. Cony wrote Anne in a letter when the senator became the first woman to run for president on a major party line, in 1964. Anne, by then living in New York, in turn wrote her own letter to the senator encouraging her in her pioneering political quest to challenge Goldwater and Nixon for the Republican nomination.

Senator Smith's skill at making average people feel important was very much in evidence in the letter she wrote back to Anne. "I am truly pleased," she said, "that you even remember me!"

"You are the most gracious person I ever met, and so kind to me when I was working my way through school," Anne responded. "How could I ever forget you?"

The admiration was apparently mutual. "I know she told me once that Margaret Chase Smith asked her if she wanted to come to Washington, D.C. and work for her," Achsah said. "But of course she never went."

Still, when she registered to vote, in the mid-1940s, Anne became a Republican. It was the party of the Conys, of Margaret Chase Smith, and of Maine's Yankee establishment, a world she had glimpsed from the kitchen where she prepared the sandwiches for Aunt Boo's teas. The Democrats—who ended Prohibition and brought the country out of the Depression, the party of Maine's Catholics and French Canadians, and the party whose leader, FDR, inspired the name of her little brother, now dead—held no appeal for Anne. She remained a staunch Republican till the day she died.

From the time she entered the Hallowell School in 1937, and for literally decades after, Anne thought often about her little sisters. Not Lee so much, who was just seventeen months younger than she and could take care of herself, but Achsah, Nadeen, and Peanut. At first, Anne, who was eleven when her mother died, and Lee, who was nine, had naturally assumed most of the burdens of taking care of the little ones. "She'd get Nadeen ready, and I'd get Peanut ready, and we'd both help Achsah and Junior," Lee recalled. "Then Anne would get the baby ready, and we could go out."

But once Anne became a teenager, with the cupboard in Mechanic Falls increasingly bare and her own ambivalence about whether she'd rather have her father at home every night or not, she began to stay away herself. She found friends and other families who were willing to take her in, and she spent less and less time with her sisters and brothers. If she felt any pull of responsibility as the oldest, she buried it. Maybe it was selfish; maybe it was survival. But by the time Anne was fourteen, she was rarely home to help out, and Achsah, then eight, had taken over many of the duties that were originally hers. Not long after came the flood, and then the fire, and then there was no home for Anne to return to even if she had wanted.

Alone in her bed at night at the Hallowell School after a long day of chores and following all the rules, Anne had plenty of time to think—too much time, in fact. She knew she had not been a good older sister. She had abandoned those three little girls, just as their mother had abandoned all of them. She felt guilty; she was guilty. There was only so much she could do for them while she was still in the Hallowell School, but she resolved to do something. Perhaps an encouraging letter and a small present might make a difference to the girls; perhaps she could make up to them some of what they'd lost.

"She just took over the motherhood job near as I could figure out," Peanut said. "She made sure she knew where we were, sending us a letter every week, keeping in contact with people we lived with and making sure we got a Christmas present every year. I know she couldn't afford anything expensive. But she would send us a shoebox with aluminum foil or tissue paper inside, and in it there'd be popcorn and candy and a couple of trinkets, like a roll of fifty pennies."

And even though Peanut barely remembered her father by the time her childhood was over, "from the time I was a teenager, Anne got me to start writing him letters."

One day after Anne had moved into her own apartment and was working for the Draft Board, but not long before the war wound down, Achsah showed up on her doorstep in Augusta with a problem that couldn't be solved by writing a letter or buying candy. She was pregnant. Of course this sort of thing happened all the time; people like to pretend that teenage pregnancy only became a problem recently, but in fact even in small towns in Maine it was quite common decades ago. Maternal mortality records throughout the first half of the twentieth century routinely list abortion—even though it was illegal—as one of the top causes of death among pregnant women. And both Anne and her sister knew lots of girls who'd married young to the wrong guy because they were pregnant, or who'd given hidden babies away to be raised by other relatives as their own, even though half the people in town knew who the real mother was.

Given the alternatives, Achsah wanted to try to end the pregnancy. And Anne happened to know a doctor who she thought could help. She took her sister to see him, but when they explained the situation, he cut them off.

"I don't do that kind of thing," he said.

Anne wasn't so easily turned away. "Well, I know you did it for someone else," she said, naming a woman who she'd heard had been to see him.

The doctor seemed surprised. He thought it over for a moment and finally said, "I can give you a shot. Maybe that will help. But that's all I'll do."

The shot did the trick. Achsah miscarried and she recovered just fine. Years later, after her own daughters were born, Anne wrote in a letter to her sister that "having an abortion was worse than having a baby." But if she knew that from her own experience of getting rid of an unwanted pregnancy, she never told.

. . .

Achsah managed to avoid getting herself sent to the Hallowell School by doing well in school and working as many jobs as she could handle—everything from delivering newspapers and picking vegetables to working in restaurants and factories. She also always managed to find someone who'd take her in. When Ida moved to another town, Achsah figured out a way to stay in Hartland by boarding with a woman named Pauline who had a daughter her age. At night after supper, Pauline would turn on the radio while they washed dishes. Pauline washed and Achsah dried, and they had a running joke: if Achsah found a little speck on a fork, she'd say, good-naturedly, "You didn't get this clean!" And Pauline would respond, "It's a poor wiper can't wipe it off, Axie!" If there was a song they liked, they'd put down the washrag and towel and dance together in the kitchen. It wasn't the same as having a mother and father who loved you, but Achsah knew things could be a lot worse.

Then, right before her senior year of high school, she wrote to Anne in Augusta and asked if she could stay with her for a while. It turned out that Anne spent nearly all her time at Ruel's apartment and was happy to have Achsah stay in her place. So Achsah went to school that fall in Augusta, worked afternoons and evenings in a restaurant, and lived at her sister's place, a nice one-bedroom near the state capitol that most of the time she had to herself.

"Maybe one night a month Anne would get pissed off at Ruel and come up there and stay in her own apartment," Achsah said. "But the bedroom was hers; I didn't sleep in the bedroom. I slept on a bedroll on the couch in the living room. In the morning I'd put the bedroll away in her closet, and at night I'd get it out before I was ready to go to bed."

Early one Sunday morning, Achsah woke up sick from something she'd eaten. It happened to be a night that Anne had stayed in the apartment. When she saw her sister throwing up, Anne told her to get in her bed, where she'd be more comfortable than on the sofa. Achsah did, and soon fell asleep. A few hours later Anne woke her up. She'd made her chicken and mashed potatoes and stuffing. It was the kind of food Achsah loved, but it wasn't what she felt like having then.

"I'm too sick, I can't eat that," she protested.

Anne fumed for a moment, and felt a rage boiling up inside her. She'd taken her sister under her wing, given her a bed to sleep in, gone to all this trouble to cook for her, and now she wouldn't eat it!

"Goddamn you," she finally screamed. "Goddamn you, you eat that!"

Achsah couldn't refuse the order now, and she forced herself to chew and swallow what was on the plate. And to her surprise, she started to feel better. "It was a good thing she did make me eat it, because I went to school every day and I went to work every afternoon, and I needed the nourishment," she said.

One day when Achsah was in the apartment, Ruel dropped by. Achsah had met him before she moved in with Anne; all the sisters knew him because he often drove Anne to visit them on weekends, in his coupe with the rumble seat. On this particular day, though, running into Achsah at Anne's place, he told his girlfriend's seventeen-year-old sister that he kept a bottle of wine in the apartment that was a certain special vintage, and he said he'd be happy to open it so Achsah could try it. She declined, but mentioned the incident later to her sister. "I've been trying to get him to open that bottle of wine for a long time," Anne told her. "He wouldn't open it for me."

When the fall semester was over, Achsah went back to finish her senior year at Hartland High, the town that had come to feel like home to her, even though no one from her family lived there. She got a job manning the town telephone switchboard and proudly graduated that June with a ninety-three average, even though her semester in Augusta had disrupted the year for her. A couple of people around town who knew that Achsah was on her own stopped her in the street when she graduated and gave her cards of congratulations with a couple of bucks inside. One person who'd loaned her thirty dollars so she could get her graduation picture taken refused to take the money back when she went to repay it. "I'm sure you need it more than I do," he told her.

But her own father had different ideas. To her surprise, at the last minute, Bill Farrell showed up at the graduation with Lee, who was married now. Achsah had already given away her reserve tickets to someone else, so her family ended up watching her get her diploma from seats in the balcony where the ceremony was held. And afterward, her father came up to the room where she was staying and asked Achsah to pay him back twenty dollars she had borrowed from him somewhere along the way.

"I'm not saying anything bad about my father and I'm sure my dad really needed the money," she said, "but there were people in Hartland who treated me better than my own relatives."

Six months after graduation, Achsah married a young man she'd been dating for a while. She wrote Anne that she planned to get a credit account at a store so she could buy some items to set up housekeeping. A few days later a box arrived from Anne. She had sent her little sister, now a married woman, a lamp, towels, and a mirror. And when Peanut married a few years later, Anne sent her the money for a new skirt, blouse, shoes, and a permanent.

Just as the letters that Lena Farrell sent her sisters had all of a sudden turned into letters from Anne Farrell, the envelopes she sent weekly from Augusta all of a sudden turned into envelopes postmarked "New York." The war was over and the Draft Board was closing down, so her job in Augusta would soon be eliminated, she wrote to her sisters. She offered no explanation of what had become of her relationship with Ruel; perhaps it went without saying that he just wasn't the marrying type. Also unstated in her letters to her sisters was the fact that it wasn't as easy for her to get a job now in Augusta. Soldiers coming home were taking back the jobs women had filled in their absence, and Judge Cony had died from a heart attack on the first of January in 1945, so Anne no longer had the benefit of his patronage. Still, she was grateful for what the judge and his wife had done for her. His obituary appeared on the front page of the *Kennebec Journal* on the second of January with a headline bigger than the one atop the story in the next column, which announced that the Germans were staging a massive offensive against Allied troops. But it wasn't the size of the typeface that caught Anne's eye; it was the description of his "human kindness" and the line quoted in the obituary from one of his eulogies, a line she vaguely recognized from a poem she'd read in school: "Truly he lived in a house by the side of the road, and was a friend to man."

But while the front-page news about the war in Europe will be remembered forever as the Battle of the Bulge, the Conys were soon forgotten—not by Anne Farrell, but by the city where they lived and entertained and owned the finest house around. By the 1970s, the property, sold when Mrs. Cony remarried and moved, had fallen into disrepair. When it was renovated for use as offices, the garden was turned into a parking lot. Still, this three-story mansion with the columns and all those windows didn't quite fit in to what State Street had become— another unremarkable street in a small American city, with car dealerships and restaurants and signs to the highway leading somewhere else, and hardly a pedestrian to be seen. The developer had a feeling there was something special about this place, and he'd hoped to get enough information to install a historical marker on the building; those sorts of things always enhance property values. But the name on the original deed, Robert Cony, didn't mean much to anyone by then; too many generations and too many newcomers had gone by to recognize the history of the fine old Cony name.

I got a letter from Anne," her father William Farrell wrote to Achsah in February of 1947. "She has found a place to stay at last, she says she is lonesome and misses her Big Coon cat and her man Ruel. I only hope she makes good. She had lots of Courage to Strike out all alone for the Big City don't you think so? She will be writing to you soon."

When Anne wrote to Achsah and her other sisters, she sent glamorous photos of herself and said that she hoped to become a model. Before she'd left Maine, Ruel had taken some formal pictures of her made up with dark lipstick, her auburn hair pulled back or swept up; she looked sweet in all these photos, but also a little bit like Judy Garland in *The Wizard of Oz*. The new photos, taken professionally in a studio against a white backdrop, were different. In one of these, she was wearing tailored clothes, cinched at the waist, with shoulder pads and platform shoes, her hair parted on the side and cascading in shimmering waves across her face, like a brunette Veronica Lake; in others, she wore a black evening gown and long gloves and averted her eyes from the camera, looking off into the distance with an aloof, regal gaze. The country bumpkin playing dress-up, staring lovingly at the camera and the person taking the picture, was gone.

Shortly after Achsah's first child was born, Anne took the train from New York to Hartford, Connecticut, where Achsah lived briefly in the late 1940s, to pay a quick visit to her newborn nephew, the first child to be born to any of her sisters. "Anne had always been neat and clean and trim and had nice clothes, but she had learned a different way to arrange her hair," Achsah recalled. "Before, you'd say, 'Yes, she's an attractive young woman,' but you didn't realize how attractive she was until she had this different hairdo. Now she really was beautiful."

But after a few small jobs and photo sessions at fashion schools and studios, Anne saw that it wasn't going to be so easy to make it big in New York. Sure, she could turn heads on the street, another pretty girl getting whistles, but she was all alone and needed a steady paycheck to support herself. She decided to seek government work yet again; she bet rightly that even without Judge Cony as a reference, her experience and clerical skills would make it easy to get a job in New York. She put together a résumé, neatly omitting her years at the Hallowell School by stitching her education in Mechanic Falls to the school on the coast where she lived with the principal's family and had been denied the poetry prize. (She never mentioned the Hallowell School to her daughters either; we only found out about it after she died.) On the application to take the federal civil service exam, she gave Ruel and Mrs. Cony as her references. And in the section of the form marked "father's occupation and present employer," she wrote, "not known." An itinerant blacksmith's whereabouts were anybody's guess and nobody's business.

Anne was hired as a clerk by the War Department on Governor's Island, a military base located in the middle of New York Harbor. Every day from her room in a residential hotel on the East Side, she took the subway down to the tip of Manhattan and then a ferry past the Statue of Liberty and the Brooklyn Bridge. Manhattan in the postwar years was a thrilling place to be, safer and cleaner than she'd imagined a big city might look like, the people so beautifully dressed, so fast in their walk and their talk, so funny, so smart, so sophisticated about the world. Yellow taxis zoomed around, an airplane was always visible above, and the Empire State Building and sleek, slate skyscrapers of Rockefeller Center could be seen from almost anywhere except the wicker seats on the subway. The United Nations was under construction and rundown tenements were being demolished all over town to make way for modern elevator buildings. Yet the city also had small-town touches: the ragman with a horse-drawn cart, the milkman trudging up and down stairs each dawn to leave his glass bottles with the pleated paper tops, the friendly shopkeepers—florists, butchers, pharmacists, bakers—who knew their regular customers by name.

Of course not everything was wonderful. There were coldwater flats, and drunken bums, and the noise from the elevated trains; incinerators and coal boilers belched black smoke into the already acrid air. In summer, there was no relief; the concrete got so hot baking all day in the sun that at night the heat seemed to pulse back out from the ground. And in winter, she couldn't even guess if it was raining or snowing or clear by looking out her tiny, grimy windows overlooking a dark alley; she got in the habit of running downstairs and stepping outside the building to check the weather.

But all in all, it was better than the backwoods of Maine, with its stinking outhouses and mill towns and hungry, raggedy children, and she was certain she'd never look back. It wasn't enough to have changed her name and gotten a place of her own in Augusta; she needed to get away entirely to have the new life she imagined. Like so many other New Yorkers, she had come here from somewhere else to *be* someone else. It was supposed to be as simple as that.

I have often thought about reversing the journey my mother took. I have always spent my summer vacations in Maine, carrying on, as an adult with my own family, the tradition I began with my parents when

I was small. And there was a time, some years ago, when my husband and I thought that maybe we should make Maine our permanent home.

Our summer house isn't suitable for year-round living; even in August, the fragile plumbing chugs and roars and burps as water is pumped from a well into the house and then back out again, up a hill to a leaching field. There's no doubt that the pipes would simply explode if used past October, when the ground begins to freeze. My sister has even posted signs in the bathroom, for the benefit of urban guests who might otherwise be tempted to use the flush as a garbage disposal: "THIS IS NOT A NEW YORK CITY TOILET!"

So when we toyed with the idea of settling in Maine, we knew we'd need to find another house, and jobs, and a part of the state that wasn't so remote that we'd go nuts. We looked at the want ads and the real estate ads, and saw right away that we could buy a much bigger, nicer home for far less money than anything we could ever dream of having in New York. In Brooklyn, I have a tiny backyard, the size of a postage stamp; so little storage space that I hate to buy more than two boxes of cereal at a time; and a desk in the living room where I write books, two steps from the table where we eat dinner and three steps from the sofa where the kids watch TV and play video games. And I know plenty of families who live in far smaller apartments than ours.

But in Maine, for a fraction of the price of my co-op, I could buy a big, beautiful, old-fashioned house, on an acre of land, just about anywhere. The job market was not quite as inviting; there were not as many options for a journalist like me and a lawyer like my husband in Maine as there are in New York. But in the end that probably wasn't the deciding factor. There was something else, something almost intangible, that told me this just wouldn't work. Maybe we are addicted, to some extent, to the noise and the hassles of urban life; maybe we secretly like the fact that our mornings are ruled by the *New York Times,* that we can't leave the house till we've read it. And then there's the matter of takeout Thai food, a staple in our New York household, the crutch for nights when the kids are sick of pasta and I'm too busy to make anything else. I couldn't live in Maine year-round, I used to joke, because I couldn't live without chicken saté and pad thai noodles.

Then one night on our last trip to Maine, my husband went shopping in Waterville, a college town of about fifteen thousand that is the nearest thing to a city we have within a half-hour's drive of our little lake. And when he got back, our old Toyota was filled with the unmistakable fragrance of basil, chili, and lemon grass. In the course of doing his errands, he had found take-out Thai food, and the bag he'd brought home was still warm despite the drive on I-95 and a half-dozen country roads. We gobbled it up, and although our vacation was nearly over, we went back to the restaurant the next day for more, instructing the waiter to tell the chef we were seasoned Thai food lovers who wanted our order as spicy as he could make it. I selfishly begged the owners to please tough out the long Maine winter and stay in business till the following summer when we could return for more.

So now my last excuse is gone. I can get my Thai food in Maine, and yet I still spend eleven months a year in New York. Sometimes, when I have circled our block in Brooklyn for the fifteenth time looking for a parking place, it does seem like it would be a lot easier to live somewhere else. But at the end of the day, inconvenience is just not a strong enough reason to abandon the place you grew up, even if the alternative is a place you love as much as I love Maine. My mother was looking for something a lot more profound than a cheap house or a place to park the car when she moved to New York, and it would take a lot more than that to get me to move to Maine. She was reinventing her life; I'm just looking to simplify mine.

After getting back to Manhattan from her job on Governor's Island, Anne would sometimes stop in a bar and have a Remy Martin. Sometimes someone sitting nearby would pick up her tab, and that was all right too if the person seemed like a gentleman. One evening she brought a bag of popcorn with her, and as she sat there sipping her drink and tossing the kernels into her mouth, she heard a friendly voice call in her direction.

"Hey, stingy!" the man said. "You gonna eat that popcorn all by yourself?"

She turned around and smiled. The speaker was a handsome soldier with big blue eyes and a cocky grin, older than she, with a neatly creased army cap atop his shaven head, a lapel covered with medals, and his right arm in a Statue of Liberty cast, pointing straight up to the ceiling.

There was no fly on the wall recording what happened next, but it's probably safe to assume that it went something like this. All charm and poise, she no doubt asked what happened to his arm, and he must have explained that he had a run-in with a bullet in Belgium in January of '45, the encounter that came to be known as the Battle of the Bulge. Something clicked in Anne's memory; she vaguely recalled a story about that phase of the war on the front page of the paper she had saved bearing Judge Cony's obituary.

The soldier gave his name—Dave. To show that he wasn't a total cripple, he probably pulled out a cigarette, popped it in his mouth, and deftly lit a match from a matchbook with his good hand, opening the cover, folding the match backward with his thumb, and striking it on the strip, making the flame in one smooth motion. He touched the light to his own cigarette, then offered one to her, which she accepted.

By then he'd likely noticed her Yankee accent, and without too much probing, he discovered she was from Maine. A few more minutes and she found out that he was working for the army's public relations department, traveling around the country giving interviews to radio stations and newspapers and giving speeches at Knights of Columbus meetings. He sold war bonds at these events, while discussing his own experiences in battle and promoting the army's new efforts to physically rehabilitate wounded veterans like himself. And no doubt he learned that she was working for the War Department, and was as interested in hearing his stories about Europe as he was eager to tell them.

Before long, another series of letters had been sent to Anne's sisters. She had married, on the Fourth of July, was expecting a child, and had quit her job.

Aunt Lee laughs as she reminisces to me about my mother visiting her in Connecticut with my sister, shortly after Nancy was born in February of 1949, at eight and a half pounds. "She tried to get the doctor to write on the birth certificate that the baby was premature," she says. "But he wouldn't do it."

I had flown down earlier that day from New York to visit Lee in the retirement community where she lives in a warm place, far from Maine's winters. The last time I'd seen her, nearly twenty years before, was at my mother's funeral. She was so sweet that day, so calm and charming, nicely dressed, her lipstick perfect, her chatter and smiles a welcome distraction from thinking about what had happened. It would have been awful if she'd cried and carried on; we were so stunned, my sister and my father and I, by how fast my mother had died that we hadn't yet gotten to the point where we could mourn, and we wouldn't have known what to do if someone else had started crying.

For some reason it never occurred to us that the people who attended the funeral might want to come back to my father's apartment afterward, so we hadn't bothered to get any food, and when Aunt Lee returned with us, there was literally nothing to eat but a package of sliced cheese. I remember pulling the yellow squares apart, one by one, prying the paper dividers off and solemnly handing them out—one for me, one for my sister, and one for Aunt Lee, as if they were the last edible morsels in the city of New York.

My mother had always kept in touch with all her sisters, but after she died, I lost track of Lee. Aunt Peanut gave me her address when I started trying to find out more about my mother's life, but Lee later told me that when she got my letter, she was afraid to open it—afraid that something awful might have happened to Nancy or me. Why else would I be writing all of a sudden after twenty years? Finally she took a look, and she was relieved to see there was no bad news, just an unusual request. Could I come to see her, and would she tell me all the stories from when she was little? Of course, she said, and I booked a flight. We exchanged photos by mail, and she promised to pick me up in her pick-up truck.

But when I arrived on her end, clutching the little head shot she'd sent me, I didn't see anybody who looked like her. I waited five minutes, thinking maybe she was late, then ten, but still I didn't see her.

I have a high threshold for panic, and I usually assume that everything will turn out fine no matter what disaster might be unfolding around me, a quality that has served me well whether I am driving in a blizzard, covering a riot, trapped in my canoe on the wrong end of our lake by a strong wind, or running to scoop up one of my children, bleeding and hysterical, from a wipe-out on the playground. But somehow, standing in that airport, all I could think was that she wasn't going to be there. I started to worry that she'd had a change of heart, that she simply couldn't bear to go through with our meeting. I paged her, and counted the minutes on my watch till another ten had passed, my heart beating in my throat the entire time. Still no sight of her. I imagined her sitting at home, eyeing the clock just as I was, wondering if she'd done the right thing by staying away. Should I call her, or just get back on the next plane to New York? After all, this was rather audacious of me in a way, calling up an old woman, out of the blue, after making no effort to maintain contact for two entire decades, and asking if I could come down with a tape recorder and ask her all kinds of personal questions. What was I thinking when I imposed myself on her this way? What the hell was I doing here? I had no right to expect her to open her heart to me, and if she stood me up at the airport, it was really what I deserved.

But all of a sudden it occurred to me that I was being ridiculous. There was one explanation for her absence that I hadn't considered. Perhaps she simply hadn't made it to the gate. Maybe she couldn't find a place to park. Maybe she'd misplaced my flight information. A hundred reasons came into mind in that moment, and I picked up my bag and started running out of the arrivals area toward the exit. As soon as I turned the corner, there she was, seated on a bench, a cane by her side, looking perfectly relaxed, as if she had no doubt that I'd come walking up any moment, clearly clueless about the anxiety on my end. I slowed myself, feeling about as foolish as I ever have in my life. Of course she was waiting for me here. This was the normal place that people meet in an airport. I'd been picked up at airports a hundred times in my life; whatever made me think there was a problem just because I didn't see her the second I stepped off the plane? There was no point in telling her how stupid I'd been, and I worried that if I told her what had gone through my mind in the past twenty minutes, she'd be offended that I ever doubted her. So I resolved to simply walk over and greet her as if none of these crazy thoughts had ever entered my mind.

But as we made eye contact, I felt overwhelmed again by a completely different set of emotions. I felt like crying. I couldn't speak. For the second time in a half-hour, my head and my heart refused to connect, and I was angry with myself for being so emotional. *Why am I feeling this way?* I wondered, unable to come up with an answer or swallow the lump in my throat. I'd approached this as I would any story, packing my tape recorder and my notebook, even making a list of questions I wanted answered. But now that I was here, it didn't feel like just *any* story; it felt like I was about to hear the saddest story in the world. And yet it was also a story I already knew. A story, in fact, that I knew by heart.

An image popped into my head of my mother, back in the days when she used to make nice dinners, serving Aunt Lee in our apartment when I was small. Then, my brain fast-forwarded to the picture of all of us standing around the kitchen without my mother, after the funeral, passing around those idiotic slices of cheese, giggling at the absurdity of it all without ever really acknowledging just how awful the life that just ended had been. And now I wondered: How many opportunities had we all missed to help my mother out of her hell in all the years that came between?

In the brief moment it took for these thoughts to pass through my mind, Lee smiled but said nothing, perhaps seeing that I was about to cry and not wanting to push me over the edge. After all, of all my aunts, she was the one I barely knew. It would have almost been unseemly for her to acknowledge that she could tell I was losing it, or presume that she could make it better by asking what was wrong. But then she leaned over and hugged me, and I knew that it was all going to be just fine. I knew why I was there; I swear I could feel my blood pressure returning to normal, the pulsing in my head and the trembling in my fingers gone the minute she put her arm around me. I took her hands and searched her face, and I felt completely calm again, certain that I had done the right thing in making the trip. I mumbled something easy, like, "It's so good to see you." Then I followed her to her pick-up truck as we began chatting about mundane things like the weather and my flight, and we drove off.

But once in the car an awkward silence took over. I couldn't start asking her all my questions right away; we just didn't know each other well enough. With my other aunts, we always pick up where we leave off; we know enough about each other's lives to have a continuing conversation, even if we haven't spoken in months or a year. But with Lee, everything was new. We were practically strangers, and it was hard to know where to begin. As I searched for the right words, she took the burden off me by pointing out features of the landscape as we passed by. "There's your pretty palm trees," she murmured, "and there's your pretty clouds. And look at that grass, so green. Isn't it lovely?"

I had never been to this part of the country before, and I had to agree it was beautiful. But it was also eerily comforting to hear her running commentary on the birds and the flowers and every other sign of the natural world that she noticed as we drove along. It's not like we were driving through a national park; we were on a highway, leaving an airport. A different sort of person would have noticed the signs and the malls. I realized that Aunt Lee's observations about the palm trees and the grass were exactly the sort of thing my mother would have said if she were driving with us.

We parked at a restaurant that she knew had a good deal for lunch and a mixed drink for a dollar. "Oh good, it's a Seabreeze today," she said after looking at the menu in the window, and I was happy to join her in having one. I noticed that her nails were nicely done in French manicure tips that she glued on herself; I suddenly remembered that when I was a very little girl, my mother used to do French manicures the old-fashioned way, with clear polish and a white pencil rubbed under the tip of the nail till it made a bright, clean stripe.

I reminded Lee that the last time we had seen each other was when my mother died. And I explained that I was trying to find out what had happened during Anne's life that might explain the awful way it ended.

"I think Anne dwelled on all the sad things," Aunt Lee replied. "And you can't brood about these things. Time lessens the pain, and you can't do anything about the past. You can only change today and tomorrow."

We ate our lunch and drank our drinks, and headed back to her modest one-story home on a quiet, nicely landscaped street.

Inside her house I noticed a framed picture of President Kennedy on one of her walls. "How long have you had that?" I asked.

"Oh, ever since it was on the calendar," she replied. I told her that my mother always had a picture of Margaret Chase Smith on the wall, and that she was a lifelong Republican who proudly voted for Richard Nixon twice.

"That crumb!" Aunt Lee exclaimed. "I bet she was sorry. He was the biggest bum we ever had in the White House."

She thought for a minute longer about my mother choosing the party of Nixon over the party of Kennedy.

"Now why'd she go do a thing like that?" she said. "Your mother was born a Democrat. We all were."

She told me how her parents had agreed to name their last child after one of the Roosevelts—Eleanor if it was a girl, Franklin Delano Roosevelt if it was a boy. And that was really all it took to get us going. For the rest of the day and evening, we sat in her living room and caught up on old times and traded stories. When I was a child, she had lived in Connecticut, and visited us from time to time. Her oldest son died of lymphoma when he was twenty and I was seven; I remembered the day, shortly after his death, when my mother left me in my father's care—a very unusual event—and traveled to Hartford to see her. No one would tell me why she got all dressed up and went away for the day, but somehow I was able to figure out my cousin's death from snatches of conversation I overheard.

"It's very hard to bury your own child, you know," Lee told me. "You always think they're going to bury you."

Lee had moved to the retirement community where she lives now shortly before her last husband died. "Then I got certified as a nurse's aide because I couldn't find any other jobs, and I worked for a while doing that," she said. "Now I'm seventy-eight. I've got a lot of health problems, but I'm okay. I've got diabetes and bronchitis and my eyes are bad. . . . I use this cane to steady myself when I walk, and I bought that blue pick-up truck, used, a couple of years ago. It's got a lot of miles on it but I hope it lasts me the rest of my life."

We talked about her childhood, how Lizzie kept things going, and how her father couldn't cope. "But I don't blame him," she added. "Alcoholism is an illness, you know. And he was an alcoholic."

I told her how heavily my mother had been drinking at the end of her life. "I never saw her without a cigarette in one hand and a cup of coffee in the other," Aunt Lee said with a sigh. "Caffeine, nicotine, and liquor. That was the only medication she had, I guess. I never smoked. Tried it once, but didn't like it. And aside from that Seabreeze we had yesterday with lunch, I haven't had a drink in three months."

When I was small, Lee used to call my mother sometimes in the middle of the night. In those days of heavy, black dial phones wired into the wall, there was no such thing as an answering machine, or the ability to unplug the phone, and somehow my mother was not willing to leave it off the hook, so it would ring and ring and ring. I remember sleepily wandering out to the living room in my pajamas to see what was going on and finding my mother sitting there in her armchair, the tip of her cigarette a little red glow in the dark and the blue smoke curling up to the ceiling, visible in a shaft of light coming through the window from a streetlight. "It's Lee," she would hiss, eyeing the phone as the rings continued. "Go back to sleep." Sometimes she would take pillows and bury the phone under them in an effort to mute the noise, but always, eventually, she would answer, and then I would get in my bed and fall into a dream with the smell of her cigarette smoke in my nostrils and the sound of her ragged voice rising and falling in the other room. I described what I remembered to Lee and asked, trying to make sense of it all, "Were you sad when you made those calls? Was it after Bobby died? Had you been drinking?"

"I really don't remember," she answered, her voice trailing off.

I nodded and reminded myself that I was here to talk about my mother, and not about her. We both turned our faces toward the television, which had been on throughout our conversation and was suddenly a welcome intrusion, taking up the awkward silence in the room. After watching for a minute, she suggested we take a break to have something to eat, and we headed into her kitchen. "Here, try this, I made this banana bread for you," she said, cutting me a piece. It was delicious, and I copied down the recipe. "You can make it for your boys," she said, referring to my sons.

Suddenly her demeanor changed and she looked at me meaningfully. "Listen, I've been meaning to ask you," she said in a quiet tone of voice. "Does your husband treat you well? I mean, he doesn't hit you, does he?"

"No, of course not," I answered quickly, a little taken aback by the question, but touched that she wanted to make sure I was okay. "He's a very good man. And we've been very lucky. We have a pretty nice life."

"That's good," she said, sitting back and smiling, apparently relieved to have a subject that had been on her mind out of the way. After a while she looked at me again.

"I'm glad you came to visit me," she said. "It's about time we got to know each other."

I was glad, too, and sorry that it had taken me so long to make the trip. In between all the stories about her childhood, and my bringing her up to date on my kids, we actually had a lot of fun. We stayed up till after midnight chatting, then started in again first thing in the morning. There was just so much to say, and she had a *joie de vivre* that amazed me, an optimism that I had never really encountered in any of the other Farrell sisters. She'd had just as hard a life, and yet, even at her current age, with all her health problems, she didn't seem to be worn down by the misery of her past. She was looking forward to a church outing the next weekend; she was excited about the prospect of getting a photo I promised to send her of my kids. For some reason, I keep thinking about the hors d'oeuvres she served me in her kitchen: a tray of olives and pickles and cold cuts and salads. It was like we were having a party, she and I, instead of a visit between a niece and aunt who hadn't seen each other for years.

It was hard to say good-bye when it was time to go, just twenty-four hours after I arrived. I wondered if I'd ever see her again. Aunt Deen lives in New York, a short drive from my house, so I see her all the time. Peanut and Achsah are up in Maine, and my annual vacations just wouldn't be complete unless I saw them each summer, just as I used to when I was small. But Lee had moved far south, several thousand miles from her native state, to a part of the country I didn't expect to get back to anytime soon.

As we got in her truck to drive back to the airport, she turned to me and asked: "Did you see how I'm growing a pineapple in the front yard? You cut the top off and plant it, and another fruit comes up. A man in a store told me how to do it, and now I grow one every year."

It takes a certain kind of person to grow something that has to be replanted every year and that bears just one fruit—a certain kind of patience and faith that what's to come is worth waiting for. My mother never had that outlook, and I'm not sure I have it either, but it was inspiring to see it in my aunt.

After I got home, I called my sister and described my visit—how much fun I'd had, how upbeat Aunt Lee was despite her circumstances.

Nancy said she wasn't surprised. "Aunt Lee," she said, "was always a bon vivant."

6

BIG SISTER

LEFT: *Nancy and Beth in coats handmade by Anne.*

RIGHT: *David, Anne, and Nancy.*
Anne is staring at her former beau, Ruel, who is not pictured.

My sister, Nancy, is twelve years older than I am, but people are always asking if we are twins, or if I am older. The only time anyone compliments the way I look is when I'm wearing something she bought me; is it any wonder that I remember more clearly what *she* was wearing on every significant occasion in my life than what I was wearing? She had on a purple minidress for my fifth-grade graduation, a flower in her hair when I finished high school, and a long, ethereal pale pink dress with matching sweater and pillbox hat when I got married, which prompted one of the guests to announce that *she* was the best-dressed person at the wedding.

She moved out of our apartment to marry her first husband when I was six and she was eighteen, and after that from time to time she would come and take me for an outing. Once when I was about nine or ten, she took me for brunch to Maxwell's Plum, just the sort of groovy place where fabulous people like her hung out circa 1970. I was supposed to go to the ballet later that day with one of my father's unmarried sisters, an event I was dreading; it was so much fun to be out with my own sister and so awful to go to the ballet with Aunt Ruth. The more I thought about the ballet, the sicker I felt; and before I knew it, I had thrown up on the table at Maxwell's Plum, right in front of all the beautiful people I wanted so much to be like. It was possibly the most publicly humiliating moment I had ever experienced in my young life, but Nancy wasn't at all perturbed. She handed me a linen napkin to wipe my face, threw a twenty-dollar bill down on the table—in an unsoiled spot, of course—and led me out of the restaurant without a backward glance, instructing me to roll down her car window in case I had to throw up again.

When I was very little, and she was a busy teenager, she was leaving the apartment one day and I started throwing a tantrum. After she shut the door, I smashed my lip on something, leaving a scar beneath my mouth. My mother always told the story as an example of how rotten Nancy was that she wouldn't stick around to play with her baby sister, but I knew that wasn't the right interpretation. It was that she was going out to have fun, and I wanted to have fun, too. The only way that was going to happen was if I got to be with her.

A few years later, I pointed the scar out to her, just to needle her, and reminded her that she was the cause of it. She blithely informed me that she would gladly pay for plastic surgery to have it removed as soon as I was an adult. That was the end of the rehashing of *that* story. P.S.—the scar gradually disappeared, and the plastic surgery was unnecessary.

And that's how it's always been. She's the cool one, and I just kind of fall in line behind, speechless but happy to be in her aura. Music, clothes, where to go or what to do—whatever she thinks is fun or good, I simply bow to her authority. I've never heard of any of the songs that she put on a CD she recently gave me, and yet, of course, I loved every one of them; it was as if she knew me better than I know myself. She's my personal shopper, too; if I need an outfit for a special occasion or a new bag, I just tell her, because I know whatever she picks out will be much nicer than anything I might choose. I don't have the patience to go shopping; I don't care all that much about the result; and I trust her taste more than I trust my own. I even borrowed her wedding dress to get married in, figuring there was no point in trying to find a nicer one than the one she'd already picked out, and not really caring all that much about it anyway. Recently a friend of mine who doesn't even know her e-mailed me to ask, "What's your hipster sister listening to these days?" She's a trendsetter even among people who've never met her.

I have also learned a lot from her over the years: that getting lost in the car doesn't matter, because you never stay lost; that you can't make a good Bloody Mary without celery salt; that people are happier when their surroundings are clean, well-maintained, and cheerfully decorated; and that I'm deluding myself to think I can keep a sofa looking nice when I have two boys, a big dog, and a couple of cats.

Along the way she's learned something from me, too: that all tofu is not bad, that I can do for her with books what she does for me with clothes and music, that it's stupid to spend a lot of time with people who are drunk, that you can still respect yourself even if you don't wash your hair every day, and that a sad story can be just as worthwhile as a happy one.

Still, on balance, I think I follow her lead a lot more than she follows mine. When we eat lobster, I watch her very carefully and crack the shells and scrape the meat out just as she does. And after I had my own children and realized how hard it is to strike a balance between love, indulgence, and discipline, I called her up to apologize for having criticized her long ago over some now-forgotten incident involving her daughter.

Which isn't to say I live my life as she's lived hers. She's into yoga, candles, and inspirational self-help seminars, while I find all of those things unspeakably boring and pointless. She must have music playing all the time, while I find silence to be a great luxury. She likes to give parties, while I don't even particularly like to go to parties. I met the man I married when I was twenty, but she's been married three times and had more boyfriends since she turned forty-five than I've had my whole life. I think my mother always thought of her as the "bad" daughter and me as the "good" daughter, but in reality, it was just that Nancy had already broken all the rules by the time I came along. Nothing I did could ever shock anyone as much as the things she'd already done, so there was really no point in even trying.

We like each other's cooking, and when we are on vacation together in Maine, we take turns making dinner because we cook such different things. Me: vegetarian, spicy, ethnic, one-dish wonders, come and get it. Her: meat, fish, traditional, hors d'oeuvres and many courses, all beautifully arranged. She likes to fill the refrigerator up with whatever looks good from the supermarket; I prefer to make a menu for the week and a list to go with it, to make sure we don't end up with a stick of butter more than we might be able to use.

And while she enjoys kayaking in places she's never been before, I think kayaks are too much work and uncharted waters too much risk. I prefer to canoe across our little lake, like I've done a hundred times before. It pleases me no end that I know just how the paddle will feel in my hand, the wood worn smooth from years of doing this and the callouses on my skin in just the right places. I like to watch the water swirl predictably to the side in little eddies as I row, and I like knowing how to fine-tune the steering without thinking about it, by angling the paddle just so and holding it steady against the momentum I've created.

Most of all, I like how the other side looks as I pass the halfway point, when the familiar green landscape suddenly comes into focus, a forest of individual trees.

One day not long ago, my sister and I spent a few hours together eating and drinking at establishments somewhat more sedate than Maxwell's Plum, but as in tune with the early twenty-first century as that was with the 1970s. We had cappuccino and chai tea at Starbucks for breakfast, bento boxes, plum wine, and mochi ice cream in an Asian garden for lunch, and French martinis and crab cakes in a tiny bar during happy hour. I am happy to report that while I was prepared to jump in with the twenty myself this time in the event that one of us was unable to keep it all down, no hasty exits were needed. Around us people chatted on cell phones, checked their pagers, and click-clacked on laptops, but my sister and I stayed focused on the decades long before any of those things were ever conceived of. She conjured up for me her childhood, like something out of a *Thin Man* movie, David and Anne playing Nick and Nora at the Normandie with their cocktails and cigarettes and comings and goings; and I compared it to my childhood, a cross between *Diary of a Mad Housewife* and *Summer of Sam*. It was as if we had grown up with two completely different sets of parents instead of the same mother and father, just twelve years apart.

"I remember being really young when I looked at both of them and saying, 'I'd rather be Daddy,' " she told me.

Not me. I remember looking at both of them and thinking I didn't want to be either one, but hoping against hope that I wasn't doomed to be Mommy.

In the 1950s, when Nancy was small and before I was born, my sister lived with our parents in a little apartment in a tenement on East Forty-Ninth Street. Every Sunday, Anne would make a big dinner, put on makeup, do her hair, and get all dressed up. David had brought home some of the full skirts that were in style—an aqua one with fringes and a white quilted one with flowers—and they looked just beautiful on Anne. Then she'd put on a fancy open-throated top, or a sweater with fur around the collar, and high heels, and make sure her lipstick was just right; she liked fire-engine red because it set off her chestnut hair and dark brown eyes.

When she emerged all dressed and pretty, David would say, "Are you ready for cocktails, Annie Farrell?" Then he'd get out the cocktail shaker, a marvel of industrial design that brought to mind sleek cars or Art Deco skyscrapers, with a silvery stainless steel top and drink recipes etched in raised capital letters onto the frosted glass cylinder; it was like making your drink inside a miniature version of the Chrysler Building. He'd drop in tiny ice cubes from a small, finely crosshatched metal tray, then pour in grenadine, squeeze a couple of limes, and add generous quantities of apple jack—a cheaper, tamer, American version of French calvados, which was a stiff apple brandy he'd learned to love while stationed in Normandy during the war. Then he'd shake it up, the ice tapping the side of the glass like a maraca, and triumphantly pour out something called a Jack Rose. It was the kind of drink that looked, from its delicate salmon color topped with white foam, like a ladies' cocktail, like something fun for those who couldn't handle the stronger stuff. But David—dressed in a button-down shirt and real trousers, not the undershirt and khaki pants he wore to work—had a light touch with the grenadine, and a heavy hand with the apple jack; one whiff of his Jack Rose made the eyes water, and the first sip would go down about as well as turpentine. A couple of sips on an empty stomach and the room was spinning, but the more you drank, the better it tasted, and the better it tasted, the more you drank.

Nancy would be handed a Shirley Temple—ginger ale and grenadine and a Maraschino cherry from the jar they kept in the fridge, and sometimes they danced to music on a record player. David taught Nancy how to do the Charleston, and he and Annie Farrell waltzed or did the foxtrot. Then Anne brought out the appetizers: celery stuffed with cream cheese and sliced olives, sliced Cracker Barrel cheddar cheese on Saltines, herring in cream sauce from a jar, and cubes of kosher salami pierced with toothpicks. For dinner, Anne made coq au vin, with rice and mushrooms and a savory sauce; or roast beef au jus, with baked potatoes, salad, a frozen vegetable, and rosé wine. She'd learned how to cook at the Conys', and everyone who came for dinner on Forty-Ninth Street raved that she was the best cook in America. Sometimes company consisted of another couple; but just as often the guest would be one of Nancy's maiden aunts. David had two unmarried sisters who didn't speak to one another and could only be invited on alternate Sundays; the third maiden aunt was Anne's sister Deen, who had lived with them when Nancy was a baby.

• • •

Deen left Maine when she was seventeen in the company of a Salvation Army captain, a woman who'd heard her play piano for the Hallowell School and invited her to be the accompanist for Salvation Army services at a post in Connecticut. But the captain had a hidden agenda, and it wasn't long before Deen called Anne for advice. "I told her this lady who was living with me had given me a black eye and that she told me she wanted to be my mother, my father, my brother, and my sister," Deen said.

"Get on the next train to New York," Anne told her. "David will meet you in Grand Central."

Deen slept on a sofa in their living room on Forty-Ninth Street while finishing her degree at a high school in Manhattan, but the apartment was small and she got the feeling that Anne—a new mother and newlywed—didn't really want her there. After about a year, Deen rented a room somewhere else, supporting herself with various jobs, first at a five-and-ten, then at the Waldorf-Astoria Hotel in the personnel department, later at a pharmacy and the Red Cross blood bank. She got a credit card from Bloomingdale's by giving out her own phone number as a reference. "She's a very nice young lady from Maine and we like her style," she said of herself when the store called to check up on her.

"I tried not to feel subservient to anybody because I had been that way all my life," she said. "I made up my mind I was going to hold my head up high and not let things get to me. I told my dentist, 'I'm showing my teeth, keep them white for me.' I wasn't going to let people treat me badly anymore."

Eventually Deen began to study nursing. Nancy remembered what a big deal it was when her young aunt began wearing a little nurse's cap and cape. Then one day someone caught Deen coughing up blood in the bathroom at the nursing school where she was studying. She was sent for a diagnosis, and when the doctor detected a mass on the membrane around her heart, he told her to write her will before undergoing surgery.

In those days hospital visiting hours were extremely limited, so Anne bought a nurse's uniform for herself to sneak in to see her little sister in the hospital. "She was really critically ill; I don't think they expected her to live," Nancy remembered. "Mommy never left me with baby-sitters, but I remember this time, I did have babysitters. She just put on that uniform and went into the hospital to see her."

After months of recuperation, Deen was well enough to work again. She was hired by an obstetrician, the doctor who later delivered me. And that was when my mother's own, long illness began.

In the summer Anne and David always took Nancy to Maine, to a lake not far from Augusta. They'd rent a little camp, the term Mainers use to describe a simple cottage that wouldn't be suitable for year-round living but provides shelter for a vacation by a lake or a hunting trip in the woods. Each year, they rented a different camp, whatever was avail-able on the lake they liked to go to, but one year, a friend from the lake called to say that one of the camps was for sale, for two thousand dollars. Anne desperately wanted David to buy it; she always said, in a faraway voice, as if she didn't think anyone was really listening, that all she ever really wanted was a little house by the side of the road. So David sent the money off. When they arrived at the house the following summer, Anne went inside and looked around and started to make a list of what needed to be done to make it liveable, fixing this and changing that. Da-vid listened for a few minutes, then walked over to see the friend who'd arranged the sale. He sold the camp back that day, just unloaded it without ever consulting Anne, and they moved that afternoon to a rental. Anne didn't say a word; there was no explanation from David and no recriminations from her. But Nancy could tell her mother was heartbroken, and completely powerless to do anything about it.

Once each summer, Anne would plan a trip to what she called "up country," where Achsah, Peanut, and their father Bill Farrell lived. She got out maps, telephoned for directions as if she'd never been to visit her relatives before (even though she saw them every year), made extra food to eat along the way, packed David's truck with the boxes of clothes she'd saved throughout the year for her sisters and their kids, and got up early in the morning to begin the trek. Inevitably David would get lost en route, or the truck would break down miles from nowhere, or a terrible thunderstorm would force him to pull over by the side of the road. It seemed to take half the day just to get to one relative's house, and then the visit could never be very long because there were always the others that had to be seen in the same trip. And the country roads they took, with no names and no signs, had to be located before dark, so the return drive back to the camp on the lake had to be under way by sunset.

Bill Farrell lived with a Dalmatian in what looked to Nancy like a barn. She and Anne and David would drive into his yard and then stand there talking for a while; they never went inside, and there never seemed to be much to say. The dog entertained Nancy by climbing a ladder, and David told her the dog had been trained to pick pockets, too. But Anne said that wasn't true, it was just that he'd once found a wallet, brought it to her father, and her father had found the wallet's owner and rewarded the dog by giving him a treat. After that, the dog thought he'd always get a treat if he could bring his master a wallet.

Grandpa Bill had a well in the yard, and because he had no electricity and no refrigerator, when he shot a deer, he'd keep the meat from spoiling by storing it down in the well. David showed the deer to Nancy, tied by the hooves and hanging deep inside the water; he thought it was cute. But she thought it was disgusting, and refused to drink water at his house after that.

The visits to Achsah and Peanut were different. They both had kids for Nancy to play with, and Anne was anxious to show her sisters what she'd brought for them. All year she saved back copies of magazines like McCall's and Ladies Home Journal, fabric and sewing supplies, and hand-me-downs or extra clothes that David brought home. When David's truck was packed to go to Maine from New York, half of what was in it was boxes of stuff for Peanut and Achsah. And when they thought they were getting close to where her sisters lived, Anne would stop at the next general store they passed—there was usually one at the crossroads of even the smallest town—and buy a gallon of milk, a half-gallon of chocolate, strawberry, and vanilla ice cream, a loaf of bread, and a bar of butter to bring to each of her sisters. When they arrived,

Anne would start buttering the bread, and by the time she was done with the loaf, the buttered slices had disappeared, eaten as fast as she put them down.

Achsah had seven children in all, six boys and a girl; Peanut had five, two girls and three boys. Today, with abortion legal, sixth graders learning about birth control in school and sterilization done on an outpatient basis, it's hard to remember how common large families like these were just a generation ago. Family planning wasn't impossible; it was just atypical. And teenage brides like Achsah and Peanut were in very different situations, both biologically and psychologically, from the twenty-first-century forty-something woman who's postponed marriage and motherhood for so long that she needs a team of fertility specialists in order to produce just one child.

Still, while it shouldn't have been a surprise that her sisters had big families, Anne cried each time she got a letter from one of them saying they were pregnant again; she was terrified that one of the births would kill them, and she knew that each child added to the burden of trying to clothe and feed a family. Once Anne suggested that Achsah give away one of her baby boys since she'd already had a couple of sons. After that, Achsah stopped including news of her pregnancies in the letters they exchanged, waiting instead until after the babies were born to inform her older sister that she'd become an aunt again.

But David often joked that he'd trade either of his girls for a little boy or a puppy dog, and he always liked seeing his nephews up in Maine. He especially admired the way Achsah's husband Francis got on with his boys. Francis had taught them all to shoot, and on one visit he invited David to pick out a rifle from his gun collection and try his hand at target shooting. David chose a weapon and looked through the sights to line up his shot. Just as he was about to pull the trigger, he heard a high-pitched scream. His soldier's instincts, still sharp and tight a decade after the end of World War II, whirled him around in the direction of the shriek. Even with his bad hand, it was easy to fire off a shot in the split second it took his mind to travel back to the woods of Belgium and the fields of Holland and the farms of Normandy, where the enemy could be nesting in the brush and civilians could turn out to be the enemy, where a child's cry in a forest could be a trap, or merely a distraction, or, if you allowed it, a dilemma.

But in the next split second he came back to the field in rural Maine, where he stood with his brother-in-law, listening to the happy shouts of their children playing nearby. David's bullet had flown harmlessly into the air, and the kids weren't even distracted by the noise. David lowered the gun, shook his head, and handed it back to Francis. He lit up a cigarette, said he was tired from all the driving, and walked into the house to lie down. He never picked up a gun again as long as he lived.

The other people they usually saw once each summer in Maine were friends of Anne's, including Aunt Boo, who had remarried since Judge Cony's death but whose second husband had also died, and Ruel, who'd never married. Achsah said that when Anne was first married to David, she used to tell him, "If you're not nice to me, I'll go back to my poppa," meaning Ruel. But David didn't seem to be jealous; perhaps he was oblivious, or perhaps he didn't care. In a photograph from one of their vacations up in Maine, David has his arms protectively over Nancy's shoulders, and they are looking away. Anne is standing a few inches from them, almost by herself, not touching her husband or daughter. She is looking straight at the camera, not quite serious and not quite smiling, but as if she has a secret that only she and the photographer will ever know. The photographer, of course, was Ruel.

Anne wasn't the type of mother who got down on the floor and pretended that dollies were her babies or that stuffed animals could talk. She didn't build with blocks, sing nursery rhymes, or play games. But there was one day when, for whatever reason, she announced to Nancy that she had something to teach her. They purchased some clay at an art supply store where a friend of the family worked—one of several little stores in their Manhattan neighborhood where they had a relative of David's or a friend working behind the counter—and together they sat at the kitchen table all afternoon, rolling the clay in long snakelike strips, then coiling the strips around and around into baskets. They glazed them and baked them, and lo and behold, perfect little pots emerged hot from the oven. That same day, they took out paints and paper, and Anne taught Nancy how to draw roses and umbrellas. Nancy felt quite honored that her mother had chosen to spend the day doing artwork with her. She wasn't sure what Anne did the rest of the time; Nancy had been sent to nursery school from the time she was two years old and it didn't seem possible that sewing, cooking, and cleaning could take up all day, every day, but she did know that a day of play with her mother was a special day indeed.

It was certainly better than a day spent by her mother's sewing machine. How Nancy hated standing stock-still, the crinkly paper patterns and inside-out material pinned around her as she held her arms up and lifted her chin on command. Sometimes she'd get nauseous, it would take so long to get pinned for a new dress; she'd beg to take a break before she had to throw up. And everything Anne sewed had to be perfect; it was not unusual for her to rip the seams out and start all over again if they didn't meet her standards. It's not hard to imagine that these standards stemmed from some ragged, mismatched outfit that she was forced to wear as a child; Deen remembers wearing hand-me-down dresses that hung to the floor, and Achsah still smarts over the clothes provided by social workers that were either hideous or ill-fitting.

One day when Nancy was playing with her mother's jewelry box, she found some coins inside. She was allowed to go to the candy store by herself, so she took the money with her and spent it. Sometime later her mother went to the jewelry box and noticed the money was gone. "Where's my silver dollar?" she asked Nancy, who had to confess that it had been spent at the candy store. "It was the only thing my father ever gave me," Anne said, and started to cry.

It seemed like Nancy was always doing something naughty, and Anne always tried to get David involved in the punishment. Anne would wait till David came home from work, then yell and scream about whatever had happened that day, and hand him a belt. He'd take Nancy in the next room and hit her once or twice, more for appearance's sake than anything else. As Nancy got older and more willful, Anne took it upon herself to do the punishing. She'd hide in the corner near the bathroom, and when Nancy emerged from the shower wrapped in a towel, she'd hit her on the legs. But one day when Anne went to smack her, Nancy put her hand up to protect her face and her mother hit her hand on the bone of her teenage daughter's arm. "You tried to break my arm!" Anne screamed. When David came home, she had the belt at her side, ready to hand to him to administer the punishment. But David was drunk and something snapped when she told him Nancy had tried to break her arm. He threw Nancy on the bed and began beating and choking her. Instead of handing David the belt, Anne began hitting David with it to get him off Nancy.

David was always there for Anne's special Sunday dinners, but on other nights, whether or not he would make it home for supper without being summoned was a crap shoot. At some point every evening, if he hadn't called, Anne would instruct Nancy to pick up the phone and dial Buzzy's, his favorite bar. Even though they lived on the East Side and went out together to piano bars and French restaurants, when David went drinking alone, he preferred Buzzy's, downtown near his office on the West Side, a workingman's bar if there ever was one. It was located on what was, at the time, a gritty corner, at Twenty-Fourth Street and Sixth Avenue, deserted after dark except for the neon beer signs in the window, and conveniently located two blocks from his office.

"Find out if your father's coming home for dinner," Anne would tell Nancy, and she would call Buzzy's and ask if her father was there, having memorized the phone number for her daddy's second home at the age when most kids are still trying to memorize their own phone numbers. Anne would never serve dinner, even if it was ready, until David walked through the door sometime after the call had been made, even if that meant serving cold meat at nine o'clock.

But sometimes for dinner, instead of an angry wait for David to return from Buzzy's or Anne cooking a big meal for company, Nancy and her parents would go out to a café or nightclub or restaurant. Nancy loved these evenings out; she loved to order off the menu, many courses, just like the grown-ups. "David, don't let her order all that—appetizers, soup, dessert! It's just going to be wasted," Anne would always say.

"It's fine, Annie," David would reply, lighting up a cigarette. "There's no sense in coming out if you can't have what you want." Then he'd turn to Nancy and tell her: "Nanny, you order whatever you want."

Her favorite destinations were the Tally Ho tavern and a French restaurant called Annette's. At Tally Ho, from the age of three, Nancy would sit, a perfect little lady, on a bench with the piano player, a black man whom everyone called Inky, sipping Shirley Temples while her parents sat at the bar. At Annette's, David and Anne would dine on frogs' legs and escargot while Nancy followed around the owner's peach-colored standard poodle; she and the curly-haired dog were about the same height.

Once a week for a couple of years, Nancy was also treated to lunch at Buzzy's, without her mother. David would pick his daughter up from school at noon, tell the teacher he'd try to have her back in time for class, and take her to the restaurant that was adjacent to the bar where he hung out at night. They had fried shrimp or burgers, and they were always waited on by a waitress named Helen, who wore a uniform with a flower handkerchief pinned on the pocket and lived in an apartment above the bar.

Helen was awfully lovey-dovey to Nancy, much more so than any other waitress Nancy had ever been served by. And although Nancy was only in fourth or fifth grade, she couldn't help but wonder if Helen was trying to show her father what a good stepmother she would be, if David would only give her a chance. David, for his part, appeared to be playing the part of the most devoted father in the world, as if to say to Helen, "This is the other part of my life, the part you don't usually see, and I'm not going to give it up." Sometimes Nancy thought she was imagining all these undercurrents, two adults trying to prove to each other how much she meant to them; other times she was sure there was a point to these lunches that had nothing to do with eating.

On weekends, David took Nancy to his office and let her play with the adding machine while he did paperwork; he gave her money to play Frank Sinatra on the jukebox at Buzzy's; he took her to a playground or sometimes to the Palisades Amusement Park, with its saltwater pool, across the Hudson River in New Jersey. Bring a friend? Fine! Go on the rides? Fine! Buy cotton candy, popcorn, ice cream, soda, whatever you want—fine! Nancy was her father's princess, and he was her hero. With Anne, everything was a problem; with David, nothing was.

Nancy was a smart little girl, so smart that she skipped three grades and graduated from high school when she was fifteen. She'd play jump rope with a girl her age who was three grades behind her, then go on a double date with a girl from her class who was three years older. Nancy was going into sixth grade but was still young enough to play with dolls when she fell in love with a doll carriage she spotted in a store one day while out with her father. It had silver medallions and whitewall tires and fenders over the tires; it was so big you could fit a real baby in it, and it was sixty dollars—a small fortune considering that their monthly rent was only forty dollars a month. David couldn't say no; he bought her the carriage. He carried it up the three flights of stairs inside their building; it seemed to take up half their tiny apartment, and it certainly cost more than anything else there. Anne screamed and screamed when she saw it and found out how much it cost, but David just didn't care. Anne couldn't have a house in Maine, but David wanted Nancy to have everything.

Often before he came home from work, Anne would complain to Nancy about him—how he was never home for dinner on time, how he wasted his money when they couldn't afford it. And when he got home from work, Anne would complain to him about Nancy—how naughty she'd been or the messes she'd made. But from an early age, Nancy could see that her father enjoyed life, enjoyed having what he wanted, and wanted Nancy to enjoy life and have what she wanted, too.

Shortly before I was born, Anne, David, and Nancy moved to a bigger apartment downtown, on West Twenty-First Street—conveniently located near David's office *and* Buzzy's Bar! But it wasn't nearly as nice as East Forty-Ninth Street had been. There, every storekeeper had become a friend. The downstairs neighbor worked in their favorite French restaurant. David's brother Sol had a little variety store a few blocks away. Anne could walk down the street and run into a half-dozen people she knew. And the neighborhood was home to both wealthy townhouse owners and working-class families.

It was different in their new neighborhood, Chelsea, which was, at the time, a rundown part of Manhattan, filled with tenements and rooming houses and brownstones that are worth millions today but that were eyesores back then. At the corner, old men passed the time sitting on milk cartons, drinking cans of beer barely disguised by paper bags. Squatters camped out in abandoned buildings, and the local playgrounds were a volatile jumble of winos, druggies, black kids from the projects on Seventeenth Street, and white kids from the Irish gangs of nearby Clinton, just a few blocks north. There was no neighborhood French restaurant. Just a dingy Horn and Hardart's Automat on Twenty-Third Street, well past its prime, and a greasy takeout place called Chicken Delight whose catchy slogan was much better than its food: "Don't cook tonight! Call Chicken Delight!"

The decade was different, too. In the 1960s, urban anonymity replaced neighborhood friendliness as an evil hallmark of life in New York City. Our building had twenty-eight apartments, but we didn't know more than three or four of our neighbors by name. Greetings were rarely exchanged in the elevator, a slow, clanking box that often broke down, and eye contact was discouraged. When you went into the big Key Food around the corner on Seventh Avenue (a store that would be burned down in the 1970s), nobody there knew your name, nor wanted to.

The new apartment was also located in a heavily Hispanic area, home to many families from the first big wave of postwar immigration from Puerto Rico. Latin music blared out of open windows up and down the block in the summer; few people had air conditioners. When I went to school down the street at P.S. 11 in 1966, I was the only kid in my first-grade class who spoke English. I remember sitting in the back of the room reading a chapter book while the teacher held up, for the rest of the class to see, common items like pencils and paper in order to teach the English words for them. It only reinforced the feeling Anne had that this was a mistake, we didn't really belong here, and we would never fit in.

All in all, it was a depressing change for her, and it came at a time when she was realizing that the glamorous life she'd once dreamed of would never happen. Nancy was a strong-willed adolescent, on the road to becoming a rebellious teenager. David was not the kind of man who was ever going to get ahead in life; he paid the bills, but that was it, and he had no interest in social climbing, or in buying a little house in the suburbs somewhere. And then she became pregnant for the second time. Two babies, twelve years apart, dooming her to start all over again with diapers and middle-of-the-night feedings just when Nancy was getting old enough to take care of herself. If she'd had any thoughts of going back to work, the responsibility of the new baby made that impossible.

She felt, understandably, frustrated and overwhelmed by her circumstances; she seemed angry and in a bad mood all the time. This was not the life she had expected, and it seemed to be getting worse, not better. After I was born, she developed a postpartum infection with a high fever. At first her doctor didn't take it seriously, and by the time it was treated, she was so worn out that she couldn't get out of bed. It was the first time she'd gone into a funk like that, lacking the energy to rouse herself for the day's chores, and it took a few months after childbirth for her to begin moving around the apartment again.

But Nancy felt she had permanently changed, that she never really recovered from childbirth the second time. She wasn't only angry now, the way she had been for some time, screaming at the slightest provocation. She also seemed miserable and exhausted.

No one had thought to acquire a crib or bassinette for me, so the big doll carriage David had bought for Nancy became mine. Nancy used to take me for walks outside in it when our mother was too sick to go out, and when people peered in, expecting to see little dollies, there I was, a real-live baby. It was about that time that Anne took Nancy to see a psychiatrist, hoping to get some guidance in how to handle her willful older daughter. The shrink said there was nothing wrong with Nancy, but he was concerned about Anne and hoped to have her come back for further treatment. She never did.

A few months later Nancy started to get sick herself. She couldn't swallow, her urine was bright red and her shit was white, but she figured she'd get better eventually, and that waiting it out was better than telling her mother. Anne always got angry when other people got sick. She blamed them for not taking better care of themselves, complained about waiting on them, but insisted on playing nursemaid. She made home-made chicken soup and brought meals in bed and drinks with ice and straws and plumped the pillows and gave sponge baths with chilled witch hazel, all the while screaming about how much work it all was. Nancy decided she'd only get yelled at if she told her mother how sick she was, so she kept it a secret. Then one day she passed out cold and ended up in the hospital for a week, diagnosed with hepatitis and mononucleosis. She was home from school for six months.

Anne and David rarely went out together in the evening after they moved to Twenty-First Street. Anne didn't like using babysitters and no longer felt like going to the cafés and nightclubs they'd gone to when Nancy was little. David seemed to ignore her in public, leaving her stranded at the bar or at a party where he knew everyone and she knew no one; and it was humiliating to be left sitting alone while he drank and joked with his friends. But one night there was a big dinner sponsored by the veterans association for the 101st Airborne Division, whose men—David among them—had parachuted into Normandy, becoming the first soldiers to hit the beach on D-Day. Anne reluctantly agreed to attend and to allow Nancy to babysit for me.

Shortly after they left, one of the other teenagers in the building came to the door to talk to Nancy. A friend of his—a rather pathetic boy, pale and fat with caked-up eyelashes, an orphan who'd been adopted by the pastor of a neighborhood Anglican church—was having a birthday party at the church, and his parents were trying to round up some kids to come. Nancy said she couldn't leave the apartment; she'd promised her mother she would stay home to babysit. But the party was just two blocks away, the boy said, and there would be plenty of grown-ups—including some nuns—there to watch her two-year-old sister. So Nancy went, taking me, all bundled up in boots and a little snowsuit. The nuns were thrilled to have a baby to play with, and the birthday boy's parents were grateful to have an additional teenager joining the small group eating cake.

Nancy didn't stay long, but while she was gone, Anne had called home to see how things were going. When she got no answer, she and David left the veterans dinner and rushed back to the apartment. Anne was hysterical when she finally saw Nancy. "I can't trust you to do anything!" she screamed. "The one time in two years I ask you to take care of your sister and you couldn't do it! You couldn't not go to one party? You can't be trusted, for anything, ever!"

Nancy didn't see that she had really done anything wrong. She was trying to be a Good Samaritan, to attend a party for this boy who had no friends, and her sister had been in the care of a group of nuns. What was the big deal? It seemed no matter what she did she couldn't win, and if she couldn't win, there was no point in trying.

Nancy was fifteen years old in 1964 and a senior in high school. She liked partying with her friends, hanging out in Greenwich Village, and spending as little time as possible at home. She had a twenty-nine-year-old boyfriend who had a motorcycle and worked in a café; in the winter he had a beard and long hair and wore boots, and in the spring he shaved his head and wore sandals. He gave her the key to his apartment, and one day, she brought him home to meet her parents. They offered him a drink, and then David took him on the side for a chat. The chat consisted of an ultimatum: If David ever saw Nancy with him again, he would have him arrested and sent to jail.

In response Nancy decided to run away from home. She took a train to New Jersey, then got as far as North Carolina hitching rides before having second thoughts. The Regents exams she needed to pass in order to get a high school diploma were the next day; a high school diploma might be useful someday. So she decided to head back to New York, take the tests, and run away some other time. The first truck driver who headed north with her had dishonorable intentions, so she ditched him in the middle of the night in the middle of nowhere, only to be picked up by a couple of Pennsylvania teenagers who were happy to drive her back to Manhattan. They dropped her off at her boyfriend's house at five in the morning; he frantically told her that her parents had to be notified immediately.

"For all I know the FBI is across the street watching me," he said. "Your father has been to the police and I promised I would call them if I heard from you."

When she finally arrived back in the apartment on Twenty-First Street, she told Anne and David she had only come back to take the Regents, and that she had to have some coffee so she could get through the tests being held that morning. She staggered in to school to sit through the exams, and was later debriefed by the police, who, at her father's urging, told her every runaway-hitchhiker horror story in the book. Then she went home.

It was then that Nancy heard, for the very first time, the story that defined her mother's life, the story that her mother thought about every single day but until then, had kept secret from her teenage daughter: How the Farrell sisters had been sent to live with strangers because their father kept them home from school. How Grandpa Bill had been sent to jail because he didn't have the money to care for them. How Anne had been sent to live with the family of a high school principal near Bar Harbor, how she had socialized the family's retarded child and won the poetry contest and had the prize taken away, how her pay had been docked because she burned a hole in the blanket trying to keep warm by lighting a candle. How she'd gone from there to Mrs. Cony's house, where she had to wash the windows and make all the food before she could go to school in the morning.

And how it had all happened because Lizzie Noyes had died in childbirth. How the hospital had sent Lizzie home a few days before the baby came, knowing that her life was in danger once she went into labor. How if it wasn't for the Catholic Church prohibiting birth control and her father keeping after her mother to have sex, Lizzie would not have gotten pregnant again.

And finally Anne revealed the part of the story that hurt the most, the part that haunted her, that made her cry and gave her nightmares. She told Nancy that when Grandpa Bill couldn't start the truck to take Lizzie to the hospital, he'd sent Anne to get help. But the snow was so deep and so soft that each time she pulled her leg up to take another step, she sunk deeper and deeper into the drifts. A few steps more and her boot stayed stuck down deep in the snow, her foot coming up covered by nothing more than a sock. Frantically she tried to find the missing boot, first by sight, carefully examining the spot where she was certain she'd pulled up her foot, then with her hands, digging and clawing and hoping to feel its familiar shape, realizing that every second she wasted looking for the boot delayed the arrival of help for her mother. Within a few minutes, her foot was soaked, throbbing, frozen; she couldn't stand it, couldn't stay there, couldn't find the boot, couldn't do anything but keep going, dragging the bootless, numb foot behind her.

She made it to the firehouse and rode back in an ambulance to the house surrounded on three sides by the Little Androscoggin River, then frozen to a white, hard sheet of ice. But it was too late. The baby had been born and Lizzie Noyes was dead in a pool of blood.

Anne started crying and Nancy started crying, and for a day or two, a different relationship existed between them. She wanted Nancy's sympathy, and she got it. Her mother had told her this story to make her feel guilty about running away, and it worked. How could Nancy be such a rotten daughter when her life was so easy and her mother's life had been so hard? But it wasn't long before Anne went back to screaming and yelling and complaining about everything Nancy did, the same bitch of a mother she'd always been, and Nancy didn't feel sorry for her anymore.

Nancy married at age eighteen, to a young man from an Italian-Irish family whose mother seemed more than happy to wait hand and foot on everyone in her family, bringing them drinks and cold cuts while they watched television. Nancy's new mother-in-law had a job and bought furniture and clothes on monthly payment plans from department stores, something no one in Nancy's family had ever done. It was a revelation to Nancy that a mother could be so hardworking and yet so uncomplaining, so self-sacrificing and yet so in charge of her household.

Nancy's wedding took place on St. Patrick's Day during a freak snowstorm that forced the bridal party to clutch their long skirts up off the wet sidewalk and step carefully in their fancy shoes so as not to slip in the slush. I was the flower girl, wearing a dress made by my mother, but Nancy's dress came from a department store, bought with the money she was earning as a margin clerk on Wall Street. The reception was held in our small apartment, and somehow a hundred people crammed into the living room, with the champagne packed in ice in the washing machine because there was no room for it anywhere else.

I stayed up later that night at the wedding party than I ever had before, an excited little girl at a grown-up reception, adored by all the guests, lapping up all the compliments for my homemade dress. And at the end of the evening, sometime after midnight, when Nancy walked down the hallway to our apartment door, to leave, with her husband, I asked someone where she was going.

"To her apartment," I was told.

"But this *is* her apartment," I replied. Nobody had thought to explain to a little girl that when a big sister gets married, she moves out forever; it was just one of those things that grown-ups assumed you knew to be so. But I had no idea that she wouldn't be living with *me* anymore. I thought that having a wedding was like having a Christmas tree or a birthday, that you dressed up and got presents but afterward everything was basically no different from how it had been before, and that Nancy would go on living in our apartment like she always had, and sometimes this man she now called her husband would come over and hang out like he always did, and other times she would go to his house and hang out like she always did. I didn't realize they would be moving into their own apartment so they could hang out all the time together, without either of their families around. When I finally realized what was happening, after she'd left, I lay down on the hallway rug in front of the door and started to cry. After having a sister all my life, suddenly I had become an only child. And now there was no one to take up the space between my parents and me.

The day after the wedding, the phone in Nancy's new apartment rang. It was Anne, calling to chat. All of a sudden, it seemed, Nancy was no longer an unruly daughter who had to be disciplined; she was now a married woman to whom Anne could unburden herself. Anne proceeded to announce that she was miserable, profoundly unhappy; that David was a terrible husband who never came home; that he was so drunk at times he peed in the dresser drawers; that he danced with other women and talked to other men but had no interest in spending time with her. She said he had what she called "body lice," and that no matter how many times she washed the sheets, she couldn't get rid of them. Nancy realized at once that her father didn't have lice, he had crabs, which he could only have gotten one way; but she said nothing, nothing during the entire conversation except, "Yeah, yeah, yeah." Finally Anne began crying, saying that David had broken her heart, that there was no joy in her life, and that everything in the world was completely hopeless.

At long last she had nothing left to say and they hung up. Then Nancy started sobbing uncontrollably, so hysterically that she told her mystified newlywed husband she wasn't sure she would ever be able to stop.

I once asked my sister if she was afraid she might wake up some day crazy like Mommy, and she said without hesitation that the thought had never crossed her mind. After all, she decided early on that she wanted to be like our father, if for no other reason than to make sure she didn't turn out like our mother.

But I never saw myself as choosing between the two. I agreed with the part of my father's philosophy that said you have to make your own happiness in this world, and I think I've done a pretty good job of making mine. But I didn't like the way he cared so little about my mother's happiness; to me, it seemed selfish and cruel. Besides, I identified, even as a little girl, with my mother's artistic soul—the part of her that painted roses and noticed the birds and recited poetry, and I wanted to be like that. I just hoped her suffering wasn't part of the package.

I know I have inherited some aspects of her temperament. I am a moody sort; even my oldest son has said he doesn't see how I can be so mean and angry one minute, and then just fine the next. It's true that when I lose my temper, I can hear my mother's rage in my own voice, but it always disappears as fast as it arrives. I'm a dreamer, too, like she was, with an ever-changing list of things that I would love to do. I resolve to write a play, learn piano, buy a sailboat; I imagine becoming a horticulturist, or a teacher, or adopting a little girl from a third world country. But I know, chances are, I won't make all these dreams come true. I'm too easily discouraged by things that don't come naturally, too practical for risk and whimsy, too quick to criticize myself and others; all that's her in me, too.

And yet I know I must avoid her fate. But how? Whenever I come across those little pop quizzes on mental health, I always take them. Not for me, but for her, as a way of determining what went wrong. I check the box for, "I am so sad or unhappy that I cannot snap out of it," and I give her extra points for feelings of worthlessness, guilt, and abnormal sleep patterns. It is reassuring to see that none of this is how I would describe myself, but by the time I'm halfway through, she's already scored so high that if she were alive, she would require immediate hospitalization. And then of course I realize the absurdity of this, and wonder if perhaps I am crazy after all, performing amateur psychoanalysis on a woman who's been dead for twenty years.

In some ways, I think of her as someone who was just too delicate for this damn world, someone whose sense of self could withstand only so much abuse before collapsing. If I'm stronger than that, it's because she made me that way. She had faith in me; I could feel it, even as a very little girl, and I sucked it in the way a hummingbird pulls nectar from a blossom. I was always certain of her love, and that was a vaccine, for me, against whatever forces had crushed her. It makes me think that if she'd had the mother's love that she gave me, she might have been fine, too.

7

ANCESTORS

The Farrell-Michaud House in Van Buren. (Pete LaPointe)

M y ancestors were ordinary people, not movers and shakers of the world, carried along by currents they probably scarcely understood, let alone could control," writes Gerard J. Brault in his book, *The French-Canadian Heritage in New England.*

Most people would probably say the same thing about their families; I can certainly say it about the Farrells. After all, momentous developments in history have a way of affecting little people in ways that are usually unanticipated and therefore rarely understood until long after the changes have taken place. And so, in a funny way, it would not be wrong to give Napoleon partial credit for the arrival of Bill Farrell's ancestor, Michael Farrell, on this side of the Atlantic sometime before 1815.

In 1807, Napoleon signed a treaty with Russia that made it impossible for England to import timber from Northern Europe. The British had long used the tall trees of North America to build their navy's ships, but now they began mining the forests of Canada even more heavily to meet every aspect of consumer demand for wood in England. Where the Spanish had failed to find gold and silver in the New World, the British would reap a fortune in trees.

But there was one problem with transporting all these trees from North America to Western Europe. What would fill the ships on the way back across the ocean? There was not enough demand for goods from Europe to serve as ballast, but there was one other possibility: turn the vessels into passenger ships for the return trip. To spur ticket sales, like any good businessmen, sea captains reduced the price of passage. As a result, it was cheaper to sail from Ireland to Canada than from Ireland to the United States. As Cecil Woodham-Smith relates in *The Great Hunger,* a history of Irish immigration, by the mid-1800s, the cost of transporting a family of six from Belfast to Quebec was one pound per person; Belfast to New York was three times as much. And that's part of the reason Bill Farrell's great-grandfather Michael bought a ticket from Wexford, a city on the southeast coast of Ireland, to Saint John, New Brunswick, rather than to Boston or Manhattan.

Why Michael Farrell wanted out of Ireland, some thirty years before the potato famine, is also not hard to imagine. He was born around 1783 amid a baby boom that historians estimate tripled the population of Ireland. Ironically, a low standard of living had actually contributed to the population growth. Because people had no hope for achieving a comfortable existence, they had no motivation to postpone marriage or parenthood; there were no dowries or inheritances to wait for, no apprenticeships to be had. Home for most families was a sod cabin, with little or no furniture; a diet of potatoes, which were cheaply and easily grown; and a fire fueled by turf, the matted grass that was there for the collecting. With no expectations for household goods or income, teenage marriage was common, and with brides young and fertile, families were large.

In addition, most of the land was owned by absentee British landlords, with leases and subleases enforced by local rent collectors, a system that kept the peasant tenants in perpetual debt. As families multiplied, they divided their rented plots into ever-smaller lots for their ever-increasing descendants, until, around the time that Michael Farrell chose to emigrate, entire families were subsisting on the potatoes grown on an acre or less. With few paying jobs to be had, increasing pressures on land and food, and a rather miserable daily existence, it's no wonder that the ticket brokers hawking passage to British North America, as Canada was called, found willing passengers in every town in Ireland.

So Michael Farrell's motivations for leaving the land of his birth are easy enough to understand; the only mystery is why he traveled alone. He would have been around thirty years old when he arrived in Saint John. Given that life expectancy for most Europeans was only about forty years at the time, and given the young age for marrying that was typical in Ireland, it's surprising that he seemed to have no family. But whether he was running away from trouble, abandoning a wife and children, or seeking a new life after losing his family in some sort of tragedy is neither part of the record nor part of the legend.

But other stories about Michael Farrell have survived, handed down like precious quilts from his grandchildren to their grandchildren, tales that in years gone by passed from an elder's lips to a youngster's ears, but that today are spread via e-mail and genealogical Web sites, from one fourth cousin to another, all of us separated from our immigrant ancestor by six generations. He was not a famous man, or a wealthy man. But his existence is still being analyzed and contemplated by his descendants, from Washington State and California, to Texas and North Carolina, to Ontario and New York City. Most of us have never met, but we e-mail endlessly about our roots; one cousin, Len Gravel, has set up a Web site just for Michael's descendants. A recent message to me from one of these cousins many times removed, Doris Lapointe, began, "I keep thinking about our Michael . . ." And surely if someone is still thinking about you more than two centuries after you were born, that is some small measure of immortality.

When I began to look for something that might explain what happened to my mother, I did not expect to go back in time any further than her parents. But the more I learned—that Bill Farrell had been in a reformatory, that his father had been an alcoholic, that his grandfather had been a prominent citizen of a town his great-grandfather helped to found—the more I wondered where the break happened. How does a family go from proud immigrant pioneer to fine upstanding citizen to alcoholic to ne'er-do-well to a woman whose youthful ambitions were replaced by a morbid hopelessness? Was it an alcoholic gene, or a crazy gene? Was it, as Brault suggested, that they had all been carried along by currents they neither recognized nor controlled—immigration to the New World, Maine's timber boom, New England's post–Civil War decline, the Great Depression, the picture-perfect 1950s and the unraveling of family life and urban life in the decades that followed? Was my mother's destiny laid out generations ago, or was she a prisoner of her time?

And what of her ethnic heritage? Where did that fit in? As far as I was concerned, it was another one of her strange, mysterious secrets—a secret I was determined to reveal. On my father's side, this question was so easily answered. They were Russian Jews. Religion, nationality, culture, language—all those elements were easy to define. But on my mother's side, it was a muddle. There was a story about an Indian in the family, but I didn't really understand where she fit in. And why was it that my grandfather had an Irish name but spoke French, when he was born and raised in Maine? He was a Catholic, but my mother hated Catholics and she wasn't one, even though my Aunt Deen was. If I wanted to understand my mother, I needed to sort it all out. And in order to sort it all out, I had to go back to the beginning, to the source of the Farrell name, the Irish blood, and the first one in the family to settle in Maine. That's why I started researching Michael Farrell.

England's colonial army was an obvious career choice for young men with few opportunities at home. And so when Michael Farrell arrived in New Brunswick, a growing community of Irish soldiers working for the British government already existed there. But their spiritual needs were going unmet. Though the Catholic Church had been active in the area ever since missionaries arrived to convert the Indians in the early 1600s, nearly all of the priests were French. Canada was originally colonized by France and didn't come under British control until the 1700s, by which time French Catholics were already entrenched. But in 1813, the bishop of Quebec received in his diocese an Irish Dominican priest.

The priest was assigned to Saint John, began to hold Mass in the City Court Room there on Market Square, and soon made plans to build an Irish church, to be named in honor of Saint Malachy, the eleventh-century bishop of Armagh, Ireland. Enter Michael Farrell, who had some skills as a carpenter, and was recruited to help build the chapel.

In the summer of 1815, Michael Farrell was sent on a canoe trip up the St. John River to find trees suitable for the church. Some days later, he arrived in the French-speaking town of Grand Falls. He ended up lodging in the home of Germain Dubé, a French farmer and widower whose second wife, Marguerite Denys, was the daughter of a British loyalist. It was the only house in the area where English was spoken, and any political resentments the Irishman Michael Farrell might have felt toward a woman of British descent were probably muted by the relief he felt at being able to communicate at all.

Besides, the Dubé home held additional appeal for Michael in the winsome form of Germain's daughter, Julia, an outgoing fifteen-year-old whom Michael had observed working on her father's farm, haying in the fields and milking the cows. Family lore has it that Michael fell in love the minute he saw her, but it's easy to imagine that her father's reaction to this budding romance might have been less than encouraging. Germain's ancestors had come from France to Quebec in the 1600s, with the first wave of settlers in the New World; he must have had some doubts about the prospects of this Irishman twice his daughter's age, who'd just arrived from across the sea with no assets, no reputation, and no family to fall back on. Perhaps Michael asked to marry Julia then and there, or perhaps he sensed that he had to prove himself in order to win Germain's approval. Or perhaps Germain simply made it clear that his young daughter would have to grow up a little and Michael would have to establish himself before a marriage could take place. Either way, when construction on St. Malachy's Church was completed in 1816, Michael came back to court Julia.

In 1820, they married in the church at St. Basile in New Brunswick, not far from the Dubé farm at Grand Falls. She was twenty years old, he was thirty-seven, and soon after they wed, he received a land grant from the British North American government for three hundred acres on the other side, the northwest side, of the St. John River. Even today, the area is wild and green, the riverbank densely forested, at least to the casual observer driving by, with evergreen trees. It doesn't take much to imagine a small ferry boat bringing people back and forth across the river; the picturesque towns that exist there today, with their tidy Main Streets, modest homes, storybook churches, and small farms, are the obvious legacy of the settlers from Michael and Julia's generation and their descendants.

Michael and Julia built a homestead on their land, along with a farm, and began having children—twelve in all, over twenty-three years. But whether Julia's husband lived up to local standards for improving his property is unclear. The condescension of a surveyor who mapped the riverside settlements in 1831 is palpable as he noted of Michael Farrell in the margins of his report: "Irish. Paid $8. House. Barn. Fifty acres poorly cleared."

Despite the surveyors' disapproving tone, Michael eventually did okay for himself. The census of 1850 valued his property at nine hundred dollars, not a bad return on an investment of eight bucks. And just as the Dubé family had offered bilingual hospitality to weary travelers, so Michael and Julia turned their home into an inn where both French and English were spoken. Julia also worked as a midwife, traveling by canoe and snowshoe along the St. John to deliver more than a hundred of her neighbors' babies. She was an herbalist as well, remembered decades later by a granddaughter, Alice Michaud Cyr, for the roots, flowers, and herbs she used to treat mumps, scarlet fever, and other common illnesses in an era when treatment by a real doctor was rare.

The town where the Farrells lived was called Violette Brook, and although it was across the river from the town where Julia grew up, it was considered part of a region of Canada known as Acadia. Then, in 1839, a boundary dispute broke out when several hundred Acadians began cutting timber on land that was considered, by the United States, to be part of Aroostook County, Maine. Ten thousand U.S. soldiers were deployed in towns along the presumed border to prevent further incursions. Diplomatic negotiations resulted in the Webster-Ashburton

Treaty of 1842, which defined the St. John River as the natural border between the two countries, ending what historians now call the Bloodless Aroostook War.

But the new boundary also meant that families like the Farrells, who considered themselves residents of one country, suddenly found themselves residents of the other. The Farrell homestead was on the side of the river that had been deemed part of Maine, and Violette Brook was renamed Van Buren in honor of the sitting U.S. president, Martin Van Buren. And so it was that Michael Farrell, an Irish immigrant who settled in Canada and married a French girl, died on American soil in 1855 at the age of seventy-two, his descendants destined to trace their roots to Maine.

Michael Farrell's children were born and lived the early part of their lives during an economic boom for the town of Van Buren, the county of Aroostook, and the state of Maine. Maine was the Northeast's very own frontier state, nearly as big as the rest of the New England states combined but with a small fraction of the population. In the early 1800s, Americans migrated there in droves from places like Massachusetts and New Hampshire, hoping to stake claims and make their fortunes in farming, lumber, and fishing. The state's very name—"Maine," to distinguish the "mainland" from the hundreds of islands that dotted its shores—was bestowed by early colonial explorers who spotted, from sea, the towering pine trees growing ashore and recognized their potential value as readymade shipmasts. And while much of Maine's best timber was in wilderness areas hundreds of miles from the ocean, its powerful rivers served as highways to carry the logs out to the sea. Tossing a tree trunk in the Penobscot, a 350-mile-long waterway that provided a direct connection between the landlocked northern city of Bangor and the Atlantic, was like rolling a marble down a hill.

By the 1830s, the lumber industry was fueling a real estate boom in Maine that rivaled Manhattan's in the late 1990s. One tale held that a visitor to Bangor in 1835 couldn't find a hotel room, so he paid seventy-five cents to lean against a signpost. Five years later, the signpost-leaning rights were sold for five dollars. In another story, two paupers escaped from the Bangor almshouse and before they were caught, they'd made eighteen hundred dollars speculating on timberland.

But the truth was in some ways even stranger than fiction: Maine's rivers at times became so filled with floating logs that tree-trunk traffic came to a halt and the water beneath literally could not be seen; the phenomenon gave rise to the expression "logjam." It was not uncommon for more than a million feet of lumber to be cut in a single day as production exploded in the 1830s; pine trees from Maine at one point accounted for a full seventy-five percent of all U.S. timber exports. As time went on, new inventions—the chainsaw, the circular saw, the peavey—aided production, and by the mid-1800s, the banks of every waterway in the state were lined with lumber mills.

Thousands of men found work cutting trees and working in the mills in Aroostook, the mind-bogglingly huge, wild county where Van Buren was located. One-fifth the size of the entire state of Maine, larger than Connecticut and Rhode Island combined, and the largest county east of the Mississippi River, Aroostook County was ripe for development. Aroostook was home to two thousand bodies of water, large and small, acre upon acre of unmapped woods, and a river valley that offered some of the best farmland in the Northeast. With the Canadian border dispute settled once and for all, Maine did what it could to encourage growth in the area. Land was sold cheaply and settlers were allowed to work off their debt by helping to build state roads in places where there had previously been no way to travel except along the river.

Michael Farrell's property became increasingly valuable as the town of Van Buren—its Main Street and roads—grew up around what had once been those acres of "poorly cleared" farmland. As adults, several of Michael's children ended up with parcels from the original land grant, and they became among the most prominent local citizens and businessmen of their day. Charles Farrell had a general store in town and also operated a lumber mill on the St. John River. John B. Farrell ran a hardware store next to his brother's store and was a classic example of an upstanding town father. He was the first town clerk, the first superintendent of schools, a mail carrier on the Caribou-Presque Isle line, and served two terms in the state legislature as well. The house on Main Street where he lived with his family stands to this day.

Michael Farrell Jr., his father's namesake, also rose to local prominence, becoming a deputy sheriff, a justice of the peace, and Van Buren's first postmaster, in addition to running his own farm and operating a ferry across the St. John. His small estate alone—including just one parcel of the larger lot his father had bought for eight dollars and later split among several children—was valued at a thousand dollars in the 1870 census. It seemed that the offspring of the Irishman whom Germain Dubé had eyed so skeptically were doing quite well.

Michael Jr., like his father before him, married a French Catholic girl from the other side of the St. John River. He and his bride, Eulalia Bellefleur, were married in the same church at St. Basile where Michael and Julia wed, in New Brunswick where Eulalia's family still lived. Eulalia was a schoolteacher, and like her mother-in-law Julia, her ancestors had deep roots in the New World. But while the Dubés were among the earliest settlers of Quebec, Eulalia Bellefleur's ancestors were from Acadia, the name given by colonial explorers to Nova Scotia, New Brunswick, and the area that was later defined as Northern Maine. Eulalia's great-great-great-great-grandfather, a Frenchman named Pierre Thibodeau, was among the first Acadians, immigrating to the New World in the 1650s. But eventually the area came under British rule, and in 1755, the English deported the Acadians, burning their homes, confiscating their possessions, and herding thousands of them onto ships to be dispersed into exile in various British colonies. Some hid; some made their way back after years of wandering; some ended up in Louisiana, to form an Acadian—or Cajun—settlement there. Eulalia's family ended up in New Brunswick, and she was born there in a town called Green River.

The wanderings of the Acadians and their cruel routing by the British were immortalized in Longfellow's poem *Evangeline*. It narrated the story of an Acadian girl separated from her fiancé amid the chaos of the brutal deportation. When the two are finally reunited, many years later, Evangeline's lover dies in her arms. I know the poem from an old, fragile book my mother owned, a book I assumed she kept and cared for because the poet was from Maine, and because the verse's famous opening words—"This is the forest primeval, the murmuring pines and the hemlocks"—conjured up a vision of the woods she loved. It was only years after my mother died, as I got to know the family history and some of my distant cousins, that I realized the story of Evangeline was connected to us. But I can't help but wonder: Did my mother know? And was that why this poem mattered? And did she leave behind this dusty little book of verse, printed in 1897, with its faded cover and stitched-together pages and black-and-white illustrations, to prompt my thoughts about it, like a smear of white paint on a tree trunk to reassure you that you're still on the trail?

Or was it all coincidence?

For the distant cousins I have met through the Farrell genealogy, many of whom have far more French blood than I do, the Acadian connection to our family is extremely important. The deportation of the Acadians was a story overtly told in many of their homes, the way Jews of my generation explain to their children first about Passover, when Pharoah enslaved the Jews, and then about Hitler, who tried to wipe them out. In fact, when I took my own children to Grand-Pré, in Nova Scotia, to a memorial built on what is presumed to be the site of the deportation, I found myself explaining it to them in terms of the Exodus story—that just like the Jews, these Acadians were uprooted from their homeland and sent wandering for years, but somehow, also like the Jews, they held on to their heritage. That identity remains strong today, both in parts of Canada and in Aroostook, where many American-born descendants of the French wanderers still speak English with a heavy French accent, and where menus are as likely to list *poutines* and *ployes* as they are french fries and pancakes. My children don't normally have any interest in historic sites; they'd rather go to a playground than look at a painting or an antique tool. But for some reason, they wanted to know more about Evangeline and what happened to her people. Had I told the story better, because it meant more to me, than other historic tales I tried to hook them on? Or is it just a better-than-average story? Perhaps they understood my explanation for how

we were connected to the story, and that increased the appeal. Whatever
it was, it was powerful, just as it had been for me when I was a child
and my mother told it to me.

Every boom is followed by a bust, and the irrational exuberance, to
borrow a twenty-first-century phrase, of nineteenth-century Maine simply could not last, fueled as it was by a limited resource, the virgin
forests. It was 1846 when Henry David Thoreau journeyed to Maine
"to see where the white-pine, the Eastern stuff of which our houses
are built, grew," as he relates in *The Maine Woods*. But already, by then,
the stateliest trees were long gone. One lumberman told Thoreau that
"what was considered a 'tip-top' tree" in 1846 would not even have
been looked at twenty years earlier; standards for harvest changed as the
best stands disappeared. Of course other woods came into vogue as the
pine forests gave out—spruce, birch, beech, and oak—but within a few
years, the reserves for each tree in turn were quickly depleted.

And just as the timber boom began to fade, the Civil War began.
Maine had virtually no blacks, free or slave, but preservation of the
union and abolition were hugely popular local causes. Mainers felt that
the state owed its very existence to the controversy over slavery, having
been admitted to the union as a free state in 1820 in exchange for the
creation of Missouri as a slave state. But the so-called Missouri Compromise was also viewed as a devil's deal, contributing to the spread of
human bondage by trading Maine's statehood for Missouri's slaves. Others saw the Missouri Compromise as a tragic formalization of an irrec-
oncilable split between North and South, an acknowledgment of two
Americas in one country and a foreshadowing of the Civil War. Thomas
Jefferson, an old man when it happened, said the Missouri Compromise
"filled me with terror. I considered it at once the knell of the union."
Harriet Beecher Stowe wrote *Uncle Tom's Cabin* while living in Maine,
and when the Civil War broke out, seventy thousand men from Maine—
ten percent of the state's total population—energetically marched off to
front lines that were hundreds and sometimes thousands of miles away.
Among them was the famous lieutenant colonel of the Twentieth
Maine Volunteer Infantry Regiment, Joshua Chamberlain, who had six

horses shot out from under him and whose men valiantly helped hold the Union line at Gettysburg.

Nearly ten thousand of the soldiers Maine sent to fight the Civil War died on battlefields far from home; many more chose not to return. The population of Maine had doubled in the forty years between the time Michael Farrell married Julia Dubé and the beginning of the Civil War, but between 1860 and 1870, census takers found the number of people living in Maine had actually decreased, from 628,279 to 626,915.

Michael and Julia's two youngest sons, Edward and Andrew, were among those who fought in the Federal Army. They were also among those who moved away from Van Buren when the war was over. Unlike some of their older siblings, neither one of them had ended up owning any of the original Farrell land grant, and when they came marching home, they found the lumber jobs that had once been plentiful were suddenly scarce. Not only had clear-cutting depleted the forests, but after the Civil War, steel replaced wood as the material of choice for shipbuilders, and steam replaced sails as the best way to power a ship. Maine's shipbuilding industry, which once helped fuel demand for timber, began to fade as well. Locally, in Aroostook, a series of fires destroyed many of the sawmills along the St. John. "Hard times," Charles Farrell, who remained in Van Buren, wrote in 1884 to his brother Andrew, "is the general cry everywhere."

Many young men from Maine—including some of Michael Farrell's grandsons—who came of age in the late nineteenth century could not find work. Some went west to work for lumber companies in Washington State, Montana, and Oregon, where the harvest of virgin forests was just beginning. Another fifty thousand people left Maine after the war to take their chances in the gold rush or to take advantage of cheap land on a newer frontier—the flat, fertile plains of the Midwest. In 1880, Maine had sixty-four thousand farms; the number decreased every year after that until, by the 1930s, there were barely half that. As a result, Maine is much greener today than it was a hundred years ago; any hiker can tell you that it's not unusual to stumble across stone foundations, unreadable tombstones, or even apples covering the ground in the woods where some old abandoned orchard is still bearing fruit. When the one-time pioneers of Maine moved on to the next frontier out West, the forest primeval started creeping back.

Michael Jr. and Eulalia had thirteen children, but their prospects were not nearly as bright as the previous generation's. Not only were times hard, but a family fondness for drink was beginning to cause some problems. Maine banned the sale of alcohol the year that Michael Jr. and Eulalia were wed, but that didn't seem to prevent the ruination of several Farrells in the second and third generations whose drunken reputations outlived them by a hundred years. Among those with a terrible weakness for liquor was one of Michael Jr.'s sons, named Michael for his father and grandfather but known throughout their French-speaking community as Michel.

As an old man, Michel Farrell, the father of my grandfather William Farrell, was said to have suffered from delirium tremens and to have seen things that weren't there. And as a young man just starting out in life, he chose to marry a woman who also liked to drink and who, in today's jargon, would be labeled a codependent. Lena Michaud was her name, and they married in 1881, two years after Michel's father died. Now several of Michel's relatives had married Michauds; it was a common enough surname for that place and time. And like the other Michauds, Lena spoke French, and was a Catholic. But there was something about Lena that set her apart from all the other Michauds, and that was the fact that she appeared to have come from nowhere. Today, with the click of a mouse or an afternoon spent in a library, anybody interested in the history of a Van Buren family can trace their ancestors back for several hundred years. Church records are plentiful; Census records are available; and even some state and town records are accessible. Julia Dubé and Eulalia Bellefleur's ancestors can be dug up as far back as the 1500s; Michael Farrell is listed as "the immigrant ancestor" of the "Farrell line" in a fat, old book on genealogy in the Maine State Archives in Augusta. But Lena Michaud appears to exist only in marriage to Michel and as mother to her three sons. Her own identity—where she came from, when she was born, who her parents were—has disappeared. Even her very name is a subject of debate: Lena or Lina? Or Delina, Adelina, or Helena? Michaud or Mitchell, Mishoo, or Misheau? Any one of those is possible; no one knows for sure.

But for all we don't know about the mysterious Lina-Lena-Delina-Adelina-Helena Michaud-Mitchell-Mishoo-Misheau, we do know this: There was a good reason she hid who she was. And that's because she was an Indian.

In school, in the twenty-first century, my children learn that Indians—now called Native Americans—were the "first" Americans, that they were noble and innocent, naively helpful to the explorers and settlers who exploited them and killed them, and worshipful of the environment that the rest of us have spent the past four hundred years destroying. Modern pedagogy holds that Columbus didn't discover America; he disrupted it. The Puritans weren't pure; they were arrogant. And Manhattan wasn't bought; it was stolen from people who didn't understand the terms of the contract. It's unambiguous, good guy–bad guy stuff, easy for a kid to get a handle on; and it comes with a ready-made slot for your emotions. You're supposed to be awed by the beautiful beadwork and well-designed teepees, but also guilty and sad about the way things turned out, with all of those tribes and their sacred animals dying. History is now being taught as if it were a series of street muggings, in which every significant development is a struggle between victim and perpetrator. In this chapter, the Indians are the victims, and the rest of us are criminals.

When I was growing up in the 1960s, of course, we learned it differently. Like every schoolchild of my generation, I was taught that Columbus was bold and brave and smart, one of the great figures of history; that the "first" Americans were the Pilgrims who came on the *Mayflower*, that unless you got here before 1776, you were an immigrant and an interloper; and that Manhattan was an insignificant island when the Dutch made their offer.

But even when I was little, there was already a flip side to these legends, a cultural nudge-nudge, wink-wink, from adults and from sitcoms and movies, and even from the basic story line in our social studies books. The under-the-table suggestion was that the way we were being taught about the Pilgrims and the Indians was a scam or a joke, and that while we all had to pay lip service to these ideas and spit them back out in our fourth-grade reports, it wasn't really what anybody thought and it was okay to make fun of it all in private. It was a little bit like religion, or Santa, or the tooth fairy, or saying the Pledge of Allegiance. The grown-ups would all pretend to believe the version we were taught until we were old enough to figure out what was really going on, but they weren't allowed to tell you outright; you had to be old enough to develop your own brand of weary cynicism. So eventually, I, like everybody else, caught on. I picked up the clues from *F Troop*, my favorite sitcom, in which the palefaces were as moronic as the redskins. And I got the idea from Marx Brothers movies, in which the big-bosomed lady with the faux English accent and the lorgnette, while clearly one of those *Mayflower* descendants, was also a pretentious fool. And I even figured it out from history itself, in which the Pilgrims were helpless idiots, the explorers were disease-bearing brutes, and the buyers of Manhattan were savvy shysters, grinning madly as they walked away from New York's first great real estate deal. It wasn't quite the guilt-inducing, solemn view my children learn, but it was not unrelated. It was just that instead of victims and perps, there were winners and losers, and sometimes the winners were jerks.

My growing comprehension of all of this was reinforced, oddly enough, by my father, whose entire family consisted of Russian Jews. I, of course, had never met any of these *Mayflower* descendant types I had read about, but I understood the concept well enough, and I knew that in New York City, where I grew up, none of my public school classmates, relatives, friends, or neighbors fit the *Mayflower* category.

But Daddy, for some reason, often made little jokes about the DAR and other blue bloods; the suggestion was that while a lot of these people lived in New England, and even in Maine, none of them were related to my mother, or, by extension, to me. He was fond of telling a little story, with a knowing little grin, that whenever one of these unnamed individuals tried to impress Annie Farrell by saying (and here he'd throw his nose in the air), "My family came over on the *May-*

flower!" she would always respond, as cool and cynical as Lauren Bacall bantering with Humphrey Bogart, "Well, *my* family was waiting to greet yours when they stepped off the boat!" So pleased was my father with my mother's alleged comeback to whatever snob was trying to put her in her place that he would always chuckle at the punchline, as if he hadn't told the story a hundred times before.

My mother never interrupted or tried to tell the story herself; it seems to me that she just sat there, smoking, a slightly detached look on her face, her head cocked to one side and her eyes narrowed. She seemed to be smoldering, or biting her tongue, or somehow feeling annoyed that he was telling this story again, but feared that if she tried to stop him, she would call more attention to it, and that would be a bad thing. Did it somehow embarrass her to have this little tidbit from her past exposed, she of so many secrets? Could it be that the story wasn't true, that she had said it once to him, in jest, but he'd now repeated it so often that she couldn't bear to set the record straight? Or was she proud at having stood up to whatever Yankee matron had tried to make her feel inferior?

Perhaps she was merely mortified that the story had been reduced to a Vaudeville routine, recited once or twice a year regardless of who was in the audience in order to get a big laugh for the star, who ended up being David, not her. Or did she feel that somehow in relating the anecdote again and again, David had managed to change the subtext of the story, so that now she had become the butt of the joke instead of the wise guy? Whatever it was, I could sense she was stopping herself from stopping him, as she sometimes did, with a bitchy, snarled, "Oh David, you know it didn't happen that way!" But it also seemed like she was trying to hide her discomfort, as if she wanted to appear nonchalant, as if she didn't want me to watch her listening.

Over time the story took on a life of its own, to the point where I couldn't bear to hear my father say it because I sensed my mother's discomfort and I knew that he did not; I would listen without listening, look away and shut my mind off, let the words roll over me so that the content didn't register, and smile wanly at the end so my father wasn't hurt.

But what I never did was ask what is obvious to me now: What did the story mean? *"My family was waiting to greet yours when they stepped off the boat."* The implication is that my mother's "family" consisted of the Indians who lived here before the Europeans arrived. The implication is so clear that by the time I was old enough to understand the story, I assumed I knew exactly what it meant. But now that I am middle-aged and my parents are both dead, the story seems to be in code, like the teaching about the Indians in school. There's another meaning, not the surface meaning, and I have yet to get it. Why didn't I ask: What tribe, how do you know your family was Indian, who told you, where did they come from? It was in my head, that story, like the definition in a crossword puzzle that I kept racking my brain to solve. If I only thought about it hard enough, maybe the answer would just come to me. But obsessing about it only deepened the mystery. There were other clues of course—fragments of conversations, tidbits related by various relatives, stories in my head that seem so bizarre I wonder sometimes if I've made them all up. Sometimes I start all over again, and approach every cousin and aunt who has ever claimed to know with a fresh question, as if it's never been asked before: Was Lena Michaud an Indian, and how do you know? But every person has a different answer, and it's impossible to reconcile the stories. She was a full-blooded Indian princess, I was told; she was the daughter of a tribal governor. She was kidnapped from a reservation and raised by Christian missionaries; she was practically a slave to the family that stole her; or she ran away from an oppressive father and voluntarily lived among the whites. She was a Penobscot, or a Micmac, or a Maliseet. Her very name was a trick, or a clue, or a puzzle: Lena, Lina, Delina, Adelina, Helena, Michaud, Mitchell, Mishoo, or Misheau. She changed it on purpose to cover her tracks. Or maybe she was just going back and forth between the Anglos and the French. Or maybe she was simply illiterate.

I was determined to straighten all this out. I would search the records, I would scrutinize Web sites, I would pore over Census forms, I would read the histories, I would interview everyone until I got the story straight. There was no way this woman was going to hide from me!

I started where everyone starts their research these days: on the Internet, from the privacy of my own home, using Web sites that had produced incredibly accurate genealogies of every other ancestor on my mother's side. There are many Lena Michauds, of course, and takers for every other permutation of her name. But using my grandfather's birthday, I was able to find the Lena Michaud who was, indisputably, his mother; she shows up in many different places as Michel's wife and William's mother. The only problem was that where she came from, when she was born, who her parents were, is all missing. It's like she appeared, fully grown, on her wedding day in 1883, with any past she might have had suddenly wiped out.

I wasn't the first person to come up empty-handed. About fifteen years ago, one of my cousins hired a genealogist who knew everything there was to know about Van Buren, a woman named Martine Pelletier, to try to find Lena. She did not succeed. Another cousin traveled to Indian Island, where the Penobscot reservation is located, to look through records there, but nothing matched our Lena. I asked all my aunts, who vaguely recalled a story about their father's mother being an Indian, but who had no specifics about where or what. Then I started all over again, with the most basic information that I had. An Indian princess? It sounded a little suspect; these tribes had no royalty. On a whim, I typed the words "Penobscot Indian princess" into a search engine, and got a message from the Penobscot Web site.

> Many people contact the Penobscot Nation asking for information from tribal records that might establish or prove Penobscot ancestry. In some instances, their inquiries are documented with solid background information but many are based only on a family tradition of Indian blood. For example, there has always been a family story that great-great-grandma was a full-blooded Indian princess.

Clearly the Indian princess theory was someone's idea of a joke, a joke that I was just now getting. But I didn't give up. Even though I didn't know her birthdate, if she was married and having children in the 1880s, she would surely show up in the 1880 Census as a teenager or twenty-something. I spent a week or so sifting through Census data at the New York Public Library and the National Archives, hunting down every person in the 1880 Census whose name might be related to hers. Although I turned up many women with her name, almost none were the right age—except for one: Lina Michaud, listed as a twenty-year-old "housekeeper" in the 1880 Census, living with a family of Michauds in Cyr Plantation, a town in Aroostook County not far from Van Buren. The Census taker noted that the family had recently immigrated from New Brunswick; I remembered one of my mother's cousins telling me that "our grandmother was a full-blooded Indian, come down from Canada." It seemed likely that this was her; the age was right, the place was right, the origin was right.

But did that mean she wasn't an Indian after all, that she was instead the biological daughter of this family she was living with? I went back to the Internet genealogies and found the family. Everyone listed in the Census as part of their household was also listed in their genealogy, everyone except for Lina. How to explain that she appears with this family in the Census, but not in their genealogy? It was as if to suggest that although she shared their last name and lived with them, she was not, in fact, related to them. Did this support the theory that she was "kidnapped" by a white family? It seemed unlikely that an illiterate French-speaking couple, the father a carpenter with seven children, would have the means or motivation to "kidnap" an Indian girl; and if he had, what would have stopped her from running away? They weren't living in the wilderness, miles from nowhere. They were living in a town, with farms and roads and neighbors.

The other theory was that she had run away from home or voluntarily gone with this family; that seemed more likely, that perhaps she was even working for them, as many families, even working-class families, often hired young women for little more than room and board to help out with the housework, cooking, and child care.

There was one more place I hoped to find some clues: the Maine State Archives in Augusta, where people like me, with roots in Maine, come from all over the country to solve family mysteries. I was the youngest person in the room by about twenty years as I took a seat at a microfilm machine and began to look at various records for Farrells and Michauds in Aroostook County. I laughed when I came across this passage in a contemporary book, *Maine: A Bicentennial History*, by Charles E. Clark; the description fit me and everyone else in that room so well.

> There are children and even grandchildren of those nineteenth-century emigrants who have come Back East, searching out ancestral graveyards and cellar holes, sniffing the surf and the mud flats, contemplating overgrown and useless orchards and forested former sheep pastures, and consulting genealogical dictionaries in the Maine Historical Society. Some of them stay, seasonally or year-round. And who can deny them the right to call this home?

Around me people gasped and whispered as they discovered divorces in the family that they never knew about or births coming just a few months after hastily arranged marriages. I spent most of my time there sifting through records from the nineteenth century, only to be disappointed; they are spotty at best. I had already discovered that there was no marriage certificate for Michel and Lena, and that her children's birth certificates did not list her birthplace or race. A cousin had told me that an arrest record existed for her, on a charge of public drunkenness, and that was easy to find but offered no further clues to her identity.

But one other document did. On a marriage license for Lena's son, my grandfather William Farrell, and Lizzie Noyes, his bride, information was required regarding the married couple's parents. Here William Farrell listed his mother, Lena, as having been born in Madawaska, which is the name of both a town in Maine and a county in New Brunswick. But more telling, perhaps, is what he left out. The marriage license asked for the "color" of the bride and groom's parents, and William Farrell left that line blank for his mother, Lena, while writing "white" for his father Michel. That omission is the closest thing I ever found to a documented confirmation that Lena was an Indian, as opposed to all the stories and rumors; I smiled at the thought that my grandfather had unwittingly left a clue for me to find, eighty years later, simply by leaving something blank.

Lena and Michel's first child, George, was born in Van Buren a not-quite-so-proper six months after they married. Their second child, my grandfather William, was born in 1886, also in Van Buren. But by the time their third and last child, Fred, was born in 1888, they'd moved, presumably because Michel could not find work in Van Buren, which was by then in the midst of "hard times," as his uncle Charles wrote his uncle Andrew. Fred was born in Caribou, not far from Van Buren, but soon after, Michel and Lena moved with their three sons to Waterville, a city in Central Maine where factory jobs were attracting an influx of unskilled French-Canadian laborers. They took Michel's mother Eulalia with them; Michel's well-connected father, Michael Farrell Jr., was dead, his property long sold and the proceeds long gone. Michel supported his family with an unsteady living as a housepainter and wallpaper hanger, but he seems to have spent his spare time drinking. Eventually William Farrell ended up in the state reformatory for boys in South Portland; whether it was his father's drinking, his mother's arrest, general neglect reported by others, or some transgression of the law that William, an adolescent, committed himself is unknown. But his fate was not uncommon in an era of so-called progressive child welfare, where middle-class reformers took it upon themselves to remove children from poor families on the slightest pretext, on the theory that they were better off in an institution than in a socially unacceptable home environment. William Farrell probably learned his trade as a blacksmith at the reformatory, but no one could have foreseen, in a rural state like Maine in the year 1900, what a poor choice of a career that would turn out to be.

His brothers fared differently. Fred went to France in World War I and married a French woman, Marie, while he was there. They had six sons, the first of whom, Jacques, or Jack, was born overseas. Fred built houses for a living, and his boys all inherited the musical gene that had William Farrell playing fiddle for country dances at the Morey Farm.

Jack and his three oldest brothers had a radio show out of Augusta in the 1930s and early '40s, playing folk and country music on fiddle, guitar, and mandolin. And when Jack came back from World War II, he took ten bucks out of his pocket and bought his youngest brother Timmy his own violin. Timmy went on to become a virtuoso bluegrass violinist known as Fiddlin' Timmy Farrell; his concerts and tapes are filled with old-fashioned waltzes, polkas, rags, and reels, and country classics like "Turkey in the Straw" and "Orange Blossom Special." But I really felt the family connection when he stood up at a bluegrass festival in Sidney, Maine, and started singing a funny song he wrote himself, "I'm just sitting here drinking, sitting here thinking, that there's nothing that I really wanna do."

The third brother, George Farrell, had a small filling station somewhere in Central Maine, but he never made much money. When he died in 1963, his widow Mary wrote in a letter that he had spent his last years in Providence, Rhode Island, even though they wanted "to get back to Maine before. But they did not have free hospital, medicine or doctors [in Maine] as they do" in Providence, so George died in Rhode Island. But Mary brought his body back to Maine; like my mother, he wanted to be buried there.

Over time all of the parcels in Michael Farrell's original land grant were sold outside the family, with the exception of one lot on Main Street, where John B. Farrell—the hardware store owner, mail carrier, and state legislator—had built his home. His daughter Emily married a man named Fortunat Michaud—no relation to Lena—around 1910 and inherited the house. She and her husband had it renovated in the style of the era and turned it into a magnificent Queen Anne Victorian mansion, with a three-story turret, tin walls, a columned wrap-around porch, and ornate interior woodwork. Today it is the grandest piece of architecture in the area. Emily and Fortunat ran a store on Main Street in Van Buren and had three children. One of them, Constance Michaud, ended up with the grand old house.

Constance grew up like a princess in a castle. She loved beautiful clothes and was engaged to be married to a wealthy Quebecois. But a week before the wedding, the groom died in a bizarre accident—cut on the neck with a razor while getting a shave in a barber's chair. Constance never got over the shock; she became a recluse, and gradually shut the door on one room after another in the mansion where she had decorated Christmas trees and played piano as a girl. In 1988, she had a stroke, and was moved to a nursing home, where she later died. The house and its contents were put up for sale, and the description of what was sold at auction suggests that the place had become a virtual time capsule for a real-life Miss Havisham, each room filled with possessions untouched by modernity: Depression-era radios, a map of the Western Front from World War I, Victorian clothing, books from the 1890s, and many other household objects that had become antiques simply by virtue of having stayed in one place for so long a time.

In 1991, a few years after the house was sold, I traveled to Northern Maine on vacation with my husband, and we stayed in a bed and breakfast on Main Street in Van Buren called the Farrell-Michaud House. I knew my grandfather had been born in Van Buren, but I didn't really know my family history, and the proprietor at the time couldn't say for sure if my Farrells were related to those who'd lived in the house or not. So I left Van Buren without realizing that the man who'd built the house, John B., was my great-great-grandfather's brother.

In the summer of 2002, I went back and met the woman who lives in the Farrell-Michaud House now, Susan Bouchard and her family. Susan is not a Farrell, but she knows more about the Farrell family than many of us who are blood relatives. The house is now restored to its early twentieth-century magnificence, with period wallpaper and antique furniture and old photos of the people who lived there once. Susan told me the story of Constance's doomed engagement, and she showed me how I was related to the former owners.

"I could imagine the family around the table for the holidays, and hear their conversations and general laughter," Sue wrote in a book about the house, *A Jewel in the Crown of Maine*. "I could imagine Constance in the Music Room playing a tune . . . or the family sitting around the fireplace listening to a radio program."

As I walked around the beautiful old house where my ancestors once lived, I could imagine it, too.

I'm not very clever with computers, so I can't seem to figure out how to use the various software programs for creating family trees. But I've drawn the Farrell tree on graph paper many times now, in tiny, careful print, using a pencil so I can erase and rewrite as I go along, then sending copies to all these distant cousins I have met. We trade names and dates, sending our branches back and forth so that eventually, everyone has one big, complete tree, all of them stretching back in time to Michael and Julia.

I can figure out, without too much trouble, how I'm related to everyone—how many times I need to use the word "great" to describe my relationship with someone from the past, or whether one of my newfound relatives is a second, third, or fourth cousin, and how many times removed. But it's a funny feeling to put my own name near the bottom of the tree, beneath all the people who've come before me. Somehow it makes me wonder what is it about them that has ended up in me. I am very musical; is that my fiddle-playing grandpa coming out? And the long, long bones of my arms and legs, with skinny fingers and skinny toes, limbs I inherited from my grandfather and my mother and passed down to my oldest son Danny—I wonder who else on the tree had those. When I was a teenager, I always wore my hair in braids, and sometimes I'd joke that I got those braids from my Indian great-grandma. But really I have no idea who my hair comes from—woolly, unruly, a perfect barometer of whatever moisture levels are in the atmosphere, tamed only by the strongest chemicals the government allows you to put on your body without immediately dying of cancer. My sister has the same hair—of course, she loves hers, while I hate mine—but there is no cousin on either side that we have ever seen with hair like this. And what about my eyes—not quite green and not quite brown? Whose are they, in a family where eyes are either blue or brown?

People often look at my older son and say, "He looks just like you!" And he really does, even though he has the blue eyes and straight hair

I don't. It's the shape of his face, and the way he smiles, things that are harder to quantify than eye color and hair but that actually matter more. My younger son does not inspire the doubletake people do when they see my older boy next to me, and yet sometimes when I look at the younger one, I see his brother there. I imagine strands of DNA swirling somewhere in his brain, instructing this facial muscle to move in just this way, that eyebrow to go up or down to form an expression of surprise or glee that is unmistakably genetic, like the familiar outline that remains on a Xerox of a Xerox of a Xerox.

Shortly after I began corresponding, by e-mail, with a distant cousin named Joyce Miller, I happened to be on business near her hometown in Texas. We arranged to meet for lunch inside my hotel at a certain place and time; I described myself as tall and thin and said I would carry a copy of a certain book so she would be sure to find me, since neither of us knew what the other looked like. About fifteen minutes before our lunch date, I went for a walk in downtown Fort Worth. As I crossed a busy intersection, her car pulled up at a red light and she immediately picked me out of the noontime crowds. I suppose there could be a million reasons I stuck out; New Yorkers never seem to really fit in when they visit other places. But she said there was an unmistakable family resemblance, and as I sat across from her during lunch, I saw it, too. It was in the shape of her eyes, and the bones of her face, and most certainly in her nose—not a big nose, not a button nose, but a straight and elegant nose with a finely angled tip, a nose I had seen on the faces of my mother and my aunts and the pictures of my grand-father, a nose I could recognize, even on a stranger.

Sometimes when I see a photo of myself, I can see that the shape of my face is like my mother's. If a Cubist artist were painting us, we might end up with the same eight-sided heads, with points on each side of the temples, cheekbones, jaw, and chin. But an abstract drawing would miss the difference, a difference that jumps out at me. There's nothing I am hiding; it's always easy for me to smile. She always looks like there's something on her mind, and it's something the person look-ing at her must never know.

• • •

Over the generations, a funny thing has happened to the Farrell reputation. The Farrell clan had risen to prosperity, respectability, and influence within a generation of Michael Farrell's arrival in Saint John, but somehow all of it had dissipated, as Farrell after Farrell hit the skids or the bottle or both. If one side of your family was the Farrells, the other side of your family was sure to be looking down their noses at them. And if anyone in the family had any doubts about whether this scorn was justified, all they had to do was make a pilgrimage, as many of them did, to see Uncle Eddie, the last resident of Van Buren to bear the Farrell name.

Eddie Farrell was a grandson of the original Michael, a son of Michael Jr., a brother to Michel, and an uncle to my grandfather William. He was the youngest of his thirteen brothers and sisters, and he lived in a tin shack by the St. John River, near the town dump. He had wild hair and a scraggly beard and he rarely bathed. He scavenged old furniture and other things from the garbage, cut firewood, and did odd jobs around town to make a little extra money, and had some kind of mysterious injury for which he received a monthly disability check from the government. His checks went to the main grocery store in town, an IGA run by his nephew, Charles Watson, who would dole out some of the money, knowing Eddie would blow it on booze, and keep the rest to pay off his tab at the store and for other essentials.

"As soon as Eddie got his money from Charlie, he'd first buy a pack of cigarettes and a glass of beer at the store and then immediately walk into the nearest bar and declare to anyone and everyone there, 'Drinks are on me!' " Watson's grandson, Matt, recalled. "He'd have the entire wad spent in an hour and be drunk as a skunk."

On very cold nights, Watson's wife would make a plate of hot food for Eddie and send her son Willie down to the shack by the river. "A little woodstove would be blazing away and Eddie would be in there all cozy, smoking a cigar and often whittling something out of wood," Matt recalled his father Willie telling him. "Sometimes on Sunday afternoons my dad's mom would send him to get his uncle Eddie and bring him back to the house for dinner. Eddie never wanted to come because he knew that he would be forced to take a bath and have his clothes washed."

Many other nieces, nephews, and distant cousins trooped over to the shack by the river to visit Eddie as well. John B. Farrell's great-granddaughter Emily remembered being secretly taken there as a child by her father, but when she got home, her mother always knew where she'd been. "You've seen Eddie, haven't you?" she'd always say. "I can tell by the way you smell!"

Eddie was, by all accounts, a sweet and gentle man, despite his eccentricities, bad habits, and nonconformism. And he seems to have been genuinely beloved by his family. Yes, they visited him to fulfill a familial obligation, and he served as a living warning to the children about the temptations of liquor. But they also came out of genuine affection for the last Farrell in Van Buren. Because really, what Eddie Farrell was was a lovable bum. Ironically, incredibly, in the town where his ancestors had been pioneers, in the place his own grandfather had helped to found, and in a part of Maine where his relatives had owned some of the finest property, most essential businesses, and one of the grandest houses around, the very last Farrell was homeless.

8

MAIL

LEFT: *Achsah, Peanut, Anne, Nadeen, and Lee at their father's funeral in 1954, the last time they were together.*

RIGHT: *Bill Farrell shoeing a horse.*

In the papers we found when my mother died was a letter dated the nineteenth of March, 1947, from the office of Maine's attorney general, addressed to her father, William Farrell.

Dear Mr. Farrell,

As I review my docket I note that you still have made no payments toward the support of your children in accordance with the court order against you which was made at the time the children were committed to the custody of the state of Maine. This is to advise you that unless I hear from you on or before the fifteenth of April whereby you make some satisfactory arrangement for taking care of this obligation, I shall find it necessary to prepare a petition asking that the court issue an execution against you. In accordance with this execution you will be ordered either to pay the amount of the execution or you will be committed to jail for failure to comply.

Yours very truly,
Jean Lois Bangs
Assistant Attorney General

The response was written by hand in a plain, legible script, on the reverse side of the paper.

Dear Lois Bangs,
Your letter received, and will say I am willing to try and help what I possibly can . . . Will you please advise me as to what I am expected to pay each month on the children to settle this bill. I paid a part of this bill by serving nine months in the Skowhegan jail and that did not improve my health or my feelings. I am not in very good health but I am willing to try if given a fair break. My age is past sixty years.

Respectfully,
William Farrell

My mother was living in New York at the time this letter was sent, and I always wondered how it ended up in her possession. Aunt Deen cleared up the mystery. "They wanted to put Dad back in jail," she said. "It was your mother who intervened and made some kind of an agreement with them."

What that agreement consisted of I was not able to find out. But maybe all my mother had to do was point out to state authorities that Bill Farrell was a destitute old man who'd already served time in jail; imprisoning him further would serve no purpose. Whatever she said, it made the problem go away, and he stayed out of jail, living out his days from hand to mouth, pretty much the way he always had ever since Lizzie died. As his diaries from that time record—diaries that we found among my mother's possessions after she died—he traveled with the fairs, did odd jobs, and took care of horses at any farm that would hire him. He had barely enough money to buy his next meal—but always enough for a bottle of beer.

Feb. 22, 1948. I came to Mr. and Mrs. McCarthy's Riding School. Put up a cupboard down cellar for canned goods. Fixed a door in the barn, jacked up a cross timber. Moved some manure down cellar. Put a ring in Socks' stall. Put one front shoe on Viking today.

March 17. Today I worked in the shop all day on horse shoes. I put 4 shoes on Conrads Poney $5.00.

March 18. No work in sight for money.

March 19. I wrote a letter to Anne + Achsah + Leona tonight.

June 16. I bought groceries. Potatoes $3.50 Eggs .77 Ham 3.14 Beer 1.30.

July 3. Pete paid me $20.00 for work in the woods.

Oct. 23. A letter from my daughter Achsah. A Baby Boy was Born to her on Monday Oct. 18 1948 at Hartland Hospital at 8:37 am Weight 6 lbs 11½ ozs.

Oct. 30 Sat. Today set a shoe over on Alert and one on Lucky. Then about 1130 am a car ran into Alert and pulled his hind shoes nearly off.

Oct 31. Today Dr. Brown and the state trooper came up here to see Alert he is Better today.

1st of Nov. Monday. Chores today I cleaned out the cellar and Looked after Alert and his Bad leg.

Nov. 10. Alert is no better as far as I can see.

21 Nov. No hope for Alert of getting any better. So Dr. Brown says.

29 Nov. Chores today and I started to dig a grave to bury a horse. I worked 2½ hours on the hole. Letter from Achsah yesterday.

30 Nov. This last day of Nov. Chores today and this PM I worked digging on a grave to bury a horse. I put the windows in the cellar. The masons plugged up the window in the basement.

Dec. 1st = Wed = Chores today and 1 hr on Horse grave. Carpenters and Masons were here today. Tonight I made 5 pairs of shoes and a knife blade.

6 Dec. Mon. Rain here today. This a.m. I went down to the swamp and finished the grave for Alert.

13 Monday. Today Dr. Brown came here about 2 pm and shot Alert. Mr. Obrien was there at the grave and so was I the gun he uses was 38 special. I partly covered the grave.

14 Tues. Today on this am chores and I finished closing the grave over Alert. I carved his name on a large pine tree by the grave.

24 Dec. Chores and I bought a few groceries $5.00 Tonight Harold sent the girls over with Christmas presents about 7 lbs Bacon, a 3½ lbs chicken a few potatoes an orange some cookies and an apple. Clothes were 2 union suits 2 pajama suits and 3 pairs of woolen socks.

Sat. Christmas. Just chores today. A pleasant day and no company. I paid Abey back his beer = 6 bottles.

27 Monday. I wrote letters to Anne and Achsah.

26 Feb. 1949. I heard from Anne in New York. She has a baby girl and both are well and happy and doing well.

Nov. 14. I went to Van Buren and got my birth certificate and saw my uncle Eddie Farrell.

8 Jan. More wine 2 fifths and no work.

13 Jan. no work and no money.

After sitting down one day to read through the diaries, I couldn't help but think that the death of a beloved horse named Alert appeared to loom as large in my grandfather's mind as any news from his family. I couldn't decide if I felt sorry for the old man, just barely scraping by and all alone in his old age, or disgusted with him for being such a bum.

· · ·

In his old age, long after his children had been taken from him and gone off to raise their own families, William Farrell became a devoted correspondent to his five daughters, beginning every letter with "Dearest Daughter," and ending each note, "Love and Best Wishes, From Dad, Wm. Farrell."

"There seems to be no end to all our troubles in Life," he wrote in one letter to Achsah. "Its Just one dam thing after another." In another note, dated January of 1953, he asked her, "Can you keep warm in your house do you have plenty of wood and groceries I sure hope that you do. I am here at the Lewiston fairgrounds and have been here since last fall, I havent worked any since last October there Is no Work here at Present I have only shod 4 Horses since last fall, I am fairly well xcept for a cold I live here in an old Blacksmith Shop I am keeping Warm so far and have been able to get some groceries up till now But it don't Look to good for the next 3 months Jan. Feb. March. Then work will begin again. Well dear if I can Be of any Help let me know and If I can come up to help you In any way I will Be glad to do so."

Achsah always wrote back right away, sometimes sending along postage and envelopes to make it easier for her dad to reply. And it was one of those very letters, sitting on a table in a shack where her father was found dead, that enabled the town selectmen of Passadumkeag to track her down on the last Monday night of July in 1954, and inform her of William Farrell's death.

The selectmen met every Monday night in Passadumkeag to discuss important matters like who owed what in taxes, and on that particular night, they decided to take a ride over to see Bill Farrell after the meeting. They'd planned to ask him when he was going to come up with the seventy-eight dollars he owed in order to stay in the shack where he was living. It was actually an old henhouse on a little piece of land near a pond, and the old man had bought the place for a dollar on condition that he pay the back taxes. He liked the place; it didn't have much by way of amenities, no plumbing, no phone, but it had a nice, deep, cold well, and it was no secret that he'd been jacking (what people in Maine call poaching) deer out of season whenever he felt like it in the nearby woods. Oh well, an old man like that had to eat somehow, and the good town fathers cared far less about state hunting laws than they did about town coffers. They didn't figure he'd have the money, and they weren't sure what they could do to get it from him; after all, you can't get water from a stone. But it was worth stopping by anyway, just to prod him; they knew he had a couple of grown children, and maybe he could borrow some from them.

The last light of day was fading and the mosquitos were out in force when the selectmen pulled up in the yard around 8:30 P.M. They noticed what looked like groceries scattered around the yard leading to his door, but didn't think too much about it. A knock at the unlocked door went unanswered, so they took the liberty of letting themselves in. There they found William Farrell slumped over in his chair, his head lying on the table. They gently shook him to see if he might be sleeping, but as they feared, he was not. His hand was cold to the touch when one of the men took it in his own to check for a pulse that he did not find. Slightly spooked and slightly humbled, the selectmen of Passadumkeag returned to their car, drove to a phone, and called the sheriff in Lincoln, the nearest city; the sheriff in turn summoned a coroner.

The selectmen also found an envelope in Bill Farrell's shack with a return address that looked like it belonged to someone in the family, someone named Achsah. A call was placed to the telephone operator of the town, who called Achsah's neighbor because she knew Achsah had no phone. "Family emergency, you're wanted on the phone," was all the neighbor said when Achsah answered the door. When she finally got to the phone at the neighbor's house, she learned that her father was dead.

The cause of death was given as cerebral hemorrhage, but as with so many other aspects of William Farrell's life, its end seemed full of mysteries. His glasses were missing, and so was his violin. A deer was down the well, suggesting to some of his daughters that he'd been vigorous enough in the days before he died to shoot and haul the carcass from the woods. And the groceries spilled around the yard—it made them wonder if there had perhaps been some sort of struggle. Peanut, whose own home was not far from where her father had been living, had actually been to see him earlier that same day, but when she saw him slumped over, she assumed he was drunk and walked out. Deen was certain, when she saw the body at the funeral home, that there was a contusion on his head covered up with makeup by the undertaker, but when she asked about it, she was told that he'd probably hit his head when he collapsed. There were rumors that he'd had an affair with a married woman in town, angering her husband; and his diaries were filled with the unfamiliar names of women he wrote letters to, shared his meager groceries with, and even, sometimes, accompanied to see a movie.

It was all so bizarre that Achsah even wrote to the town selectmen, asking that they investigate whether foul play might have been a factor in her father's death. But the chairman of the board simply responded with a letter describing the circumstances under which they found his body, and ended with a polite, "I am very sorry about your father's death and offer my sincere condolence."

The funeral was held four days after the body was found. William Farrell's daughters knew he would have wanted a Catholic burial, but the local parish church said he hadn't paid his Easter duties and therefore could not be buried on consecrated ground. So Anne's husband David bought a plot in a different graveyard on an out-of-the-way street in Howland, a town in Northern Maine not far from where William Farrell died. It was a peaceful, shady spot on a hill under a pine tree; Anne thought that she herself might someday like to be buried there, so David bought a second plot as well. He also insisted on taking a picture of Anne and her sisters, reunited for the funeral for the first time since they were kids. "You girls don't know if you'll ever be all together like this again," he said.

And he was right. They never were.

My sister found the photo not long ago, and I made copies for the aunts, mailing them to Peanut, Achsah, and Lee, and delivering one in person to Deen, who lives not far from me in New York City. I pointed out to her my favorite feature: Even though all the sisters were different heights and wearing different outfits, their hems all hung precisely the same fourteen inches from the ground, like a uniform.

Aunt Deen smiled as I ran my finger across the line the five hems formed. "We all look so thin," she murmured. Then we went through them one by one, noting Achsah's pretty suit, Peanut looking so young, Lee's cute pocketbook, and Deen with her arms around the others.

Then we got to my mother. Her hair was unkempt, pulled unattractively off her face and hanging limply on her shoulders, her blouse was carelessly unbuttoned on top, her jaw was closed tight, and she didn't have even a hint of the smile that the other sisters wore.

"Your mother," Deen started, then sighed, not knowing how to put what she wanted to say. Finally she nodded and said, "She looks troubled."

My Aunt Achsah lives in a small house on the edge of a field surrounded by woods. I almost never see another car once I turn on to the quiet road that leads to her, a road that in my childhood was dirt and gravel but that has since been paved with blacktop. The cows at the farm that I pass on the way always stare curiously at me, their big mouths steadily chewing as I drive by, one of the few vehicles to disturb their reveries. They always make me think of the cows who surrounded Achsah when she was a little girl on the Morey Farm, stranded atop the woodpile, too terrified to climb down until a grown-up came to the rescue.

Aunt Achsah doesn't leave her house anymore; a lifetime of smoking has damaged her lungs so badly that she doesn't dare breathe outside air. Instead she stays tethered to an oxygen machine, with clear plastic tubes inserted in her nostrils as she sits on her sofa, right next to the television and just a few steps away from her kitchen, bedroom, and bathroom. She also has diabetes and is easily tired. The phone rings often, with calls from Deen, the occasional old friend or neighbor, and one or the other of her seven children. Two of her children—my cousins—still live in Maine and are near enough to make her breakfast almost every day and keep her well supplied with groceries; a home health aide also helps out for a few hours every week. I like to stop by, too, whenever I am up in Maine; she always has a story to tell me, or a forty-year-old letter from my mother that she's come across, or a new thought on an old subject that we've discussed before. Like me, Aunt Achsah enjoys good food, so we usually start off by sharing something tasty; she likes my husband's meat loaf and mashed potatoes, so once each summer I bring her a dish of that. When we are done eating, I sit across from her, next to a shelf covered with small framed photos, including my mother's high school graduation picture, and we begin to talk. She has an amazing memory, and I have found that any fragment of information she gives me, whether it's a date, a description of a place from long ago, the name of someone she only met once, or a type of food no one makes anymore, always turns out to be precisely right.

Aunt Achsah has also become, in the twenty years since my mother died, the person I most closely associate with her. I see the physical resemblance in small things: her nose, the Farrell nose, and the shape of her eyes, but it's really not the way she looks that brings me back; it's her mannerisms. It's the involuntary shudder she makes when something is distasteful ("Yucky!" as she puts it), or how she coughs her laugh out of her open mouth, a rumble from her chest that begrudgingly turns into a guffaw, or the way she snaps her head from side to side when she is annoyed by someone acting, as she says in her Maine accent, "smat"—"smart" without any trace of an *r*. She is a medium for connecting with my mother; she is as close as I can come to making contact, and she seems conscious of what's expected.

"There was no one like your mother," she always tells me whenever I visit. "She was a really special lady." They're words she knows I'm hungry for, and I lap them up gratefully.

Sometimes she has a letter for me she's unearthed, something my mother wrote many years before. Sometimes it's a picture, or just one more story I have never heard. "Hey," she'll say, "did I ever tell you about the time your mother was living across town, at the Connicks', and she came home on Sunday?"

I don't remember this one, so I shake my head.

"Well, we had potatoes, but I guess my father gave her the money to get mayonnaise and eggs to make potato salad, and I remember we sat out there and thought we were having the feast of a lifetime," she said, smiling at the thought of it. "Imagine that was the feast of a lifetime! Egg-potato salad for dinner, and we thought we were *so* lucky."

We laugh together, and I say, as I often do, how much I admire the way she persevered. Long after rocket ships had headed into space and most Americans had TVs, she was still pumping water to wash dishes, building fires in a woodstove, and using kerosene lamps. She didn't get electricity until 1951, and she didn't get plumbing till 1968, by which time her oldest kids were in college. Her life in Maine in the 1950s and '60s was not all that different, if measured by the lack of amenities, than the way she'd grown up in the '20s and '30s. I wasn't even sure that the lives of her ancestors, back in Van Buren in the previous century, were all that much worse.

As if to illustrate, she relates, with a smile, one of her favorite anecdotes, an example of multitasking that puts a yuppie working mother like me to shame.

"I had seen the time when my kids were little where I had a kid taking a pee in a jar, another kid taking a shit in the pot, and another kid sitting on the potchair with a bunch of newspapers underneath," she says. "If three of them had to go, what else are you going to do?"

I think about the routines I hate, and feel like a spoiled princess in comparison. I hate unloading the dishwasher, and sorting the socks. I hate serving dinner and not getting to eat mine till it's cold because I have to get up a half-dozen times to deal with the phone, a spill, a special request from a child, a missing condiment, or whatever else has to be attended to before I can get the fork in my mouth. I hate being so busy on any given evening with work or chores or meetings that I don't have time to play a game of cards with my boys. I hate staying home with the kids when they are sick—just like my mother did! And I hate wishing that I had more time to write at the same time that I wish I had more time to spend with them. But all of that is so *dumb* compared to what Aunt Achsah had to do. It's so dumb I can't even bring myself to tell her.

Instead, I just say: "I don't know how you survived. I don't know how you got up in the morning to have another day. Sometimes when I am feeling sorry for myself, I say, 'Aunt Achsah had seven kids and washed the diapers in melted snow.' So what's so bad about my life?"

"Well, I'm glad you sympathize with me," she says, then recounts to me the accomplishments of her children, five of the seven having graduated from college, their careers ranging from high-paid consultant to superintendent of a school district. I tell her the way her children turned out is all a testament to her own hard work in raising them, but she throws the credit right back to them. "I am proud that they did all they did," she says, "and that they earned their own way."

We drift, as we often do, back to her own childhood, this time to her father's death. I express surprise that she and her sisters showed him so much love as adults, that they stayed in touch and weren't angrier over the neglect that led to their being taken away by the state.

"He was our father, after all," she says, then adds that their correspondence was so regular, she was certain she'd get a letter from him even after he died. "I kept telling myself, 'You're going to get a letter from your father. You're going to get a letter from your father,'" she recalls. "And then I'd say to myself, 'You can't, you dummy, your father's dead!'"

But she knew he'd received her last letter, because it was the one the town fathers used to find her, and she just couldn't stop herself from expecting a letter back.

Then later that week the mailman brought what she had somehow known was coming: A parting message from her father, written, as always, in pencil, in his familiar, legible script, addressed to "Dear Daughter Achsah," and signed, "Love to you + Family, From Dad, Wm. Farrell." It had been mailed before his death and delivered afterward, a message from beyond the grave, loving and at the same time unnerving.

It was the final good-bye from someone who had no chance to say it, to someone who was more than glad to hear it. It almost made me jealous; what I wouldn't give for something like that.

9

NUTS

David in his uniform.

A few hours before my mother slipped into a coma, Nancy told me that she thought we ought to be touching her, that it would give her some comfort as she let go of life to have her hands held or her head gently stroked. But when we approached the bed, she didn't really seem to want us there. Instead, she just kept moaning, "David, I want David." All the misery he had brought her over the years didn't matter; in the end, she was madly devoted to him.

But why? I tried to put myself in the shoes of a country girl in the big city, just after World War II, meeting this handsome soldier and listening to all his war stories for the first time. She had no idea that she'd be listening to them for the rest of her life. She only knew that he was a hero, that he was fearless, and that now he wanted to have fun. She never imagined when they first married that his buddies from World War II would always be his first priority—more important to him than she was, more important than his children. But even after she realized how low she was on his list, she never really understood why.

I didn't either, growing up. And when I went back through my mother's life, trying to find the seeds of her despair, I kept coming back to my father. He wasn't a bad man; to the contrary, he was brave and gallant and funny and kind. Yet he could have done so much more to make her happy, and it seemed that he chose not to. He just didn't care about the things that made her miserable—where they lived, and how much money they had, and how many hours he spent away from home, working or carousing or partying with his army buddies. He had survived this terrible war, and now he was going to enjoy life; she could come along to the bars and the veterans' reunions, or she could stay home and be miserable.

She decided to stay home, and I understood why. Because when she went with him to these events—and I attended a few as a girl—he ditched her for his friends. He'd come for one reason, and one reason only: to talk about the war with the only people in the world he knew for sure would care—other paratroopers.

A friend of my husband's family, someone who never met my parents, told me she understood what my mother had gone through. Her husband also served during World War II; she knew him before he went overseas and still remembers his serial number, sixty years later, because she wrote him a letter every single day.

"We all had high hopes that when the war was over we'd settle down and live happily ever after," she told me. "But his happiest moments seemed to be when he had a reunion with his buddies. I was there like the other wives. We tried to fit in. They were all nice people. The women, we sat together and talked about kids or recipes—not that any of that appealed to me at the time; my son wasn't born yet. But we just tried to be the best possible wives. We felt it was our role, if not our duty. After all, these were war heroes.

"But coming home, and being one of the ones who survived, didn't seem to comfort my husband at all, except when he was with his buddies," she added. "I couldn't get him into my world, and he knew I couldn't fit into his."

Somehow her husband, like my father, could only feel whole in the company of other veterans. All through the war, they talked about resuming civilian life, but once they got home, they couldn't stop talking about the war.

I don't remember my father ever reading me a story from a book. He didn't need to. He had too many stories in his head. He told stories from Greek mythology, like the story of the Trojan Horse, and stories from the Old Testament, like the story of King Solomon and the infant with two mothers. He told stories from his childhood, like the day he watched the cops shoot a horse that had slipped on the ice and broken its leg. And stories about food, like his favorite store-bought lunch, a nickel-a-*shtikl* and a two-cents plain, which translated to a five-cent stick of salami and a seltzer that cost two pennies. There were also stories about his relatives, a huge extended clan of Russian-Jewish immigrants. My favorite was the one about his grandfather, a lazy old codger who pretended to be deeply religious, cheated his wife at cards, and made wine in the bathtub during Prohibition. He then put a kosher label on the bottles, wrapped them in blankets, and delivered them to customers in a baby carriage.

But none of these stories were as fascinating to me as my father's stories about his adventures as a paratrooper in the 101st Airborne during World War II. What made these stories so compelling was their moral ambiguity. Sure, the Americans were the good guys, and the good guys wanted to do the right thing, but the way my father told it, it wasn't always clear what the right thing was. Battlefields were confusing places, and split-second decisions had to be made all the time that determined life and death for both soldiers and civilians. Is the man next to me in black face in the dark friend or foe? If my buddy gets wounded, do I stay with him or keep going? If I know the road is loaded with Nazi machine guns, do I order my men to try to take them out, knowing some of my friends will die in the process, or do I try to find another way? It became chic and commonplace to air personal moral conflicts like this after the Vietnam War, but I never knew anyone else who talked that honestly about World War II. My father's stories weren't in black and white; they were in shades of gray, and I think about them still.

The war story he loved to tell more than any other was the one about a seven-year-old girl he found crying inconsolably in the fields of Holland. She'd somehow wandered away from her family and ended up on the front lines. My father had to decide; stay with his men, or break the rules, desert the mission, try to bring the child to a safe place, and then hope that he could find his way back to his division, alone, without being captured or shot?

He decided to help the child, whose name was Wilhelmina. He carried her to a convent he'd remembered passing along the way, and the nuns there promised to try to find her family. (There is a large Catholic population in the southern part of Holland, where they were fighting.) He then managed to rejoin his buddies. After the war, the girl's family contacted him, and Wilhelmina became pen pals with my sister. Many years later, my father traveled back to Holland, and a reunion was arranged. Of course by then, Wilhelmina was all grown up. In fact, as my father told it, she was a head taller and a hundred pounds heavier than he was, and greeted him with a bear hug that lifted him off the ground.

Elsewhere in Holland, he and some other soldiers found a huge cache of guilders in an abandoned house. They buried the money in a graveyard, intending to recover it later. But they never did make it back, and it wasn't clear whether my father told the story with regret, for having failed to reclaim the loot, or with guilt, for having taken it in the first place. Either way, he wanted his listeners to know that this sort of thing routinely went on; it was simply a fact of war. Anybody who claimed different was either lying or a fool.

In another story, he told of shooting a woman point-blank after finding her in a barn in the countryside in France surrounded by communications equipment. He spotted her when he left the line of march to relieve himself, and in the seconds he had to figure out what she was doing, he convinced himself that she was working for the Germans, transmitting information about the American troops passing by. He took out his gun, shot her dead, and rejoined the march. But he agonized for the rest of his life over whether he had done the right thing.

My father also liked to tell of how he'd killed a Nazi POW. The incident began with a crude joke on the part of some of the American soldiers. They called my dad over as they interrogated the German, an officer, and told the Nazi that my father was Jewish, apparently in order to taunt him, as if to say, "One of those people you despise is now your master." The German looked at my father, hissed *"Jude schwein!"* and spat in his face. Without taking a moment to think about what he was doing, my father said he pulled out his gun and shot the man dead. Now, shooting a POW in cold blood is an offense for which he could have been court-martialed. But the ranking American officer told the others that no one was to ever discuss what had just happened. And no one, except my father, telling us, ever did.

He told all these stories to me in our tiny kitchen, on the nights when he made it home from Buzzy's at a reasonable hour. We sat at a metal folding table covered with a plastic, felt-backed tablecloth, my mother on one end, my father on the other end, and me in the middle. I still remember the chairs we sat on; they'd come from the Vanderbilt Hotel, the same place we'd gotten our blankets, and they had laminated beige wicker seats and backs, attached to dark wood legs and trim with round metal studs. You couldn't sit down at the table until all the cooking was done, because there was no room to stand in the kitchen once the chairs were pulled out and we were seated. My father's chair butted up against the stove; mine butted up against the sink, and my mother's was next to the refrigerator. A round fluorescent light buzzed above our heads, and there was barely enough room on the small table for our plates, cluttered as it was with the toaster, a radio that my mother kept tuned to an all-news station, 1010 WINS, and round, clear glass cookie jars where my mother kept snacks like chips and crackers.

My favorite dinner was roast beef with baked potatoes; my mother would always cut the tender blackened end piece for me, and she'd let me soak my potato in the juice from the meat. I had to have milk with mine; she liked rosé with hers, and Daddy always had a beer—Ballantine or Schaefer—poured from the can into a glass mug with an inch of white foam on the top.

When everyone had everything they needed, we'd settle down to eat and the stories would begin.

"You know," he'd say, apropos of nothing, considering it was 1966 or so and his audience consisted of a five-year-old and her mother, both of whom had heard the story many times before, "I didn't wait to be drafted. I signed up to be in the army."

He'd chew his roast beef thoughtfully and cut another forkful from the slice on his plate, using his silverware with his paralyzed claw of a hand as if nothing were wrong, a feat that we took for granted but that took months of practice after the war.

"Why did you do that, Daddy?" I would ask, dipping my meat in a pool of gravy between the lines left in the potato by my mother's fork. Of course I knew the answer by heart, but asking him questions as he told the story was part of the ritual.

"Why?" He'd sip his drink, slurping the beer out from under the head and wiping the foam off his upper lip with the back of his good hand. "I wanted to kill Nazis, that's why. I wanted to kill Nazis because the Nazis were killing Jews."

He'd pause to let the gravity of that sink in, then add: "The army gave all of us dog tags that said what our religion was, but I threw mine away." Then he'd lean down conspiratorially and lower his voice to tell me a big secret. "In case the Germans got me, I didn't want them to know I was Jewish," he said. "If they found out you were Jewish, they'd cut off your *balls*."

I looked at him with big, unblinking eyes and nodded solemnly. I didn't know what dog tags were, or balls, but the message was clear. The Nazis were bad people. If they'd caught my dad before he got them, they would have hurt him bad.

My mother never said much during my father's dramatic narrations. She just sat at her end of the table, keeping track of the food (did more

meat need slicing, more butter for the potatoes, a refill on a drink?).
When everyone was done, she cleared the plates, did the dishes, dried
them one by one (it was forbidden in our house to let the dishes air
dry in the dishrack), put them away, and then rewarded herself with a
smoke.

My father would finish his story by saying, "Oh well, war is hell,"
then drain his beer mug and leave the table. I'd parrot him, saying,
"War is hell," but I did it so softly that no one could hear; after all, *hell*
was a bad word, and I wasn't supposed to use it. Then I'd go off to
my room and play with my dolls, several of whom were named Wilhelmina. Later, when I was ready for bed, he'd head out for his nightly
rounds, a restless tomcat on an after-dark prowl. I would lie awake for
what seemed like hours, imagining that my stuffed animals were coming
to life or singing every song I knew. Eventually, before my father got
home, I'd fall asleep, only to wake up again, briefly, when he stumbled
in later.

In all my childhood, I only remember having one nightmare, where
the Nazis were chasing me through the woods to the edge of a cliff. I
was about to fall off when I woke up, drenched in sweat, my heart
pounding. Clutching the covers and still afraid, I looked around in the
dark until I was sure I was in my room. But there was no need to call
out for my parents. I could tell I was okay.

Before I knew how to read, I could sing "Oh, how I hate to get up
in the morning!" and "Mademoiselle from Armentieres, hasn't been
kissed in fifty years!" (That it was a World War I song didn't stop my
father from belting it out now and then.) I knew that shit on a shingle
was what soldiers called the creamed-beef-on-toast rations they despised,
and that the best way to avoid kitchen duty was to make sure your rifle
was always disassembled and in the process of being cleaned. This trick
has actually come in handy at every job I've ever held: If you don't
want to get stuck doing unpleasant tasks, make sure that, on your own
initiative, you are always deeply involved in something that seems important, and the boss will look for someone else to shovel out the
latrines.

As a kid, I liked watching *Hogan's Heroes*, a comedy about a Nazi POW camp, and my favorite comic strip in the Sunday *Daily News*, "Dondi," was about a World War II orphan who had no whites in his eyes, just big round black coals. Even as late as seventh grade, I remember playing games with my twelve-year-old classmates in which we divided up into civilians and American soldiers and pretended we were hiding from the Nazis. It all seems incredible to me now; how could I have been so preoccupied with World War II twenty-five years after it ended? I guess I was trying to make sense of the drama that continued to haunt my father, and when you consider that World War II was closer in time to the 1970s than the Vietnam War is to today, it doesn't seem all that strange.

But as I grew up, I tired of my father's stories and started to tune them out. I was sick of hearing him fight World War II over again every night at dinner, and like my mother, I was sick of him spending all his spare time and money reliving his glory days in the company of his former war buddies. "All the friends I have in this world are from the war," he always said. There was always some meeting, or dinner, or reunion, or trip that he wanted to attend so he could carouse with his old pals from the 101st. In the early days, my mother would accompany him, but eventually she stayed home, not willing to be abandoned at the bar while he backslapped his buddies and flirted with their wives. The only place we ever vacationed as a family was Maine, but every year my father found the money to take himself to 101st events all over the country, and sometimes all over the world, as anniversaries were observed in Holland and Belgium and France. We often felt that the 101st meant more to him than his family, and I'm not sure he would have disputed that. Fighting in World War II was the most exciting thing that ever happened to him. His everyday life buying and selling sewing machines, eating roast beef for dinner, and taking his daughters to the park just didn't rate in comparison.

I was only fourteen when the Vietnam War ended, but I bought into the antiwar sentiment, carried it around in my head, sang all the great antiwar songs when I played my guitar. I couldn't be "antiwar" and at the same time pretend to care about my father's war. I never argued about it with my father; he refused to actually discuss any of the issues related to Vietnam. "Your country is your mother. Your mother, right or wrong; your country right or wrong," is all he would ever say when Vietnam came up, and that was the sum total of his opinion. There was to be no dialogue on the subject, because nothing else mattered, as far as he was concerned. Whatever the U.S. military did in response to orders from Washington, D.C. was to be supported, unquestioningly and wholeheartedly, by the American people, and our soldiers were to be treated with respect and gratitude, regardless of the war they fought in.

But it wasn't just a matter of solidarity with other veterans that formed his views. It was much deeper than that. My father was unshakably patriotic. He loved the flag and the Pledge of Allegiance. He loved to sing "The Star-Spangled Banner" and "America the Beautiful" and "The Battle Hymn of the Republic." He took his hat off and shed a tear or two whenever he heard *Taps* played at the many military commemorations he attended; he saluted anyone in uniform he might pass in the street, and bought a drink for anyone in uniform he might find in a bar. But it wasn't just some bullshit lip-service game that motivated him. Saying the pledge or singing the national anthem really meant something to him. It was an expression of a profound loyalty that engaged his heart and soul; it was an attitude toward America so entirely unlike the snide cynicism of my own generation that I can hardly begin to do justice to the difference. This was the country that had given his family refuge from the czar and the pogroms; this was the country that had taken on Hitler and won; this was a country where anybody who was willing to work hard could make a living and have a decent life. "Your mother right or wrong, your country right or wrong" meant not just blind obedience, but also love, loyalty, and gratitude, both to your family and to America.

But none of this was fashionable when I was growing up in the '60s and '70s. So just as I became old enough to actually understand the history of what the 101st had done in World War II, I stopped paying attention to my father's stories. Sure, I knew the words to "Mademoiselle from Armentieres" and I knew the story about the lost Dutch girl, but I didn't know what D-Day was.

By the time I was ready to find out, my father wasn't around to explain it. So I went to the history books, and read about the people and places whose names were so familiar to me that they seemed more like part of my family heritage than the account of a world war: the beaches at Normandy, the road to Eindhoven, the siege at Bastogne, and of course, General Anthony McAuliffe's storied—yet inscrutable—one-word reply when asked by the Germans to surrender: "Nuts!"

The 101st Airborne was created a few months after my father enlisted in 1942. The 101st "has no history, but it has a rendezvous with destiny," said its first commander, Major General William Lee, when the division was activated. Its mascot was a bald eagle, the fierce yet patriotic image that decorated the soldiers' shoulder patches, and its paratroopers developed a reputation for toughness that earned them the nickname "Screaming Eagles."

But the idea of an airborne invasion, carried out by thousands of parachutists jumping into enemy-held territory, was untested and controversial, and the military was unsure how best to use the division. It seemed that every army official in Washington had to personally witness demonstration jumps before a consensus could be reached on the next step. Training exercises were conditioning the men to operate like guerilla fighters despite sleep loss, limited rations, and miles of marching carrying seventy pounds of gear. The soldiers knew they were being prepared for something important. But what?

My father's impatience during his months of training—convoy drivers school, antitank school, parachute school, demolition school—followed by months of daily drills was palpable. He wrote to his sister Helen's husband, Bernie, a naval officer, in December 1942, from Fort Bragg, North Carolina:

> Every time I visit the latrine, I hear a new rumor. Some have us in Africa before X'mas. Others that we will leave for maneuvers in Texas shortly. The one that seems most likely is that we will remain here as a showoff outfit. Every time some two-bit brass

hat arrives, we are called out for regimental parade, or to make an exhibition jump. Isn't it sickening. Almost a year since Pearl Harbor and I have to play and show off for some jerk. No fooling, I'd give up my jump pay to join those jumpers in Tunisia. A lot of them were my buddies in Jump Training school. They are a fine lot of soldiers. If I hadn't gone to Demolition School, I would have been with them.

He adds a tip: "When doing tough physical duties, skip the meal preceding them. We usually have a long run, calisthenics and hand to hand combat in the morning. All I have is a cup of coffee for breakfast, and as yet, I have stayed away from the medics. That is more than most of the guys can say." Only one in three men passed the rigorous training to serve in the 101st, which included a 140-mile foot march in three days. My father was initially turned down because of his age—he was thirty-one—but he persuaded the authorities to give him a chance. In the end he proved he was just as tough as the younger guys, and he made the cut.

Once the invasion of Italy was under way, it became clear that the 101st was being readied to help open up a second front in Western Europe. In August 1943, the 101st began to be shipped out, first by train to New York, and then aboard troop ships for the crossing to England. There they were quartered at camps in the south of England, a bucolic region of farms and villages and an awesome, ancient cathedral in Salisbury that had been built three hundred years before Columbus reached the New World. But for many men, a day or two on leave in London made the effects of the war seem real in a way that it hadn't been back home in the States: bombed-out buildings, darkened city streets, air raids, and long lines at the grocery stores.

They underwent months of training at the British camps. Finally, on the night of the fifth of June, 1944, five hundred planes carrying sixty-six hundred paratroopers from the 101st began to take off, forming neat black grids that filled the sky, every three planes flying in a V. The 130-mile flight across the channel was to take an hour.

Their mission, arriving six hours ahead of the planned seaborne invasion by five thousand troop ships, was to capture roads leading inland from the invasion beaches, knock out enemy batteries overlooking the site where the ships were to land, and prevent German reinforcements from arriving. The paratroopers were essentially an advance team, deployed to do as much damage to the enemy as they could, and secure as many routes as possible, before the main force arrived.

But the neat plans from some military man's drawing board for entire units of the 101st to carry out these objectives disintegrated when the airborne armada neared the French coast. First they hit a bank of fog, then they came under intense attack from Germans on the ground. What had been envisioned as an orderly parachute drop turned chaotic. The bombardment from the ground was so heavy it turned the night sky as bright as day. Planes left formation and veered off course; some were hit, some missed the coast altogether, a few turned back. Men jumped too soon, or their chutes failed to open; some drowned while others landed miles from their targets in peaceful pastures amid herds of cows. One of my father's buddies recalled hitting the ground and looking up to see a huge white stallion, crazed by gunfire, running wild. "I wanted to get on his back and swim back to England," the soldier said.

There was no way the soldiers could form full units, as they had been instructed to do; they were scattered over too wide an area. They ended up forming small bands and carrying out virtual guerilla warfare instead of taking the enemy like a steamroller. Each soldier had been issued a toy cricket, a small metal clicker that they were to use when trying to find their comrades; there was no sound they were more grateful to hear than that little *tap tap*. My father always told us he lost his clicker and was nearly fired on by his comrades in the dark as he tried to imitate the clucking sound with his tongue before simply shouting his name and pleading, "Don't shoot!"

Ironically, the wide dispersion of the airborne troops, while unintended, contributed to their success. American soldiers had appeared from nowhere, and yet they were everywhere. There was no way for the Germans to successfully counterattack. Many paratroopers had no idea where they were and where the enemy was. But the Nazis were even more confused, and that could only help the 101st.

My father's plane, a C-47 that was fifth in line in the takeoff grid, was among those hit as they neared the Normandy coast shortly after midnight on the sixth of June. He managed to land safely, hitting the swampy ground near the village of Carentan, just south of Utah Beach, and quickly rounded up eight others; he believed they were the only survivors from his plane.

As the only noncommissioned officer in the group, he took charge, forming the eight men into a line, with four on one side of him and four on the other. German machine guns were firing from the ditches as they reached a crossroad, and under his direction, he and the others crawled up on their bellies till they neared the sound of the gunfire. He ordered them to ready their grenades, and on the signal of his whistle, they let the grenades fly toward the machine-gun fire.

"Just one vital question: Did you get them?" asked an interviewer with the BBC when he returned to England in August of 1944.

"Yes, sir," he replied.

It was four days before he and the other survivors found the rest of their unit. About two weeks into the fighting, he was interviewed by a war correspondent and the quotes were picked up by a newspaper back home, the New York *Journal-American*, and conveyed to his parents.

"I put seven slugs in one Jerry," he boasted in the dispatch. "He just covered his head with his hands."

His father—undoubtedly as proud as he was relieved to hear that his son was still alive—told the paper: "That sounds like Dave, all right. He was always a boy to attend to business."

He fought in France for thirty-five days. The battles for the four bridges leading to Carentan left the strongest impressions in his mind, because, as he recalled later, "They were covered with dead and wounded."

Before returning to England in early July, the farmers of Normandy introduced him to calvados, a brandy made from apples. It was his favorite drink for the rest of his life, and in later years, he liked nothing more than to use it to break the ice when meeting young members of the 101st who had fought in Vietnam. One of these Vietnam vets told me he had been a little reluctant to meet the 101st World War II guys. "These were the Bastards of Bastogne, the heroes of all these campaigns," he explained, "and unfortunately we were not able to bring home that same glory from Vietnam." But after a few minutes with Dave, he knew it was going to be okay. "I felt like the Prodigal Son coming home," he said, adding: "And then he introduced me to calvados."

My father was awarded a Bronze Star Medal and a presidential citation for the work he and his men did in silencing the enemy machine gunners in Normandy. But four of the nine men who carried out the mission that night died, victims of a mortar shell that landed in their midst. "The hardest thing was that you had to just keep going, even if the man next to you went down," my father always said. "You'd pat 'em on the head, make 'em comfortable, try to call the medics, but you had to keep going."

When the fortieth anniversary of the D-Day invasion was observed, my father was interviewed by the local NBC affiliate about his role in the campaign, and he said, in the tape that aired on TV, "I love hand grenades!" Fifteen years later, when I was working as a journalist myself, I happened to take a seat at a news conference next to the anchorman who'd interviewed my father, a man named Chuck Scarborough. I introduced myself and said I was certain he wouldn't remember my father, but that I wanted to thank him for the wonderful job he'd done putting the story together so many years before. To my astonishment, Scarborough said, "Was he the one who said, 'I love hand grenades'?" Apparently the phrase was unforgettable.

Only half of the 101st soldiers who jumped into Normandy went on to the next campaign. The rest were wounded, captured, or killed, along with ten thousand other Allied soldiers who died on D-Day. When you visit the American cemetery in Normandy today and view the endless rows of crosses, their symmetry interrupted by the occasional Star of David, it is impossible to not be awed by their sacrifice. "Think

not only upon their passing; remember the glory of their spirit," reads
the inscription on one of the monuments there.

Nearby, in Sainte Mere Eglise, the old stone church bears a permanent memorial to the paratroopers: a sculpture of a soldier, his parachute
caught on the roof on the church, his body suspended helplessly beside
a stained-glass window. A real soldier died there, and the evocation of
his last moments is jarring to the day-tripper blithely driving today
through the picturesque countryside, with its neat stone buildings and
apple orchards advertising homemade calvados for sale.

This is the world my father helped to liberate. The invasion he took
part in was successful, but it came at a terrible price.

Next, "We hit Holland, or Holland hit us, I'm not sure which," as
my father said in a WOR Radio interview shortly after the war. The
drop zone was behind enemy lines near the city of Eindhoven on the
seventeenth of September in 1944, and the plan for what was to be
called Operation Market Garden was simple enough: The paratroopers
were to create an "airborne carpet" by securing roads for British tanks
to use en route to the German border. The 101st was to take a third
of the hundred-mile corridor, including various bridges across rivers and
canals.

As in Normandy, anti-aircraft fire greeted the planes carrying the
paratroopers. Flak entered the plane my father was riding on before
they were able to jump. His sergeant was hit, and he was promoted on
the spot to take over his duties. Most of the other men on his plane
ended up safe on the ground, according to plan; the flat terrain made
landing easy, and the jump was carried out in daylight, avoiding the
confusion of Normandy.

But the landing was the only part of the mission that went well.
While some bridges were quickly secured with little opposition, others
were blown up by the enemy before the Americans or the British could
get to them, forcing Allied engineers to build temporary bridges on
pontoons across the waterways so their tanks could get through. And
while the British had planned to meet with the Americans in Eindhoven

by nightfall of the first day, they were thirty-six hours late, delayed by unexpectedly heavy fighting along the way. The Brits finally reached the city, which was at the southern end of the corridor, and after hours of street fighting, Eindhoven became the first Dutch city liberated under Operation Market Garden.

The mission had been envisioned as a fast one for the paratroopers: Secure the corridor, get the tanks through, in and out in a matter of a few days. The Allies had even hoped the invasion could end the war, a hope that turned out to be naively unrealistic. The Germans were much more heavily fortified than had been expected. And as it turned out, the 101st ended up setting a record for continuous battlefield service. Defense of the corridor, dubbed Hell's Highway, wore on for over two months as the enemy repeatedly regrouped and counterattacked.

"I was a jack of all trades but master of only one: the bazooka," my father recalled in the WOR interview. "We used them constantly for seventy-four days." Bazookas—portable armor-piercing rocket launchers—were used to destroy the German tanks that kept cutting into the corridor like wire cutters on a chain-link fence.

Sometime during those seventy-four days, my father's family received a notice that he was missing in action. But by a strange coincidence, they knew the message was wrong. My uncle Tan, who was in the air force, happened to be in the telegraph office at Bakersfield when a wire came across quoting my father. The wire stated that my dad had been listed as missing in action but that he had just emerged from an enemy zone, leading fifteen German prisoners. His family had not yet been informed that he was MIA, but thanks to my uncle's serendipitous reading of the wire story, by the time the MIA notice arrived, the family already knew it was outdated.

While the 101st succeeded in holding on to their section of the corridor, the Dutch operation overall was a terrible failure. British paratroopers at the northern end of the planned route failed to take their objective, a bridge near the city of Arnhem. They were hampered by bad weather, communications failures, and a lack of reinforcements, and by the time they abandoned the fight, only twenty-five hundred of them made it back to Allied territory. Fifteen hundred were dead, and sixty-five hundred had been taken prisoner by the Germans. The disaster was memorialized in *A Bridge Too Far*.

The southern part of the corridor, however, remained in Allied hands, and as the 101st pulled out in truck convoys in late November, the roads were lined with grateful Dutch villagers shouting the date the soldiers had arrived: "September seventeenth!" My father never forgot the goodwill of the Dutch people, and of all the places he saw during the war, Holland remained his favorite. He admired the Dutch underground resistance, which had provided the Allies with important information about the Germans' locations and strength, and he was charmed by the hospitality of Dutch civilians in various towns who offered to share what little they had—food, beer, and chocolate they had squirreled away during those hungry years of Nazi occupation. But I wonder if his affection for Holland also had something to do with the little girl he saved. A soldier does not often have the opportunity to do a good deed like that; mostly his orders are to do things that, outside the context of war, are murderous and evil. It was not something he had earned a medal for, but I believe that in my father's mind, bringing that little girl to safety, and knowing that he had saved one innocent person's life, meant more to him than all the Nazis he killed put together. Some years after the war, he and other veterans of the Dutch campaign were granted an audience with Holland's Queen Wilhelmina. He brought home from that trip many trinkets, and from then on the apartment of this tough paratrooper was incongruously decorated with Delft blue pictures of windmills and little wooden clogs.

If you travel today out of Bastogne, Belgium, to the Ardennes forest, which forms its eastern border with Germany, you pass by a simple brown-and-white sign bearing the words LE BOIS DE LA PAIX—the peace woods. The arrow points to a grove of sycamore trees arranged in such a way that if you were to view it from the air, you would see the outline of a mother and child, the UNICEF symbol. The trees were planted by children from Belgium, Germany, Italy, and other European countries on the fiftieth anniversary of the Battle of the Bulge, in the hope that war would never scar Europe again. At the base of each tree is a small wooden plaque bearing the name of an American soldier, and one of those plaques is dedicated to my father, who fought there in the snowy winter of 1944–45, when it seemed that the war might never end.

The 101st was sent to Bastogne in response to news of a massive German offensive. The Nazis had broken through the Ardennes on the morning of the seventeenth of December, 1944, penetrating sixty-five miles into Allied territory. The Americans were losing ground by the hour, and they decided to use their headquarters in Bastogne, a town that was the crossroads for eight roads and a railway, as the centerpiece of their defense. The paratroopers were to be brought in to hold the line.

At the time, the Screaming Eagles were recovering from the Dutch campaign in a muddy French camp in Mourmelon-le-Grand, not far from Reims. The encampment was ancient; it had literally been used by Caesar's troops, and more recently during World War I. But the food was good, and recreation was plentiful during the few weeks they had there to relax. Team sports got under way and many of the men got passes to Paris, including my father. Hoping to glimpse a historic site there, he stopped someone on the street to inquire, in his schoolboy French, *"Ou est Le Bastille?"* The Bastille, of course, *n'existe pas!* It had been destroyed by a mob in the French Revolution, as the passerby explained to this ignorant American soldier, who got a laugh out of telling the story years later.

All R&R in France abruptly ended when orders came to move out to Belgium. There was no preparation this time, as there had been for the other campaigns, no deliberations, drills, or studying of maps. This time the soldiers were handed ammunition and provisions and unceremoniously herded onto trucks. They arrived in snowy Bastogne that night, many of them not even dressed in winter clothes.

"We were told [about Bastogne] at breakfast one morning," my father recalled in the WOR interview. "By lunch we were en route.

By dinner we had entered Bastogne. And if we'd had more time for a midnight snack, you could say that by then we were surrounded."

That the Allies held fast in Belgium despite the bad weather and shortages of food, medicine, and ammunition is now history. "Our greatest enemy was not the German soldier," my father wrote in response to a letter from a Belgian museum where an exhibit was being prepared on the fortieth anniversary of the battle. "It was with shouts of joy when on the twenty-third of December, our C-47 aircraft found a clearing in the skies and parachuted much-needed supplies to us so we could take the offensive."

Until then, the outcome of the battle had been unclear. The Germans outnumbered the Allies four to one. Radio Berlin at one point reported that the 101st had been wiped out. Night bombings had left few structures standing. Correspondents who saw the hills littered with frozen bodies called the campaign the Alamo of Europe. My father was stationed in the village of Champs during the battle, his mission as leader of a twelve-man antitank unit to help keep the enemy from taking the road to Bastogne. Again, he worked the bazooka, and he received a presidential citation for coming up with a new way to test the weapon under battlefield conditions.

At various points, the Screaming Eagles were completely encircled by enemy troops. By the morning of the twenty-second of December, they were literally under siege. The Germans, so cocksure of victory, sent four men with a white flag to McAuliffe demanding surrender. "There is only one possibility to save the encircled U.S.A. troops from total annihilation," the note read. "That is the honorable surrender of the encircled town."

The story, as it has been recorded, goes that McAuliffe laughed when he read the note and said, "Aw, nuts!" Then he sat down with a pencil to write his reply and after a moment turned to his aides for help in phrasing the response. A colonel in the room suggested that he use the remark he'd initially made: "Nuts!"

When the missive was delivered back to the German emissaries and one of them translated it for the others, the enemy commander was confused. "Is the reply negative or affirmative?" he asked the Americans who'd brought the piece of paper from McAuliffe.

"The reply is decidedly not affirmative," he was told by one of the Americans, who added, "If you don't understand what 'Nuts' means, in plain English it is the same as 'Go to hell.' "

Now, it's not every day that you hear someone say "Nuts!" when what they really want to say is "Fuck you!" My sister and I have spent many hours giggling over what McAuliffe might have actually said that was unprintable, and wondering how long it took the army's public relations guys to write the press release in which they finally came up with "Nuts!" Maybe what he really said was a vulgarity related to male anatomy, and "nuts" was a coded way of rendering the story palatable to the American public. Whatever it signified, the 101st always commemorated this historic event with a so-called Nuts Night Dinner at West Point, and it was almost always scheduled for the first Saturday night in December. My mother's birthday was the fourth of December, and there was nothing she wanted less than to celebrate it with a bunch of drunken veterans. So many a year, she stayed home alone on the night that should have been hers, and David went off by himself to relive his glory days.

Of course, McAuliffe's confidence in his men paid off. The 101st managed to hold on to Bastogne against all odds, and General Patton arrived with reinforcements the day after Christmas, routing the enemy and turning the Battle of the Bulge into a decisive victory for the Allies. Hitler, who had been assured by his military advisers that the Germans would take Bastogne, reportedly remarked, upon hearing of the Allied victory, "I should like to see the German general who would fight on with the same stubborn tough resistance in a situation that seemed just as hopeless."

The 101st was officially relieved of duty from Bastogne on the nineteenth of January, 1945, the day before my father's thirty-fourth birthday. He told WOR he was "feeling somewhat victorious" as they started to pull out. After all, he had managed to survive three of the goriest campaigns of the war, while all around him, men less lucky fell and died in the most gruesome ways—hit by flak aboard the transport planes, drowned in the tangles of their parachute cords, blown to bits by hand grenades and shells, shot full of holes by machine-gun fire, struck dead with one bullet from a sniper's gun, bleeding to death in the ditches of Normandy and the foxholes of Holland and the snowy woods of Belgium. But as the 101st left Bastogne for redeployment in Alsace-Lorraine, my father became one of those bloody soldiers he had seen fall so many times. He was hit by machine-gun fire.

When he regained consciousness, he was in a hospital in Verdun. He had lost a lot of blood. He had gone into shock. He couldn't quite figure out what was going on, but his arm was in a cast and his head was in an oxygen tent.

From there he was transported to Scotland, to a hospital where the residents turned out one day with a bagpipe band to serenade the wounded soldiers. My father always said he thought perhaps he'd died and gone to hell as he listened, in his woozy state, to the deafening cacophony of the well-meaning pipers.

Then gradually he realized he'd been shot. His right arm, the arm he used to write and eat and dress himself, was paralyzed. Any thoughts he might have had of becoming a career military man were dashed. Any thoughts he might have had of returning to a normal life in the States, resuming work buying and selling the heavy machines that he needed both arms to lift, were now in doubt. He was a cripple, at age thirty-four.

There was only one thing left to do: make friends with the nurses, and find someone who could bring him a drink and a smoke. By the time his sister Helen's husband Bernie, a navy officer stationed nearby, found him in his hospital ward, he was having a grand old time, flirting with the Red Cross girls and appearing unconcerned about what lay ahead. He maintained that attitude for the rest of his life. Live for the moment. Accept the hard knocks without dwelling on them. Enjoy whatever comes your way.

It was a fun way to live, without worrying about responsibilities to other people, without planning for the future. It gave my father the aura of a man who was completely carefree; it added to his charisma and charm. It's probably part of what attracted my mother to him. But while a man like that is fun at a party or in a bar, he doesn't necessarily make a good husband. The very same qualities that enabled him to go on with life after the war without feeling bitter about his fate—a blind devotion to enjoying life, even if it meant spending every last cent in your pocket or blowing off dreary obligations—also made it impossible for him to get home in time for dinner each night. He wasn't about to buck Annie Farrell up when she was feeling down, or buy her that little house by the side of the road she'd always wanted. He just wanted to go out on the town and have a good time.

My father was a corporal by the time he left the army, and he received a Purple Heart for his injury, the last medal to add to the Bronze Star Medal from Normandy, three bronze campaign stars, the French croix de guerre, the Dutch Order of William, the distinguished unit badge, the combat infantry badge, and the presidential citations. He spent fifteen months after the shooting in hospitals in Europe and New York, a guinea pig in the fledgling fields of neuroscience and rehabilitation. He ended up with an arm that would never quite straighten out, and a hand whose fingers were permanently curled into a fist; the muscles and nerves had been severed and shortened by the bullets and a series of surgeries.

Although he relearned mundane tasks like how to tie his shoe, light a cigarette, and write and eat using the injured right hand, he never regained any feeling in it. He never bothered covering it up in the winter, since he couldn't feel the cold, and he occasionally suffered cigarette burns because he couldn't sense the heat as the butts burned down to the end. But in most respects, he was able to use the arm normally, and frequently people who'd known him for years never noticed there was anything wrong with it.

In fact, in some ways, his mental recovery took longer than his physical recovery. He had nightmares for years after the war, and would jump out of bed in the middle of the night, assuming a combat stance on the floor of the bedroom, certain that he was back on a battlefield in Europe until my mother shook him awake to tell him that he was safe and sound in an apartment in Manhattan.

. . .

Five years after the Vietnam War ended, I hitchhiked from Ithaca to Boston and got picked up by an army convoy. I rode in the Jeep at the front with a sergeant who told me how, when he was in Vietnam, he used to take prisoners up in a helicopter and interrogate them, and if they didn't answer the way he wanted, he would push them out the helicopter door.

Somehow this seemed really different from my father's story about killing the Nazi POW. I thought about telling the sergeant that what he'd done in Vietnam was disgusting and appalling and that he should be in jail, but I didn't have the nerve; after all, I just wanted to get where I was going. So I smiled and nodded and when the convoy was about to turn off onto a road that was out of my way, the sergeant was nice enough to use his CB radio to find a truck driver to take me on the rest of my trip.

Here's what I learned that day: In CB lingo, I was a hoofer. And compared to my dad, I was a coward.

Toward the end of his life, more than thirty years after he was shot, my father told me and my sister the truth about his wound. He hadn't been shot by the enemy. He'd been hit by a fellow American, a private whose gun accidentally misfired as they left Belgium for reassignment in Alsace-Lorraine. This particular soldier was a kid from Appalachia, practically illiterate and so poor he'd told my dad he never had a pair of new shoes till he went in the army. He'd worshipped my dad, and served him as an unofficial aide, cleaning his boots and sticking by his side in every battle. My father was a poor shot, but this soldier, from years of hunting in the woods, had an eagle eye with a gun, so my father welcomed his company on the battlefield. It was ironic that the same soldier whose shooting ability had earned my father's respect was to be responsible for the accident that destroyed his right arm. My father did not appear to hold a grudge against him; he knew it was an accident, and he knew how remorseful the other guy felt. But the other soldier's shame kept him, for the rest of his life, from ever fraternizing with his

old war buddies; he never attended the reunions or the trips or the meetings. And my dad, himself embarrassed that he'd been hit under such in-
glorious circumstances, allowed everyone around him to think that he'd
been hit by some mysterious hold-out of a German, instead of admitting
that he'd nearly lost his life to one of his own, in an accident.

A few years after my father died, my sister received an envelope bearing two colorful Belgian stamps and a blue-and-white airmail sticker.
In it was a photograph of the plaque bearing my father's name in the
peace woods, and a picture of the young, scrawny tree—just a head
taller than a man—planted next to it. There was also a card, from a
Belgian couple my father had mentioned to us once or twice but whom
we had never met.

"Your father was one of our liberators," they wrote. "Believe me,
we remember their sacrifices. So when we visit Bastogne, we spend a
moment in the peace woods in honor of all our American friends. Your
father was a great man. He keeps a large place in our thoughts."

If I'd had any doubts about the veracity of my father's exploits, I
suppose that note should have put them to rest. But I couldn't help but
wonder: How many of his stories were exaggerated, and how much
was real? Although I accepted them unquestioningly as a child, as an
adult, what he claimed to have done seemed in some ways incredible,
the stuff of fiction and film, not real life. Besides, so many years had
passed since I'd heard him tell them. I wasn't sure I could trust my
memory or his.

So I read books about the battles he took part in. I examined his
army records. And I scoured every clipping, letter, and tape I could find
that related to his service.

The evidence I found corroborated everything he'd said. He was in
all those battles; he was honored for taking out the nest of German
machine gunners and several other actions deemed heroic; and a woman
named Wilhelmina does turn up in a clipping from a Dutch newspaper
about a visit he made to Holland on the anniversary of Operation Market Garden. The events he agonized over, killing the POW and the
Frenchwoman in the barn, don't appear anywhere, but I've read enough

about what happened to believe that they were real. There was no mercy in the heat of battle.

But was he really a hero? He didn't use that word to describe himself, but I'm sure if anyone had asked him outright, he would have said the real heroes were the ones who didn't come home. They were the men who threw themselves on hand grenades to save their comrades; they were the ones the Germans picked off, one entire row of soldiers after another, as they tried to scale heavily fortified embankments in Normandy.

Yet he liked the adulation he got from all his stories, and he certainly did nothing to discourage the impression that he'd been brave and fierce, an impression that I think was probably correct. That's how all the men in the 101st were; if they weren't the toughest, best-trained soldiers in the army, they wouldn't have been Screaming Eagles.

Still, I wonder: Were there times when he cowered, or times when he cried? Was he haunted by the four men lost to the mortar shell under his command? And did he feel guilty that he survived, when so many of his comrades were buried beneath those crosses on the French coast? All the research in the world can't answer those questions, and we never thought to ask him. His stories were all action, no emotion; he never talked about what it felt like to do what he had done.

One weekend I watched all the great war movies about his battles, looking for some scene that reminded me of him. But I didn't find it in the old films—*The Longest Day, Battle of the Bulge,* or *A Bridge Too Far.* It was *Saving Private Ryan,* the one he never saw, that got the details right. A Jewish soldier taunts Nazi POWs with his Star of David; another soldier tries to save a child. And at one point, the captain wonders how he'll ever tell his wife back home what the war was really like.

It made me think, for all his stories, that Daddy couldn't tell us, either.

10

KHAKIS

LEFT: *David's parents, Baile and Grisha.*

RIGHT: *David, second from bottom, with his brothers and a cousin.*

I thought it was pretty funny when khaki pants came into style for yuppies and computer nerds and corporate types doing casual Friday. In my mind, khakis will never look right on a college student trying to dress up or a lawyer trying to dress down. Because in my mind, khakis will be what my dad wore to work, and he didn't wear them to sit at a desk all day pushing papers or staring at a lit-up screen. He wore them to lift greasy sewing machines into his truck, and to unload dusty bolts of fabric taller than he was, and to push dollies stacked high with boxes of zippers and buttons and thread along Sixth Avenue. That's where he worked buying and selling garment factory equipment and where he eventually opened his own little store. His khakis were always streaked with black grease, and the pockets always needed mending from where his keys and wallet poked through. There was nothing upscale about those pants; they were as utilitarian as the white cotton undershirts he wore to absorb his sweat, the T-shirts that self-conscious teenagers and wanna-be toughies today call "wife beaters." But my father would have been appalled by that label. As my sister once said, Daddy was definitely a chauvinist, but he was also a gentleman.

That combination appealed to my mother. Annie Farrell was drawn to my father's grit, and bewitched by his charm and *joie de vivre*. But while they were a perfect match in some ways, they were a terrible mismatch in others. They both liked to live it up—he, because at heart he was a hedonist who lived for the moment, she, because a night on the town, dressed up in her best clothes, eating good food, represented everything she'd never had as a child. But when the night was over, she yearned to go home to a comfortable house in a nice neighborhood with nice furniture and a little garden. He, meanwhile, couldn't care less. As long as he had enough money to go drinking when he pleased and fishing when he pleased, he didn't need anything else.

I was born in 1961 on my father's fiftieth birthday. Nowadays it's common for older men with young third wives or fertility-treated older wives to have babies. But when I was small it was quite unusual. Anytime he took me to the playground, someone was bound to ask if I was his granddaughter. This question never insulted him; to the contrary, he seemed to think it a testament to his manhood and vigor that he could father a child at his age. Once again, life had begun anew for him, just as it had when he enlisted in World War II, a thirty-year-old with nothing to show for himself, and just as it had when he married my mother after the war, an unemployed cripple, all bluster and no prospects. Now, at the age of fifty, with a baby on his knee, he could still believe that his best years were ahead of him, not behind him.

But having a father who was fifty years older than I also meant that he was not just from another generation, but from another era. He taught me to do the Charleston, the dance of his adolescence, when my friends' parents were teaching them to do the twist, the dance of their adolescence. And he sang me to sleep with Stephen Foster ballads like "Old Black Joe," songs whose lyrics had already been deemed racist and were banned by the time I was in elementary school. But I didn't care that he seemed a little out of synch with the times. It just added to my impression that he was somehow larger than life. He seemed, to me, to have stepped out of one of the black-and-white "million-dollar movies" I used to watch every day after school on television. My dad was Errol Flynn and Marlon Brando and Humphrey Bogart all rolled into one; he was a swashbuckler, a war hero, a street-tough, a Casanova, and a working-class stiff who worked hard at hard work and was proud of it. He was fearless, and while not a big man—five-foot-eight, 145 pounds—he never backed away from a fight, not with the Nazis and not with anyone else. When he was in his mid-sixties, a mugger twice his size came after him with a knife after he rolled out of a taxi late one night in front of our apartment building, three sheets to the wind. The mugger grabbed his wallet as he drunkenly fumbled to put it in his pocket, and then took off. But David's army training and street smarts kicked in, along with a refusal to be made a fool of. A burst of adrenaline wiped away the effects of the booze, and he even took a moment to do something clever: He took off his jacket and quickly wrapped it around his crippled arm, the arm that had been shot during the war, thinking that he could block the mugger's knife with that limb if he had to, and be no worse off for it. Then he ran down the block after the guy, tackling him from behind and taking him completely by surprise. He sat on the hoodlum till the cops arrived, and relished telling the story for the rest of his life.

Life to my father was one big gamble, whether he was jumping out of airplanes with the 101st in France, Holland, or Belgium, or betting away his life savings in Atlantic City, as he did after my mother died, or chasing down a bully twice his size and half his age. He took risks without considering the consequences; he wasn't determined to win, necessarily, but he *was* determined to have fun and live large and do as he pleased—as long as certain rules for honorable conduct were never violated.

He frequently imparted these rules to whoever would listen—his children, the guy sitting next to him on a barstool, an army buddy or a pretty mommy he met in the park while ostensibly watching me. The first rule, delivered to his children on a daily basis as he lit up the Chesterfield nonfiltered cigarettes to which he was horribly addicted, was "Do as I say, not as I do." He said this without apologizing; it didn't matter that he was a hypocrite. What mattered was that, as our father, he had to make sure we didn't make the same mistakes he had.

He also had a code for money: Tip generously, pay your bills on time, and make good on your debts. Tipping well was a small way he could be a big man; it meant that he would be remembered by every bartender, hatcheck girl, and waitress in town. Paying all his bills was a way of giving himself permission to fritter away whatever money was left; if the rent and the utilities and the groceries were taken care of, nobody could fault him for blowing the rest of his money on the horses or a round of drinks. And as for borrowing, because he always spent every dime in his pocket and he never owned a credit card, he often came up short for big-ticket items, like a new truck or a large gambling debt. Fortunately he had sisters and brothers—and later, daughters—who were far more careful with their money, and most of what he borrowed he was able to pay back.

"Nobody likes a stool pigeon!" was another of his favorite admonitions, usually uttered as my sister and I went off to school for the day. The way he talked, you would have thought he was a mobster with a web of illegal cronies instead of a middle-aged Jewish guy who sold sewing machines, warning his little girls against the evils of being a grade-school tattletale. But the contrast between the tough talk and the life he lived was all part of the charm.

Then there were rules regarding loyalty. Blood is thicker than water, he liked to say, and apparently that meant that no matter how much his sisters and brothers bad-mouthed him as the black sheep of the family, he would call them every Jewish holiday with a hearty "Good *Yontif!*" and visit them every Sunday with his children. I especially liked visiting my Uncle Sol. I liked the way his pipe smoke made his apartment on the Upper East Side of Manhattan smell like the woods, and even though he could be serious and stern and judgmental of my father, he was often silly with me. Whenever he called early on Sunday mornings to see if we were coming over for brunch, he'd say, "I have a television-telephone and I know what you're wearing! Pajamas!" I was little enough to be amazed by this, and I couldn't wait to see him and his wife, my Aunt Rose. She was the Jewish mother I never had, a big lady who would sweep me up in a hug and pinch my cheek with her knuckles and feed me all the Jewish food my mother never served, like matzoh with eggs and bagels with lox.

Daddy also had no pretensions, and no patience for the pretensions of others. On Saturdays I used to go to his office, on Sixth Avenue between Twenty-Fifth and Twenty-Sixth Streets, and help him balance the books for his business. Today the area is a booming yuppie neighborhood, complete with a Best Buy showroom, a Starbucks, and million-dollar high-rise apartment buildings. Busy thirty-somethings in expensive leather jackets hurry by chatting on cell phones and sipping decaf lattes as they glance at the antiques offered at an outdoor flea market. But in those days there was hardly a pedestrian to be found, except for the men walking in and out of Buzzy's, and very little residential housing of any sort. It was a gritty, gray commercial district; few of the businesses were retail, so there was no need to make them look pretty, and there were no regular shoppers—just truckers, auctioneers, and businessmen, mainly from the garment district, loading, unloading, buying, and selling the factory-grade equipment my father handled. When he and his brother Sol opened up a small store two doors down from his office, they didn't even put a sign on it. They didn't need one. They *were* the business. My father's name was all he needed for his work, and that's what was lettered on the side of his truck, and on his letterhead, invoices, and cards.

When I went in to help him on weekends, he'd dictate to me who'd been billed and for how much, who had paid and who still owed, and I would enter the names and numbers neatly in a big accounting ledger, then run the totals on an adding machine. At one point when I was in junior high school, I started putting a dash through the center of my sevens. I had seen other students and my teachers do it in math class, and it seemed very sophisticated to me, a way of adding a little elegance to a mundane row of numbers. But about a week or so after I started doing this, when we opened up one of Daddy's ledgers, he squinted at a seven with a line through it and put his finger on that spot on the page.

"I can't figure out what that is," he said. "They're all over the books! Who could have done that?" He seemed genuinely puzzled, knowing that he hadn't done it and never imagining that I was the culprit.

I explained to him that, in fact, it had been me who was crossing all the sevens.

"Why?" he asked.

I was flummoxed for a moment; why indeed? I couldn't articulate to him what that little dash through the seven represented in my mind. To me it seemed so pretty, so feminine, so classy, so elegant! By writing the number that way, I somehow felt I was closer to becoming the kind of person who *would* write the number that way. But I couldn't say all those things to my dad. I knew he wouldn't get it. "I don't know," I finally mumbled. "I think maybe that's how they do it in Europe."

He slammed the cover of the ledger shut and seemed peeved in a way that he almost never was. "Well, we're not *in* Europe," he said harshly. "We're in America. So do it the way we've always done it."

I felt absolutely ashamed of myself. It wasn't just that I was a silly teenager playing dress-up with a column of numbers; it was that I had somehow betrayed the very essence of what mattered to my father. I had tried to be someone who I wasn't, and that was a violation of another of his rules: "To thine own self, be true."

Like his five brothers and sisters, Dad was born on a kitchen table in a tenement apartment on the Lower East Side of Manhattan, on the corner of First Street and First Avenue, over a candy store. Today the area is part working class—a turf shared by Hispanic, Chinese, and a few Orthodox Jewish families—and part hipster, an urban frontier of vintage clothing stores, cutting-edge bands playing in dark, noisy bars, and young whites with multiple piercings looking for a grittier identity than the ones they were born with in some quiet suburb of New Jersey.

But a century ago, the neighborhood was teeming with European immigrants, and New York was in transition, from a nineteenth-century city with gaslights and horse-drawn pushcarts to a twentieth-century metropolis with electricity and cars. The small apartments were dark and stuffy railroad flats, with one room opening up into another, built before housing reform mandated a window in every room, and large families crammed their children two or three to a bed, rug, or sofa. When one child in the family got sick, mothers put all the kids on the fire escape to get fresh air and sunshine; even uneducated immigrants understood their apartments were breeding grounds for illness.

The streets were filled with the sounds of a dozen different languages—Yiddish, Italian, Polish, Russian, Greek, and many others—and every family had stories to tell about hunger, violence, and poverty in the country they'd come from. My father's relatives were no exception. His parents, aunts, uncles, and grandparents belonged to a large extended Jewish family that fled Russia in the early 1900s, to escape the marauding pogroms by Cossacks who terrorized Jewish families, and the mandatory conscription of Jewish men to serve, for years on end, in the czar's army. Legend had it that my grandfather Grisha decided to leave after being ordered to fight in the 1904 Russo-Japanese War. His reaction at being told to report for duty, we were always told, was simply, "What is Japan?" One story held that his wife, our grandmother Baile, tied sheets together and threw them over the wall of his locked barracks, enabling him to climb out and run away. As a child I had a recurring fantasy that if for some reason I were ever held captive someplace with a window or a wall, I could always manage to get out as long as I had sheets on my bed and hands to knot them with.

As young girls, Baile and her sisters had to be hidden in attics and cellars whenever the pogroms—which were state-sponsored terror campaigns against the Jews—were under way. Any Jewish girl found by the Cossacks would certainly be raped, maybe even killed. While Baile and her sisters never met that fate, her favorite brother Phil lost the girl he loved in one of the rampages; her breast was sliced off by a Cossack's sword, and she died. He carried her picture in his wallet for the rest of his life, much to the consternation of the woman who became his wife and their three daughters, but he did not allow that early sorrow to turn him into a mournful man. On the contrary, he loved life, perhaps because he knew better than anyone how precious it was, and he became the party boy of his generation, setting an example my father famously emulated. Phil loved my father like his own son. In fact, in later life, Uncle Phil and his nephew David—known in the family by his Yiddish name Duddy—became notorious drinking buddies.

Baile and Grisha had six children in Russia. Grisha left for New York first; Baile and the children were to come later. But by the time she arrived, all of the children were dead—five wiped out in a cholera epidemic in Odessa, with the sixth, a baby boy, dying soon after the boat got to New York. A weaker woman might have taken her own life, or fallen into a catatonic despair, or become so enraged at the injustice of it all that no one could bear to be around her. A weaker man might have blamed his wife; after all, he'd left his children in her care. But instead, they soldiered on and started over, as if the past no longer mattered and life was beginning again. Their optimism was rewarded: Baile's first pregnancy in New York resulted in a healthy set of twins, named Sol and Lee. What better way to reconstruct their family than to start off with two children at once! It was an omen, perhaps, of the bounty that awaited them, a sign that all the horror they had suffered in the Old World was to be compensated by the blessings of the New World. Next was another girl, Ruth, and then, in 1911, my father, David, named for the baby who died after Baile arrived in New York. Helen was the next child, and finally, Nathaniel, nicknamed Tan, twelve years younger than the twins, his oldest siblings. It was as if they had reconstructed the family they lost, their six dead Russian children reincarnated as six healthy Americans.

Like many immigrant families of that era, they were poor, but not miserable. They used a potato with holes in it to hold candles at Chanukah because they couldn't afford a real menorah, but they didn't go hungry too often. At home, they all spoke Yiddish, but my father and his siblings learned English quickly at school and had no accents as adults.

Still, they flavored their conversation all their lives with Yiddish expressions. Certain types of human behavior, in fact, could only be adequately described in Yiddish, and so it was from my father that I learned six words for crazy, each of them meaning something different: *Moishe Kapoyr, meshugge, farmisht, tsedrayt,* and *fartootst. Moishe Kapoyr* was the name of a comic strip character from the *Jewish Forward* in the 1920s, and when I was a little girl and acting very silly, my father would affectionately call me a *Moishe Kapoyr. Meshugge* was a dismissive term reserved for grown-ups whose opinions and actions were so absurd they could not even be considered offensive; it was an insult, but in an offhand way, used to describe a fool who was acting stupidly. *Farmisht* was mixed-up, *tsedrayt* was slightly more seriously confused than *farmisht,* and *fartootst,* on a sliding scale of lunacy, was a little crazier than *tsedrayt.* My father also reverted to Yiddish for nicknames, put-downs, and as a way to characterize arguments: I was his *bobbe* or *bobitchke,* a diminutive for sweetheart or darling baby; my mother's nagging was nothing but *hakin' a chaynik*—banging a teakettle, and when she started in on him, it made my father want to bang his *kop en vant*—hit his head against the wall. Someone who had treated him unfairly in a business deal was a *gonif,* or thief, who should go to *Boiberek,* which was a very far away place indeed. And if you burped or greedily inhaled your food, you were nothing but a *chaseleh*—a little piggy. I learned to count in Yiddish, and to say the days of the week, but beyond that and those few choice expressions, very little was imparted to me, and that seemed partly by design. Because the only time my father actually conversed in Yiddish were occasions when he didn't want me to know what he was saying—either because he was mulling over a big family crisis with one of his siblings, or when he was yelling at our landlord, who pretended to be a very pious Jew and refused to answer the phone on the Sabbath, but who was too cheap to provide adequate heat and hot water in the winter.

Since my mother wasn't Jewish, she couldn't cook the food my father loved from his childhood. So if he wanted borsht, tongue, hard pickled green tomatoes, *kishka,* which literally means intestines, or *schav,* a cold vegetable soup, he headed out to a deli. But he didn't care about keeping kosher, and he happily ate ham or shrimp if my mother made them.

His own mother had broken her kosher rules for him when he was small. If Duddy wanted milk with his meat, a combination forbidden in a kosher house, Baile would sneak it to him. His sisters and brothers, as adults, cited this as proof that he had been their mother's favorite, and he did not dispute it.

Perhaps it was because he was named after the baby who died on the boat that he had a special place in Baile's heart, alone among her six living children. Perhaps she had known it would be this way from the moment he was named, for *David* in Hebrew means "beloved," and the biblical King David proved an apt role model for who my father became: a boy who slew the giant Goliath, a mighty warrior, and a ladies' man.

Or perhaps it was because his ready grin and mischievous ways reminded her of her fun-loving brother Phil. Baile adored Phil so much that when he died of a heart attack in the early 1950s, no one could bear to tell her, not even Phil's daughter, Millie.

"It would have hurt me too much to hurt Aunt Baile by telling her about my father," Millie said years later. "He meant too much to her."

Then, one day, a full six months after Phil had died, Baile, by then well into her seventies, appeared on Millie's doorstep. Millie and her family—her husband and three sons—were just pulling up in front of their house on Long Island when they noticed a small silvery gray shape atop the metal box where the milkman left milk by the side door. As their eyes focused on the spot, Millie realized what it was. "That's Aunt Baile," she said.

Millie was astonished to see her. Baile lived in the city and would have had to take trolley cars and trains and buses and then walked a long distance to get to their suburban home all by herself.

Yet Millie also realized immediately why her aunt—a tiny woman with a kind, round face, a kerchief over her hair, and a long old-fashioned gray dress—had come.

Baile stood up from the milk crate as Millie ran to her.

"*Mein bruder,* Phil," the old woman said, the Yiddish phrase for "my brother" giving way to English as she searched her niece's eyes. "He's dead?"

Millie had no choice but to admit the truth.

"It's all right you didn't tell me," Baile said softly after a moment. "I know you meant well."

And then Millie made tea for her aunt, the Russian way, served in a glass with a sugar cube between the teeth that melted as the hot liquid was slurped into the mouth—a *glezele tay* was what they called it. Millie explained to Baile that she had only been trying to protect her, that no ill will of any sort had been intended. Baile nodded, and patted her hand, and together they cried.

Even as a little boy, Duddy always had a twinkle in his eye and an angle on a good time, and Baile seemed to like that about her son. In her old age, she had a heart condition and was forbidden by the doctor to engage in strenuous activity, but she insisted on going every day to a community center where there was Jewish folk dancing. "If I have to die," she told my father, "let me die dancing." No wonder one of my father's favorite songs was "The Immigrant Cousin," a Yiddish ballad that told the story of a young girl from the Old Country whose cheeks were red as pomegranates and whose feet "were made for dancing." The word for pomegranates—*pomeransen*—rhymed so neatly with the word for dancing—*tansen*—that the lyrics became an unforgettable evocation of his mother.

Still, while Baile may have had an appreciation for her darling son's proclivities, that didn't make the heartaches he brought the family any easier to bear. Indeed, perhaps she loved him so much because she worried about him so much. David was the child who got into so many fights at school that his teacher finally gave him a pair of boxing gloves. David was the child who the others reported had stripped off his clothes and jumped in the Hudson on a hot summer day, then encouraged his little sister Helen to do the same, somehow teaching her to swim in the process. David was the child who didn't want to study, dropping out of school after the eighth grade while four of his siblings went on to college. David was the child who woke everyone up when he stumbled in late at night after an evening of teenage carousing, dooming his little brother, Tan, with whom he shared a bed, to a sleepless night while David snored off the booze he'd scored at some Prohibition speakeasy.

Some mothers with children like that throw their hands up in frustration, bang their *kop en vant,* cry and scream and curse a boy so full of mischief, while praying to God that somehow he will turn out all right despite all evidence to the contrary. But some mothers, like Baile, simply give in. And so she succumbed to the charms of her devilish *boychik,* with his thick curly blond hair and defiant blue eyes, while never forgetting his flaws. On her deathbed, she made his five brothers and sisters swear that they would look out for him after she was gone. Little did she know that the caretaking had already begun. When his flapper girlfriend found herself pregnant, David's big sister Ruth lent him the money to get her an abortion. And when he needed a job, his big brother Sol hired him—several times—but always ended up firing him.

Although Sol and David were the only two of the six siblings who did not go to college, they were in most other respects about as different as two brothers can be. Sol, at the tender age of eight, went out and got himself a job, working for the cocoa delivery man. The driver stayed in the horse-and-wagon, while Sol ran back and forth with the bags of cocoa, bringing them to customers' doors. In exchange, his mother got free cocoa, and he got a hearty lunch that his mother could not always provide: a tall glass of milk and three fresh buns from a bakery. It was a worthwhile trade-off.

Sol left home after two years of high school to work in variety stores, Woolworth's-like five-and-dimes that sold hardware, dry goods, household necessities, toys, and other small, inexpensive items. He eventually opened up his own store, called Jay's, on Second Avenue between Forty-Ninth and Fiftieth Streets, right around the corner from where Anne and David lived when Nancy was small.

But many years before that, he was managing stores for other people, and a few times, he hired his hard-up brother David to help. One of these jobs, in Providence, Rhode Island, ended when Sol found Dave

in the basement, lolling about with a beauty queen—Miss Rhode Island—instead of taking inventory. On another job, Sol told all the
workers that the boss needed them to report for duty on Saturday night.

"I can't be here Saturday night," David told him. "There's a dance
I want to go to."

"If you don't show up for work Saturday night, don't bother coming
back," Sol said.

David didn't even stop to weigh the pros and cons; for him there
was no dilemma. "I'm going to the dance," he announced. "See ya!"

Sol was understandably peeved and embarrassed; his own brother had
mutinied! But years later, in telling the story, Sol ruefully added, "I'm
sure he had more fun than I did."

For David was also the child who didn't want to work, the child
who preferred to run away from home and travel the country after
leaving school at age fifteen. He adopted the whitebread-sounding name
of Jack Dudley to thwart any anti-Semitic kooks he might encounter.
He got by on whatever odd jobs he could find, ranging from chauf-
feuring left-wingers and union leaders around the Midwest in the politically volatile late 1920s, to singing with an itinerant light opera
company. He had a beautiful deep voice, and his favorite show was a
light opera called, not surprisingly, *The Vagabond King,* a perfect description of his own lifestyle.

By the standards of later generations, such freewheeling behavior
might not seem so unusual. But free spirits were not that common
among immigrant Jewish families in the 1920s; they aspired, through
education and hard work, to middle-class lives, and most of them
achieved it within a generation. David was an aberration, the one who
didn't seem to care about respectability or getting ahead in life. He just
wanted to do as he pleased, and as long as he didn't hurt anyone, he
didn't see anything wrong with that.

After he was wounded, he underwent a series of operations on his
paralyzed right arm, then worked as a poster boy for the army, giving
public talks about his combat experiences and his rehabilitation while
selling war bonds. But after a few months of that, as soon as he was

strong enough, he went back to work. He didn't want to go to school on the G.I. bill; he had no interest in being a white-collar worker. He wanted to be his own boss, so that he didn't have to punch a clock or kowtow to anybody or take sick days or vacations according to someone else's rules. So he went into the line of work he'd learned from his father—buying and selling garment-factory equipment. He inherited his father's contacts and customers, and he knew how to take inventory, run an auction, and bargain in Yiddish. And if having a bum right arm cut into his ability to make a living, there was some compensation: a monthly disability check and free health insurance from the Veterans Administration, which had deemed him sixty percent disabled.

He married my mother in 1948, on the Fourth of July in the veterans' hospital on Staten Island where he was still periodically undergoing treatment. Although she signed a piece of paper converting to Judaism so they could be married by a rabbi, his relatives all refused to attend the wedding. My mother carried a chip on her shoulder about this for the rest of her life; she excluded herself from my father's weekly outings to see his siblings, never spoke to them on the phone, and regarded most visits by them to us as terrible impositions. This did not endear her to my father, who treasured his family above all else.

But somehow my mother did manage to win over her mother-in-law Baile. In the years before Baile died, Anne visited her often and nursed her when she was sick, prompting Baile to tell David that his *shiksa* wife was the best daughter Baile had, even though they could barely communicate. (Baile spoke little English.) Baile's daughters Lee and Ruth were career women, too busy to help their mother; besides, they were ashamed of how old-fashioned she looked, an old lady with a kerchief over her head lighting candles in the dark. Baile's youngest daughter, Helen, lived far away in the suburbs of Washington, and now that her husband was finally home from the war, they could at last live a normal family life with their two children; she could not be expected to help her mother in New York. But Anne had just one baby and lived in Manhattan; she was available, willing, and able to help nurse Baile. She even bought her mother-in-law a brass menorah so that the old lady could finally stop using a potato to hold her candles at Chanukah. Eventually I inherited the menorah; we use it every December to celebrate the holiday with my children.

The best thing about my father's self-employment was his willingness to close his business down for two full months every summer and take us to Maine. As a child, I took this for granted, even though I didn't know anyone else whose family did it. But as an adult, it amazes me. I now live in a world of middle-class yuppies, a world where both children and adults are manically overscheduled, and where everyone is obsessed with achievement, status, and material goods. I've thrown perfectly workable computers out with the trash because we bought a better model; my five-year-old has his own Walkman. Our neighborhood is very safe, so safe that I do let my children go trick-or-treating, and I let them play outside without worrying about the Gypsies or anybody else. Vacations in this world are about Disneyland and snorkeling and skiing and sightseeing, not about doing nothing, and I admit being guilty of taking a few vacations like that myself, and wishing I could afford to take a few more. If a vacation is about doing nothing, doing nothing for most people I know lasts for a week or two at most—maybe at an expensive beach house with the kids—but never the entire summer. I remember, as a young adult, meeting someone who was self-employed and saying, "Lucky you! You get to take the whole summer off." The person stared at me like I was crazy and then explained that someone who is self-employed could *never* afford to take the whole summer off. There would be lost clients, lost income, lost accounts; people would think you were lazy or not committed enough to what you were doing, and they'd take their business elsewhere.

Of course my father was self-employed in a different era and in a different social class. In his world, being your own boss gave you the right to do nothing whenever you pleased. In fact, the whole point of going to Maine was to do nothing. My father had no projects he tackled, no great sets of books he read or lists of things to do; he simply drove us up to whatever rustic camp we'd rented that year, and spent the summer fishing in his little blue boat with the outboard motor. By the end of the summer, we had no money; we were eating the fish he

caught every night, and the string beans we picked at the farm of a
friend of my mother's. When we got back to New York, his September
veteran's disability check would arrive so we could pay the rent, and he
would start all over again, going to auctions, making deals, and getting
his khaki pants black from lifting the greasy machines onto his truck.
He never got ahead of the game, but then again he didn't want to. It
was okay with him that he was starting, each fall, once again, with
absolutely nothing. He was certain it would turn out all right, just as it
had when his parents arrived here, penniless and heartbroken from the
deaths of all their children, just as it had when he landed on the beach
at Normandy and heard the Germans firing their machine guns from
the ditches as he made his way up the road, just as it had when he woke
up in that hospital in Europe and realized he had no feeling in his right
arm.

And maybe all of that helps explain why he sold back the little house
he once bought in Maine just hours after arriving to see it. There's no
question that he had no interest in spending his vacations as Annie Farrell's errand boy, fixing window screens and painting bedrooms. It
would have cut into his fishing time, and besides, his bad hand made it
difficult for him to do chores like that anyway. But I think there was
more to it than that. He really didn't want to own anything. He didn't
want to be tied down. He didn't want the responsibilities involved in
keeping up a piece of property and being forced to return to the same
place every year no matter what. He wasn't interested in the notion that
lakefront real estate was a good investment, or that it was actually far
cheaper to buy a summer camp than to rent a different one every year.
If it so happened that they could come to Maine again and again each
summer, that was good. But the idea of a long-term commitment scared
him. He wanted to come and go as he pleased, when he felt like it.
Having an actual address in Maine to call his own took away some of
what made his annual sojourns there so appealing. After all, he had
rejected all the trappings of middle-class life by closing his business and
spending two months doing nothing. Anne, meanwhile, wanted a little
house to call her own more than anything else. But she couldn't have
it if David said no. He was in charge, he had the money, and if he

said no, there was nothing she could do about it. In one way, what he had done by selling back the camp was completely in keeping with his live-for-the-moment free-spirit existence. But in another way, what he had done by selling back the camp was selfish and cruel, because it denied his wife a small luxury that would have meant the world to her.

Back in New York after Labor Day, my mother's depression gradually returned, and as she sunk further and further into her gloom, my father spent more and more time at his favorite hangout, Buzzy's Bar. It was just a block or two from his office, and he'd been drinking there since the 1940s. In fact, my sister suspects that part of the reason he wanted to move from the Upper East Side to downtown Manhattan was so that he'd be nearer home when he rolled out of Buzzy's, completely plastered, in the middle of the night.

Sometimes when my father went to Buzzy's he took Aunt Deen's little gray poodle, André, who lived with us for a while when she couldn't keep a dog in her apartment. André only had one eye; the other was sewn up, like a missing button on a teddy bear, from the time he'd been hit by a car. But he was a smart and agile dog, and my father trained him to jump on the barstool at Buzzy's and lap beer from a saucer.

But there were other times, especially on weekend afternoons if we'd been at his office or in the park, when my dad took me to Buzzy's. In my memory, Buzzy's is a place as familiar to me as the flat, gray front steps of the building where we lived, a place I knew so well I could have gone in blindfolded and still found my way around. I knew which stools had been taped up to keep the stuffing from coming out of the vinyl covers. I knew where the bartender, Jimmy, had to move behind the bar to get the ice and the soda and the beer. And I knew exactly which table in back we'd been sitting at when I blew air into the straw of my chocolate milk, creating a volcano of brown bubbles that spilled over the edge of the glass, onto the table, and all over my mother's lap, forever staining a white skirt she happened to be wearing one day when we went to Buzzy's for lunch. I don't remember her ever coming to Buzzy's with us again; after that, I sat at the bar with my dad.

I loved to perch on the rotating seats, dangling my feet far above the floor while Jimmy fixed me a Coke with a cherry in it. He always told me it was a drink he'd invented just for me, and he called it a Girl Scout. But one day when I was playing in the park with a little boy, my father struck up a conversation with the boy's mother, a redheaded divorcée, and then he took us all to Buzzy's. Jimmy, I noticed, made the exact same drink for the little boy that he always made for me, only he called it a Boy Scout. I was devastated, though I tried to hide my disappointment. Here I thought he'd invented the Girl Scout for me, but it was just a gimmick that he told every kid who sat at the bar. I have been suspicious of bartenders and their happy talk ever since.

One day after my own children were born, a colleague said he'd had a little time to kill while out with his daughter one day and that he'd taken her to sit at a bar with him, intending to buy her a soda while he had a beer. The bartender told him it was illegal for minors to be seated at the bar, and that he'd have to find a table. My friend was astounded by this, and I was, too. What was the world coming to when you couldn't even take your kid to a bar anymore? Some neurotic yuppie probably thought this up, the kind of person who assumes that you can't be a good parent if you take your child with you when you go out drinking.

Then I thought about it for a minute and realized whoever thought that rule up was probably right. I wouldn't dream of taking my children to a bar, and I'd probably be reluctant to let them play with the kids of anybody else who did. I'd become the kind of person I was brought up to despise, a person who worried about what other people think, who saved money for the future, who knew the difference between the good fat in olive oil and the bad fat in whipped cream. I was the kind of person my dad would have made fun of, the kind of person who wears khaki pants to sit at a computer.

Actually, I realized after a moment, my dad wouldn't have made fun of me. He wouldn't have cared. He would have just done his thing, and whatever I did would have been okay, too.

. . .

There was a picnic every D-Day in a state park for 101st veterans and their families, and while all the other guys stood around drinking beer and telling stories, this was the one time that my father made a different choice. Instead of fighting the war all over again with his cronies, he organized games for the kids. He saved trinkets all year—key chains and stuffed animals and other small items he came across in the course of his work—to give out as prizes. And while his buddies played baseball with one another, a game he could no longer play because of his arm, he led their kids in races and tug-o'-war and relays and contests.

The truth was that he loved children. He loved to be around them, he loved to play with them, and he wanted every kid he ever met to be happy. He took me to the park every Sunday, and when the ice cream truck came around, he bought cones for every kid in sight. Occasionally a drunken bum would stagger into the periphery of a game of hopscotch or jump rope as I played with my friends, and there was my dad, handing the guy a buck to get lost. He took me to see Charlie Chaplin movies and Gilbert and Sullivan shows and baseball games, once a year to see the Yankees and once a year to see the Mets. He taught me to ice skate at Rockefeller Center, and he taught me to swim in the lake in Maine. And when his friends sent him a beautifully wrapped basket of fancy nuts each year at Christmas, he handed it to me with a promise that we would feed them all to the squirrels the next time we went to the park.

He grilled me on multiplication tables whenever we went fishing, and he showed me how to play poker and pinochle and blackjack and gin. He taught me the words to songs that nobody knows anymore—"Grand Old Flag," "Drink to Me Only with Thine Eyes," and "The Daring Young Man on the Flying Trapeze." Together we watched his favorite TV shows, *Mannix* and *Kojak*, and together we watched my favorite shows, *The Mary Tyler Moore Show* and *All in the Family*, and when the shows were over and I had brushed my teeth, he kissed me goodnight and headed for the door for a night of carousing on the town.

I've always been a light sleeper, extremely sensitive to sound; in fact, for many years, I thought I was an insomniac because it was so hard for me to fall asleep unless I was surrounded by complete and total silence—the kind of silence you only get in the woods of Maine. (Fortunately, as an adult, I've discovered ear plugs and the white noise provided by air conditioners, and I've slept soundly ever since.) I would always wake up when my father rolled in from his late-night adventures, roused from my dreams by the rumble and boom of the elevator door, which was right next to our apartment, as it opened and closed to let him out. My eyes would open, blind at first in the darkness, then gradually adjusting to whatever light was coming in from the street through the window. I'd hear his footsteps, unsteady of course, make their way to our door. Then metal on metal as he fumbled to place the key in the lock, the *click* as it turned, and the *creak* as the door opened, accompanied by a shaft of light from the hallway briefly and faintly illuminating my room. He'd head for the bathroom, then fall in his bed, and I'd shut my eyes and gradually drift back to sleep.

But one night the scenario was different. He got off the elevator, came to the door, put the key in the lock and opened it, but the door hit something and wouldn't budge. He pushed again, rattling against whatever was keeping him from getting in, and then appeared to give up. He rang the bell, and my mother sprang from her bed, as if she'd been coiled like a snake ready to pounce. In hushed, urgent tones, I heard her speak, then his muffled voice back at her, through the door, but I didn't know what they'd said.

Then I realized what had happened. She had put the chain lock in place across the top of the door. If he was going to stay out that late at night, she didn't want him to come home. I heard his footsteps again outside, going back to the elevator. He went to a hotel that night, and she went back to bed, but I'm not sure that either of us got much sleep.

The lockout didn't change his ways, of course, and she never did it again; there was no point. But it changed the way I saw what was going on, because now I knew that she had tried to draw the line, and he just didn't give a damn. In fact, he told the story over and over, to his brothers and sisters and in his office, like it was a big joke. Hadn't Annie Farrell pulled a fast one on him? What a clever gal, to think of locking him out that way as punishment for a bad boy! But was it going to change his behavior? Absolutely not. He always ended the telling of that particular tale with another of his favorite little sayings:

"I've given up smoking, drinking, gambling, and chasing women." (Dramatic pause.) "The only thing I haven't given up is lying."

It always got a laugh out of his audience. But there was one person I knew who didn't think it was funny: my mother. And I was starting to agree with her.

After my mother died, a woman named Renée started turning up on a daily basis in my father's apartment, and my sister and I gradually realized that she'd actually been a part of his life for many years. She claimed that she'd met him when she was eighteen; she claimed to be my sister's age; she claimed to have been born on my mother's birthday. She was a secretary for a company my father sometimes did business with, and let's just say she made a better companion for him at Buzzy's than either I or André the dog had ever been. Renée was also black, which didn't bother us, but made us wonder why my father had been so angry when my sister married a black man after divorcing her first husband.

Renée was not my father's only girlfriend, of course; the body lice episode that my mother had burdened my sister with years before proved that. But perhaps the most memorable of the stories about his extramarital escapades was a nurse who was nice enough to have sex with him when he was in the veterans hospital in New York. He was hospitalized for about a year when I was twelve for a urinary tract infection that nearly killed him because he waited so long to have it treated. When the infection finally cleared up, he was told he would either need to be catheterized for the rest of his life, or undergo re-constructive surgery. He opted for the surgery, but before he left the hospital, he wanted to make sure he hadn't lost any of his sexual abilities. An accommodating nurse agreed to help him test the system out before he went home, or so he told my sister the night my mother died. Apparently he wanted this particular story off his chest before Annie Farrell left this earth; he took Nancy out to a bar near the hospital where my mother was dying so he could unburden himself to her and make his final good-bye to his wife with a clean conscience.

In the decade before he retired, my father actually managed to save up some money. It was the 1970s, a terrible time for the U.S. economy, with high interest rates, high unemployment, and high inflation. The garment industry and other manufacturers were laying off workers and closing factories all over the country in order to relocate in third world countries where labor was cheaper. This proved to be an incredible opportunity for my father. He could buy all kinds of goods dirt cheap, and still make a profit selling them. When a street-level business space came available at 763 Sixth Avenue, a few doors down from his office near Twenty-Sixth Street, he opened up a store there with a friend and his brother Sol—the same brother who'd fired him after the Miss Rhode Island episode. The three of them, like understudies from *The Sunshine Boys*, argued and haggled, smoked and puffed and coughed, told stories and talked in Yiddish, and bought and sold enough goods to actually make a good living. Shortly after I graduated from college in 1981, they closed the store and my father retired with about a hundred thousand dollars in the bank. He had made about twenty thousand of the money shooting craps in Atlantic City one weekend shortly before my mother died. Of course, the casinos started courting him; they wanted to get their money back, and they knew that eventually they would. So they gave him complimentary stays in their glitzy hotels, sent limousines to fetch him, and offered free helicopter rides from Manhattan to the Jersey shore. He felt like a king, and he momentarily forgot what every gambler eventually realizes: At the end of the day, the house always wins.

Within a matter of months, he was completely broke. He'd gambled his life savings away, the entire hundred thousand dollars, certain that his luck would turn at any moment as he bet more and more money on the craps table. He never got the money back; his retirement savings were gone. And when he'd cleaned his own account out, he then started borrowing to keep going, quitting his gambling only after he was three thousand dollars in the hole. He shamefacedly asked me to help him pay off his debt. I had a job by then, and had started saving up to buy a place to live. But there was no way I could say no to him. I gave him the money, even though my Uncle Sol told me I was a fool to do it. Dad promised to find a way to pay me back, but with no retirement income aside from his Social Security and disability checks, he couldn't.

He limited himself for the rest of his life to a three-dollar-a-day habit at Off-Track Betting. The local OTB parlor was a sad and smelly place on West Twenty-Third Street, with linoleum floors, stainless steel counters, and flourescent lights, where clouds of smoke poured into the street when you opened the door to come in. Small TVs hung from the ceiling, broadcasting a nonstop loop of horses pounding down the tracks somewhere. The OTB parlor also happened to be located three doors down from a synagogue with a dwindling congregation. When they lacked the minimum number of men to hold a prayer service called a *minyan*, they'd send someone in to OTB to round up a couple of old Jewish guys, including my dad, who'd shove his racing form in his pocket, put his tweed hat with the feather in it on his bald head, and go next door to help out, because, well, why not? It was a *mitzvah*.

There was one story my father liked to tell that wasn't from the war or his childhood or the Bible or Greek mythology. He said it was a story that his father had told him, and that he believed had been handed down for many generations, perhaps from some ancient exile of wandering Jews. The story concerned a tradition from a certain tribe that when the oldest person among them began to slow the group down, his child would have to take him to the top of a mountain and leave him there to die. In accordance with the custom, one day a young man led his ailing father to the top of a mountain and bade him farewell. It was customary for the old person being abandoned to behave stoically, so as not to make the young person feel guilty. But in this case, the old man began to weep.

"Father, you are not supposed to cry," protested the young man.

"I am not crying for myself," the old man explained between his sobs. "I am imagining the day your son will bring you to the mountaintop, and I am crying for you."

As my sister likes to say, we took our father to the mountaintop on the twenty-second of February in 1993. He was eighty-two years old when he died in a Veterans Administration nursing home. *Taps* was played at his memorial service in the chapel there a few weeks later, and the army provided a headstone for his grave in Maine that lists his years of military service.

Dad's decline was precipitated by a stroke that he had when I was pregnant with my first son, Danny, but he held on to this world just long enough to meet his little grandbaby. Danny seems to have inherited his grandfather's outgoing manner and fun-loving personality, along with his blue eyes and ready grin; he's generous, loyal, and good-hearted, and he has more friends than anyone I know. I can easily imagine him and his grandpa fishing together in Maine or eating hot dogs at a ball game. My younger son, Nathaniel, is named for my dad's little brother Tan, a professor of economics of whom my dad was enormously proud; but it's little Nathaniel's grit and fearlessness that reminds me most of my dad. This kid could scale a sheer brick wall or climb a metal fence long before he knew how to read, and he told us one day that he'd taken care of a bully at school by twisting the kid's arm behind his back. Yeah, yeah, I know, as the parent, I'm supposed to tell him to "Use your words!" But all I kept thinking was, here is a boy after his grandpa's heart.

How I wish Danny and Nat could have heard firsthand all those stories their grandpa told so well! I know that no matter how hard I try to write them up and make sure I get every detail straight, I can never do them justice. But Dad was suffering and sick and ready to go when he died, and that made it easier to bear. At his memorial service, everyone agreed that he'd lived a full life with few regrets. His brothers and sisters might have shaken their heads over his bad habits and his lifestyle, but many of my cousins told me that he was the uncle who had taught them that having fun and enjoying life is just as important as working hard and being successful.

We were not surprised when one of his best friends from the war, Schuyler Jackson, another D-Day veteran from the 101st, died just four days later. Helen Briggs, the Red Cross nurse who was assigned to their group during the war, put it this way at the funeral: "David was lonely up there, so he came down and got Sky."

It took me a long time to get over being angry at my father after he died. I felt he hadn't done enough to try to help my mother. I hated the gambling and booze that turned him pathetic, especially in his old age. And I hated the womanizing that I believe contributed to my mother's sad state.

But gradually I was able to let go of all that, and I tried to hold on to what was good. I focused on little things, like the time we stopped in a Howard Johnson's on the way to Maine, where the waitress announced to no one in particular that the previous customer's tip "sure was on me." My father dug into his pocket and left her a five-dollar tip on a bill that wasn't much more than that. Or my Aunt Deen describing how "gallant" he had been toward her brother Bill Jr., taking him to the hardware store and letting him buy whatever he wanted. "Bill may not understand money," my dad told Deen afterward, "but he knows how to pick out expensive tools."

Eventually I realized that there was really a lot to admire in the man— his *joie de vivre*, his generosity, his optimism, his bravery, his disdain for obsessions with wealth, achievement, and material things, and his loyalty to family, friends, and country. He was a World War II hero who bought drinks for the Vietnam guys, a city boy who was happy to give his country girl wife two months in Maine every year, a cripple who didn't let a bum hand get in the way of pulling his own weight, and a father who bought ice cream for every kid on the playground.

After he died, it was hard to know what to keep to remember him by. My sister saved his medals, of course, and we still have his fishing tackle box up in Maine, along with a handsome photo of him in his army uniform. As I cleaned out his apartment, I was about to put the cocktail shaker in which he'd mixed up Jack Roses in a box of kitchen supplies to give away, when it occurred to me that the shaker actually might be worth something. I knew of an antique store that specialized in vintage bar accessories, and figured that one day I'd drop by and see if I could sell it. But somehow I never did, and as time went on I felt more and more like the cocktail shaker was the perfect way to remember him. It's from another era, elegant yet utilitarian, and he brought it out for all the parties and social gatherings that he loved. It's on a shelf in my apartment now, and I think my father would have been happy to know that I kept it.

11

MAD HOUSEWIFE

David and Anne, on the town.

M y earliest memory of my mother is my earliest memory of riding the subway. We are in the tunnel, in the dark, on a No. 7 train, but sunlight suddenly fills the car as we emerge onto an elevated track outside. She is all dressed up, sitting in front of a window, wearing her favorite chocolate-brown knit wool suit, the one with the Chanel-style jacket and straight skirt, and a jaunty fur-trimmed beret. The seats on the train are woven wicker instead of molded plastic. We are going to the 1964 World's Fair, in Flushing Meadow Park in Queens, and I am three years old. Everything seems very civilized, and we are going to have a good time.

But sometimes I wonder if this really happened, or if I am just putting little bits of different things I know to have been true into one large false collage, one pretty dream about a pretty mommy and a pretty train. I cross-examine myself: Why would we have gone on the subway, when we owned a car? How could I have such a clear picture of what she looked like sitting against the window, unless I was sitting across from her, and why would I be sitting across from her instead of next to her if I was three? Did she really own that suit so long ago, and why was she wearing such a warm hat with no coat? Were there really wicker seats on that line in that year, or am I grafting something I saw in the Transit Museum onto my own impossible memory?

And if it all seemed so civilized, well then, I wonder sometimes if maybe it just never happened.

When my mother was depressed, she lay on a small bed in a small room in the back of the apartment with an old, dirty shade drawn down to the bottom of the windowsill. She wasn't sleeping; she was just lying there, covered up with a shawl. She didn't like to answer the telephone or watch TV and she didn't seem interested in the routines that get most people up and around even if they don't have jobs to go to: a cup of morning coffee or reading the paper the same day it's published or getting the mail or taking a shower. One day when she was lying down, my friend Linda came over to play guitar and sing songs with me. We hadn't seen my mother all afternoon, but suddenly she was standing in the doorway of my room holding a crystal wine glass and a teaspoon. She tapped the glass with the spoon, and when the bell-tone stopped sounding, she said that was exactly what Linda's voice sounded like.

But does that seem really, truly crazy, or merely charmingly eccentric? In the strange little world I lived in, in Apartment 6RE (for R-ear E-ast), we never thought my mother was crazy. Crazy was Son of Sam, the serial killer who heard voices and killed people. Crazy was Sybil, the girl in the movie with the alternate personalities. Crazy was Mr. Waddington, who lived upstairs from us and was taken away by the cops to Bellevue after he sat down in the hallway by the elevator, took all his clothes off, and said that the CIA had put electrodes in his dog. My mother slept a lot, and her house was a mess, and she said my friend's voice sounded like a spoon hitting a crystal goblet, but that didn't mean she was *crazy*.

In fact, because she didn't hear voices or undress in public, it was hard to convince other people that there was anything wrong with her at all. When I tried as a teenager to describe to my father's sister, Ruth, what it was about my mother's behavior that was so disturbing, she laughed. "You make it sound like *Diary of a Mad Housewife!*" she told me. I didn't think it was so funny. Ruth was a successful businesswoman who never married and who lived in an apartment on Sutton Place South, a very prestigious Manhattan address; to her, my mother was simply a lazy housewife. Just as Ann Landers advised lonely widows to put meaning in their lives by helping others, Aunt Ruth told me that my mother would feel better if she volunteered somewhere with people who were worse off than she was. I didn't know how to explain to her that, actually, I didn't really know anyone worse off than she was.

Somehow it wasn't enough to tell people that she lay in a bed for days on end while insisting that she couldn't sleep, or that when my father ordered her to throw away the newspapers she'd been hoarding, she merely divided them into piles and stuffed them under the beds, or that she went through a period of reading that was so manic, I used to pick books for her out of the library by sheer size—the fattest ones, as many as I could carry home, three times a week. None of that sounds so bad.

And when I say she gave up housekeeping, people wonder: Why didn't the rest of us clean it? Why didn't we hire someone to clean it? I'm not sure I know the answer, except to say that somehow we bought into her hopelessness, and we gave in to her hysterical insistence that no one except for her was allowed to try to make order of the mess we lived in, even though she herself was in no condition to do it. Soon the apartment was overrun with cockroaches, and when I turned on the kitchen light at night, dozens of them scurried across the walls, running for cover. I made a game of it: How many could I smash with the palm of my hand before they all disappeared?

I was so blasé about killing roaches that when a big one crawled out of a girl's bookbag one day in school, to the horror of everyone in the room, I earned the girl's undying friendship by nonchalantly squishing it under my thumb while everyone else scurried around for a tissue or a newspaper. But one little roach didn't bother me. At home, it was so bad I had to let the toaster run a full cycle and kill all the bugs that ran out while it was heating up before I dared to put the bread in. I remember looking in my glass of orange juice one morning to see a tiny roach swimming around. My dad took a look, picked the roach out with the fingers of his good hand, and downed the glass. "How much orange juice can one little roach drink?" he asked with a grin. If I hadn't already thought my dad was the bravest man I knew, now I was sure.

The roaches also left their little cocoa-colored eggs all over the bathroom, and when there was a hatching, swarms of them skittered around the tub and the tiles and the sink. Neighbors used to stop me in the elevator and beg me to persuade my mother to allow an exterminator in, because they knew they'd never clear up their own roach problem until she cleared up hers. But she wouldn't let the exterminator in, just like she wouldn't go to the doctor, just like she wouldn't throw the newspapers away. She'd dug herself into a hole, and she refused to come out.

When she was in her manic phases, staying up all night trying to make order out of the mess, she would sometimes quote one of her favorite Maine poets, Edna St. Vincent Millay, by saying, in an oddly cheery tone, "My candle burns at both ends!" But Millay had another poem that I don't think my mother knew, and that one was a perfect description of how she was the rest of the time: "Alone, alone, in a terrible place, in utter dark without a face."

At some point my father left. He put a bed in his office, and a TV and a fridge, and he took his clothes there and stopped coming home at night. He had to do it, he said; she just kept yelling and screaming at him. Finally one day he turned around and told her to shut up. "Nobody tells me to shut up in my own house!" she screamed. "Get out!" He didn't need to be asked twice. Besides, the house was so disgusting it was a relief to leave. He brought her booze and cigarettes and food, and he called each day to check on her, but this way he was free to come and go as he chose.

One day when I was away at college my sister, Nancy, decided to go clean the apartment out. "You'd be sitting on the sofa and the roaches would be climbing on the sofa," she told me. "I told her I was sorry, there was nothing she could do to stop me, but she couldn't live like that anymore."

Mommy was already drunk and pouring herself another drink when Nancy grabbed the bottle and emptied it in the sink. Nancy then went to work clearing out the spice cabinet; none of the little containers had been opened in years, and she just threw them all away. But every little can or bottle she put in the garbage, Mommy fought her physically to keep, hitting her and screaming at her. Finally Nancy called Aunt Deen. "You have to come over," she said. "I'm trying to clean up and you have to keep her off me, because she's being violent and nobody can live like this." Before Deen arrived, Nancy opened up a blue trunk that we used to keep toys in to find it full of old newspapers, and as she began to pull the newspapers out, she realized it was actually Roach Central, a huge nest where dozens of them were scurrying around.

"I was spraying them with roach spray and she was screaming, 'You can't do that!' and I just said, 'You're crazy, I'm throwing everything out,'" Nancy recalled. For weeks after, Mommy called her every day to complain that this had been thrown out and that had been thrown out, but Nancy knew she had done the right thing.

The roach problem lessened, but it still wasn't eradicated—until after she died. Then, within thirty days, the bugs were gone, completely and forever. My father was neat and clean and put Borax around and had the exterminator in. It was as easy as that.

For a short time, in the mid-1970s, my mother agreed to undergo shock treatments. This was billed as the cure-all for manic depression, which was what she was told she had. She never saw a therapist, and she took no medication; she just went to a hospital a few times when I was in high school, and electrodes were fixed to the sides of her head to deliver electric shocks. When she regained consciousness, she had no idea who she was or where she was; my father said that afterward, she didn't recognize him.

The shock treatments worked—at least temporarily. And while I don't really understand how shock treatments alleviate depression, it was clear that they made her forget. Forget that her own mother had died in a pool of blood during the Depression in rural Maine. Forget that I was going to a friend's house after school, so that she panicked when I wasn't home by 4:00 P.M. And forget that she hated having been a housewife every day since 1949. She started getting dressed up at night and going out with my father to bars and restaurants and shows. She told me she really liked *Saturday Night Fever* because of the beautiful dancing; she even went to 101st events and came home saying she'd had a good time.

She became a regular, with my father, at an expensive Italian restaurant on Eighth Avenue, a few blocks from their apartment, called Chelsea Place. It had potted plants and strings of twinkling lights, the waitresses sang "Happy Birthday" in operatic style, and whoever was playing the electric piano by the bar pulsed out a steady diet of disco hits. The entrance to the restaurant was a false storefront on the street for an antiques store that didn't really exist. You walked straight past the overpriced rocking chairs and the old dolls displayed on the walls to the rear door of the store, and when you stepped over the threshold, you were in the restaurant, feeling like you were an elite member of an exclusive in-the-know club. It made my parents feel good to hang out there; after a few weeks, everyone on the staff knew their names and effusively served their favorite drinks—Remy Martin for her, Jack Rose for him—without being asked.

A couple of times they asked me to go with them. To me, they seemed strangely out of place there, buffoons for the other patrons who were so chic and young and in the know. It was like a time warp in which Nick and Nora had stumbled out of their hotel suite, all dressed up and drinks in hand, and into Studio 54, where they were so stunned by the loud music and the attention from people half their age that they didn't know enough to leave. My parents seemed to be trying to recapture the cocktail society life they'd briefly led, long ago, when my sister was a little girl. They were oblivious to the fact that the world had changed and they no longer fit in. I decided not to tell my mother that the matron stationed outside the ladies' room had cheerfully let a man go in, and that for the longest time he stood there spooning cocaine out of a large leather pouch around his neck, then cutting it with a razor blade into neat lines by the sink. I assume the matron had enough sense to direct my mother elsewhere when such things went on; drinking excessively and chain-smoking were normal for my parents' generation, but drugs were completely unacceptable.

After a year or so, however, my mother's enthusiasm for accompanying my father on his nightly rounds degenerated. It was replaced by a hyperactive mania for meaningless tasks, like staying up all night to wash the walls or clip dozens of articles out of her stash of newspapers to mail off to people who probably didn't want to read them. She claimed she couldn't sleep, for days on end. The sleeplessness eventually turned into exhaustion, and the exhaustion gave way to a catatonic hopelessness. Whatever good the shock treatments had done wore off. We were all exactly where we started.

About a month after my sister's daughter was born in 1983, she brought the baby for our mother to see for the first time. Mommy put Nancy's hand on her abdomen and said, "What do you think this is?" There was a huge lump in her belly.

"It's a tumor," Nancy told her. "Why are you asking me? Why don't you go to a doctor?"

But she wouldn't, and as Nancy says, it was very hard to make her do what she refused to do. "I think she wanted to die," Nancy said. "You can't have lumps like that and not know what the deal was. She was determined not to do anything about it. And what could you say to her—that if she got all better, she'd have a great life back?"

Two months later, she was dead. The autopsy said she had breast cancer that had metastasized all over her body. And that was when we realized that she'd been drinking to numb the pain.

I think your mother had a great disappointment in life," is how my Aunt Deen explained it. "She was deserted by your father. She used to call me up and cry. She said, 'He asked me for a divorce. He stayed out all night drinking, then came home and urinated in a drawer, thinking it was the toilet.' She was defenseless. He would take her for these shock treatments, and then he'd go out with his friends and drink and spend money. She never got the support she needed from her family."

She paused and then continued. "Your poor mother was a mother to everybody. Everybody sat on her, everybody dropped on her, but she never had the pleasure in life to have someone she could go to and put her head on. She just had a breakdown. She had too big a load to carry. She smoked herself to a frazzle. She had some self-destructive behavior to begin with, and your father didn't help.

"She was a wonderful, wonderful sister. She was the most decent one of all. But she was the only one who didn't have anyone to cry on. The rest of the family, we dragged on her. She saved piles and piles of stuff for Peanut's kids and Achsah's kids, and that's why Achsah treats you and your sister like queens—because you are Anne's daughters."

Your mother didn't want to go to the doctor because she said your father needed the money," was how Aunt Lee explained it.

"But that's crazy!" I said. "My father would have paid for her to go to the doctor."

"I know," she said. "But remember that time she got hurt by somebody in the grocery store? They banged their cart into her heel, and she never went to the doctor, and she was walking around with her foot purple for so long, and it hurt her and hurt her and hurt her."

"But why didn't she just go to a doctor and get it treated?" I asked.

"She said she couldn't afford it. And yet your mother would take care of everybody else. Bring them food and everything else. She took care of them when they were sick, but nobody took care of her."

"It's ironic, isn't it, that she had what seemed like an easy life—only two kids, she didn't have to work. Yet all her sisters outlived her," I said.

"But she didn't have anyone to confide in," Aunt Lee replied. "David would come home late. He had his fun out all night, and she was left home alone. She just stayed home with you girls."

In a manic phase, my mother happened, one day, to see an art appreciation show on TV. The show was part of a series that offered college credits via public television. She submitted a neatly typewritten essay to the professor, by mail, and as was her habit in those pre-Xerox days, she kept a carbon copy. Here is what she wrote:

> In the small New England villages where I went to school, the town fathers felt if they provided a place where a child could learn the three Rs, they had more than done their duty.
>
> Only a few people had radios, television was beyond anyone's wildest dreams, and the nearest movie house was fifteen miles away by trolley car. I recall one teacher who brought in her radio in order that her class could listen once a week to the Walter Damrosch program [a classical music appreciation program broadcast during the Depression]. There were other teachers who tried to enlarge our narrow world by reading a chapter once a week from a book by a famous author or a few lines of poetry by a great poet. There were still others who shared some personal treasure with us; however, these sterling characters were few and far between.
>
> For those who have leisure and money to pursue their interest in the finer arts and have always had access to them, they may feel that the rest of us don't care about such things. However, this is not always the case; the daily struggle to keep a roof over one's head, to feed and clothe one's body, and to care for your family becomes paramount. Unless one is endowed with tremendous physical stamina and good health, it is often that one collapses in exhaustion at days' end and with a prayer that comes with the dawn you'll be able to rise for another go at life's battle for survival.
>
> Being a wife and mother in my opinion is an art in itself. Many women may be natural born wives and mothers; but, as for myself, I have had to work very hard at it and it has been a full-time job for me. Now I intend to let some things go and take the time to develop ideas and interests of my own.

She never completed the course.

• • •

One of the few friends my mother had was a woman named Ruth who lived upstairs from us on Twenty-First Street. She was a furniture designer with three children. The youngest, Sarah, was about my age and we often played together. Ruth did a lot of her work at home, but sometimes my mother would babysit for Sarah if Ruth had to go off to a meeting or presentation. Then, at the end of the workday, Ruth would come and sit in our living room. She and my mother would have a glass of sherry, talk about their families, and read the "Suzy Says" column in the *Daily News* together, giggling over the gossip about celebrity parties, the fashion no-nos committed by various starlets, and the extravagant lifestyles of the rich and famous. They chatted about their children, and Sarah and I made up songs and put on little shows to entertain them.

One night when I was in elementary school, my mother asked me to sit at the kitchen table with her. She made a pot of tea and gave me a piece of store-bought cherry pie. Then she told me that Ruth and her family were moving down South, to be near the headquarters for the company Ruth worked for. She began to cry as she told me this, and I realize now, looking back, that she really never had another friend after Ruth moved away.

I looked Ruth up not long ago and flew down to visit her. Her home is beautiful, and filled with the furniture she designed. We had a good laugh remembering "Suzy Says," and Ruth pulled out a copy of the latest *W* magazine to show me that the real Suzy, a writer named Aileen Mehle, is still hard at work penning a monthly column on celebrity gossip. Ruth's two sons, both older than I am, had me in stitches over dinner as they reminded me about a neighbor who used to fill our building's elevator with nauseating cigar smoke. And I oohed and aahed over photos of Sarah's two small children.

Before I got on the plane to fly home, Ruth handed me a treasure: an envelope filled with letters my mother had sent her in the decade after she left New York. I already had some letters she had written to my Aunt Achsah over the years; my aunt had saved them and given them back to me, one at a time, as birthday presents after my mother died or whenever I would go to see her. One day I sat down and read the letters, all of them, at once. After asking everyone who knew my mother how she ended up the way she did, I was hoping she would be able to explain it, in her own words, through these letters sent over the course of twenty years to her sister and her friend.

February 1961

Dear Achsah,

Just a few lines to say we had another daughter, Beth, born Jan. 20. I have been sick and running temperature ever since. Am feeling better today. How you ever had 7 I don't know. I have had it with my two. Sorry I haven't written to you before, but haven't been well for a long time. Don't see how you can work and do all that needs to be done in the house for your seven . . .

Love, Anne

August 1961

Dear Achsah,

How did you make out with those new jackets? Do they fit any of the boys now? I always think about writing. Beth hangs on and fusses so much. Am writing this with her in my lap. Will never figure out how you did it with your seven. Beth seems to be afraid here in the apartment and howls unless someone is constantly in the room . . .

Love, Anne

February 1962

Dear Achsah,

I read in the paper yesterday, soot is 68 tons per square mile in NYC. No wonder I'm always cleaning filth and my house is always dirty.

Love, Anne

February 1964

Dear Achsah,

I scrubbed my kitchen walls down last week, took me three days, cleaned kitchen cupboard over sink, washed my spread and David's and chair cover, living room windows and curtains and around window frames. I was exhausted over weekend. Did a three-hour ironing on Saturday that had piled up all week. Am trying to make some towels and pillow cases now as I have some scraps of material I want to get rid of and am low on cases and towels. There is so much to do in a house. As hard as I work my house is always a mess and I'm never caught up. Will get a package of things out to you as soon as I possibly can.

Love, Anne

July 1966

Dear Ruth,

Delighted to receive your letter and hear that things are working out well for you in the South. New York City is not exactly Monaco. Bus and subway fares have gone up. The hospital attendants have gone on strike. Our combined newspaper is still on strike. Even the welfare clients are organizing to strike for their rights. As the natives in Maine say after a trip to this big city: "It's a great place to visit, but I wouldn't want to live there." Frankly I'm starting to feel the same way. What's the good of being a stone's throw from Broadway when one never gets to bask in its glow. Have been trying to talk David into pulling up stakes and stop killing himself.

Ten cans of bug spray have made only a small dent in the roach population. They are feasting like Holy Romans on frosting sugar, crackers, flour, cereal, and various other goodies. The heat and humidity has encouraged them to flourish in spite of all my good efforts to discourage them.

Love, Anne

March 1970

Dear Ruth,

Another bomb factory in East Village blew up, killing one of the makers. Isn't it terrible, what's going on?

I'm so tired, couldn't get up until 11 o'clock today, was hoping for a few decent warm days.

David bought a portable TV for Beth. The one thing bought for years and I can't even have a say about it. Sometimes he makes me so furious.

Looks as if it's going to be another of those weeks slipping away without my accomplishing anything.

It's nearly 7 P.M.—not a word from David about dinner until he just popped in the door.

Love, Anne

May 1970

Dear Ruth,

Feeling so ragged have hardly made the beds this week . . . The whole country has gone mad! All the colleges here are closing with the confrontations, bombings, strikes, and memoriums. When and where will it all end?

Love, Anne

June 1970

Dear Ruth,

Last night someone laid on my bell right outside the apt. at 1 A.M. I had finally just closed my eyes. Don't know who it was or what they wanted—a couple of men and I didn't dare even peep through my door spy. I said I'd call the police if they didn't get away from that door and out of the building—they left cursing!

Tonight somebody bombed the police Hdq. at 240 Center St.

Some police we got, can't even protect their own Hdq. Shows how much protection Joe Citizen is going to get, doesn't it?

Love, Anne

July 1971 (from Lake Cobbosseecontee in Maine)

Dear Ruth,

The weather has been perfect here. Hot sunny days and wool blanket nights. The dock has a beautiful ladder. Beth is able to swim without her life jacket though the water is very deep here. This is truly one of the most beautiful spots on the lake. I hope this gives me a new lease on life. Haven't called any of my friends in town—just resting as the days are speeding by all too soon. Hardly seems possible we've been here two weeks yesterday.

We get up late for breakfast—before I get the dishes washed it's time for lunch. Swim for a bit and it's time to think about dinner.

Beth caught a bass so big it broke her line. David has had very good luck and we've had some delicious fresh fish to vary our menu.

Bought 4 quarts of strawberries and made a couple of quarts into jam much to Beth's delight . . .

Will be back in N.Y. all too soon.

Love, Anne

September 1972

Dear Ruth,

Your letter was a great shot in the arm. Don't know how you manage all that you do! I had just finished clipping out more Suzys and was going to at last write you a note.

Guess you have gathered from the absence of my letters that I'm in a very depressed state! Don't know if I'm getting senile or have just lost my mind completely. Used to have hope that a better day would come but now know that nothing's going to change. I get sick of patching up this and getting along with that old piece of junk . . .

When you don't hear from me you know I'm at a low ebb.

Love, Anne

July 1977

Dear Achsah,

It's going to be quite lonely around here when Beth leaves for college at the end of August . . .

I keep thinking I'll write then when I start working with all that's going on here my time disappears and I get so exhausted I stagger then I finally have to sleep. Hope things quiet down a bit this summer.

Have to get stamps at P.O. as am down to my last couple. Takes so much time to shop for groceries in this city. They burned the Key Food Store on 8th Ave. between 21st and 22nd Street down Mem. Day weekend so have to walk further to other stores. Did lot of my shopping there as it was close.

Love, Anne

July 1980

Dear Achsah,

Robbed twice last week and really shook up about it. Thurs. night in front of David's place!! Sat. night right in front of my building—keys, glasses, etc. gone! Didn't hear from David all week. Thurs. at 5:30 called and asked me if I wanted to have dinner with him. We had dinner and a couple of drinks and came home at 1 A.M. Said he wanted to go back to his office. Not a soul on block. He bends over to put key in door to go up to loft. This face in my face on silent feet of a cat, sneakers, wrenched my purse from under my arm off my shoulder and out of another bag I had it in. I said, "David, someone just stole my purse!" He

said, "There is no one here!" I said, "He ran around corner between two buildings." We looked but he was gone with the wind
in the dark of the night! Went upstairs and called 911. Police
emergency number. A recording comes on telling you to look up
number of precinct in phone directory. We didn't even know
what precinct we were in . . .

Stay well! I'm going to get to Maine somehow even if I have
to crawl! I'm damn sick and tired of being a prisoner here.

Love, Anne

I asked Ruth if she thought my mother knew about my father's
girlfriends. "I don't think so," she said. "She certainly never let on if
she did."

Then I asked if she had any insights into why my mother ended up
so miserable as a housewife, why she hadn't tried to go back to work.
She explained that for women of my mother's generation, there were
no easy answers. Ruth was younger, and graduating from college after
World War II, she expected to have a career. Her husband and she split
up when the children were young; she worked from home for several
years but as her designs received more and more recognition, she moved
up in the company, and eventually became a vice president.

For my mother, there was no clear path. "As the years went by, first
with Nancy, then with you, she just realized that was as far as she was
going to go," Ruth explained. "She didn't have the means of getting
out of her situation. She was clearly capable of a lot of things, but I
don't think it was just a matter of getting a job."

I often wonder if my mother's mental deterioration was inevitable, or
if the time and place in which she lived her life triggered or exacerbated
her breakdown. She chose to leave Maine; there could be no good life
in a place where she had suffered so much. Yet she was a country girl
at heart, and all her life, she looked to the natural world for healing
and rejuvenation. There was no happier moment for her each year than
our arrival in Maine for our summer vacation, and no sadder moment

than returning to New York. Perhaps if she'd had a nice little house in the suburbs, with a garden and robins hopping on the lawn, far from the soot and crime of Manhattan, her mental state would have been different. Or maybe not. Maybe she would simply have found something else to obsess and be miserable about had she not had New York City's demise to focus on, against the backdrop of the social upheavals of the 1960s and '70s. But either way, the where and when of her story matters. It mattered to her, and it mattered to me and everyone else my age who grew up then and there. And when I look at the big picture, I sometimes think it's no wonder she was so depressed.

In the '70s, every supermarket had a generic aisle, and everything in it was in white packages with black letters. My mother liked to shop there, and so did I. There were corn flakes and cigarettes and toilet paper and beer and spaghetti, and it all cost less than the same stuff in other aisles, where the packages were all in color. It was better than the store brand in a self-punishing kind of way. We'd been a bad country, we'd had a bad war, the whole world hated us, and we didn't deserve brand names in pretty boxes. What we deserved was inflation, recession, and generic packaging. "Everything looks worse in black and white," Paul Simon sang in "Kodachrome," and he was right. But it felt good to buy those generic things, good in the same way that I imagined it was good to give up nylon stockings and sliced bread during World War II. Generic was the opposite of gourmet and designer and upscale, and that was fine, because in the '70s, there were no yuppies.

When I was a teenager, there was only one good reason to go to Times Square: to buy tickets to Broadway shows at the half-price TKTS booth, which opened in 1973. My favorite show was *A Chorus Line,* and I saw it three times. I liked to sing "One Singular Sensation" with my friend Adraine as we walked down the street, arm in arm, kicking our legs up. "One smile and suddenly nobody else will do" was an anthem for our friendship, and we didn't care if grown-ups were staring.

But other than the theater, there was nothing in Times Square that a normal person would want to see or do. I remember one day in 1975 I met some friends for a boat ride, and as I walked across Forty-Second Street to the Hudson River pier, I was propositioned six times in five minutes. Garbage was blowing around, X-rated signs blinked everywhere, and except for my tormentors, the place was practically deserted, like a science fiction movie after the final conflict. I didn't hear the term "crossroads of the world" used to describe Times Square until I was much older; if I had, it wouldn't have made any sense to me. The Times Square I knew was not the Times Square where a soldier kisses a girl in a mass celebration marking the end of World War II; it was a Times Square where a girl might get grabbed by a dirty old stranger with evil intentions.

A block west of Times Square was Port Authority, the city's main bus terminal, and it was also seedy and scary. My mother and I went there one night in 1978 so I could catch a bus back to Cornell, where I went to college in upstate New York. We got there a little early, and my mother asked a police officer inside the bus terminal if he could recommend a place in the neighborhood to have something to eat. "Lady," he said, shaking his head, "I wouldn't go out there after dark, and I've got a gun."

When I was eleven, my Hebrew school teacher told us that some Christians had killed a lot of Jews by giving them showers. I had no idea what he was talking about, and of course ran home to tell my mother, who was appalled by that particular version of events and promptly took me out of Hebrew school. I didn't figure out what the Hebrew teacher was talking about until I read Leon Uris's novel about the creation of Israel, *Exodus*. My father always said he joined the army to fight Nazis because they were killing Jews. But I didn't really get it, didn't really realize what had happened to the Jews, until I read Leon Uris. In social studies I wrote a report on ancient Egypt, made a diorama of the Great Wall, and drew a timeline to show when the Mayans built their pyramids, but it was 1973 and I had never heard anyone talk about the Holocaust.

. . .

My mother didn't let me walk to school by myself until the sixth grade, and I read nearly every day in the paper of someone being killed or wounded because they valued their money more than their life. You had to make sure when you left the house that you had ten dollars for a mugger as well as ten cents for a phone call. Less than ten dollars and they might kill you. I took great comfort in the advice of a woman I knew who'd outrun a would-be attacker: If someone comes after you with a gun, give up your wallet, because if you try to get away, you could get shot from a distance. But if someone has a knife, just run. What's the guy going to do? Throw the knife at you? Made a lot of sense, I thought.

Every night, the Channel Five *Ten O'Clock News* would be on in our living room. Seconds before the newscast began, a voice on the TV would ask, "It's ten P.M. Do you know where your children are?" And every night, in my mind's eye, I would see a mother in some remote corner of far-off Bronx or distant Queens who, upon hearing these words from the TV, would look around her living room to take stock of her family, and suddenly realize that one of her children was missing. She would search the apartment, and then the building, and then start crying and praying while calling 911. And then the police would arrive and try to determine if little Julio or lovely Sheila had run away, been abducted, or simply disappeared into the night. Thank goodness, I always thought to myself, for that ominous little reminder from the Channel Five *Ten O'Clock News*; without it, how many lost children might go unnoticed until it was too late?

When I started kindergarten at P.S. 11 in 1966, we said the Pledge of Allegiance, sang "My Country 'Tis of Thee," made ashtrays out of clay for Father's Day presents, and had to show the teacher that our nails were clean before she let us dance to a forty-five RPM record of "Georgy Girl." By the time I got to fifth grade, a kid had stabbed me in the shoulder with a pen, drawing blood; when the teacher told his mother what he'd done, she beat him up in front of the rest of the class. A substitute teacher told dirty jokes to keep our attention, and there were fewer and fewer kids for whom English was a first language. In sixth grade, in 1973, the principal's voice came booming over the loudspeaker one day instructing us all to get under the desks to avoid being hit by stray bullets from a gang fight in the street.

In seventh grade I escaped to a school called Hunter. You had to take a test to get in but it was free; that meant we were all of us smart but none of us rich. In my old school, we'd had to go to the bathroom in pairs because you never knew what awful thing might be lurking in those dirty little toilet-paper-less stalls. At Hunter, it was so safe you could go to the bathroom by yourself.

One day in 1975 my social studies teacher interrupted our studies of federalism and held up that famous front page from the *Daily News*: FORD TO CITY: DROP DEAD. New York City was on the verge of bankruptcy, and President Ford had no interest in bailing us out. I had this image in my head of the island of Manhattan teetering on the edge of a flattened world, about to fall off. I was sure that anyone with any sense had already moved to the suburbs—maybe some place like New Rochelle, where Dick Van Dyke and Mary Tyler Moore had lived in their sitcom, or Brewster, where Marlo Thomas's parents had lived in *That Girl*. The way I saw it, Marlo had made an awful mistake leaving her parents' big, beautiful house, practically in the country, for that little tiny apartment in Manhattan where she undoubtedly had roaches and scary neighbors.

In the city where I grew up, the FMLN was always planting bombs and some vital group of citizens was always on strike—teachers, cops, transit workers, garbagemen—paralyzing the city in various ways. But I was sure that in Brewster and New Rochelle, not only were the streets and the buildings always clean and safe, but no one ever walked off the job. And I was pretty sure that kids in those places went trick-or-treating.

After the fiscal crisis, the subways got so bad that you had bragging rights as a macho New Yorker just by commuting twice a day. Every surface was obliterated by graffiti, and every ride was beset by catastrophe—fire and smoke, doors stuck open, doors stuck closed, rats and roaches, criminals snatching chains and weirdos jerking off in the corner seat. I took the subway to school starting in the eighth grade, and it was normal to be stuck in a tunnel for fifteen minutes without a word of explanation from the conductor, lights out the whole time. All anyone could do for comfort, sitting there in the dark, was to run a fingernail in and out of the little hole shaped like a Y that was carved into every subway token. Nowadays, of course, the trains are clean and reliable, the conductor tells you what's going on, and the lights almost never go out. And all of that is very good, because there is no little Y to stick your fingernail in; everybody uses MetroCards.

Sometimes I would take the city bus to school if I wasn't in a hurry. What I remember most about the bus was the Lysol Lady. She was a tall, thin black lady who always had a large clear plastic bag over her head, and inside the plastic bag she was always spraying Lysol at her own face. She paid her fare so the driver had to let her on, and she never took a seat. She would just stand there, holding a pole with one hand and spraying Lysol with the other. You'd hear "Pssssh, pssssh" and smell the faintly chemical smell and look up to see her remarkably calm face breathing in those fumes. I used to stare at her and stare at her; something about her, and something about the way everyone on the bus ignored her as she stood there poisoning herself, reminded me of my mother.

I graduated from high school in 1977 and that summer was the most unbearable of my life. Maybe it was because I couldn't wait to get away from my parents and go to college; maybe it was because of the blackout and the looting that followed, or maybe it was because Son of Sam was on the loose. Not only were our politicians incapable of balancing a checkbook, not only were our citizens so deranged that they destroyed their own neighborhoods when the lights went out, but now there was a mass murderer writing wacky letters to the newspaper and shooting at couples parked in lovers' lanes. I felt lucky to be escaping to college; surely I was leaving the worst place on earth.

My mother died before the city turned around, before crime went down and real estate went up and museums went from being cheap and empty to being expensive and crowded. To her, Tab was an evil-tasting diet drink and not a computer command, CDs were bank accounts for a bear market, there were only two Barnes & Noble stores in all the world, and Pintos had exploding gas tanks instead of four legs.

Some of what has happened since my mother died would have upset her as much as the campus unrest, crime, and bombings of the '70s. I'm thinking about crack, AIDS, 9/11, and Al Qaeda. Other things would have mystified her: ATMs, e-mail, dot-coms, faxes, microwaves, rap music, and decaf cappuccinos. She missed both the bull market and the return of the bear market, along with the Clintons, the Bushes, and Giuliani. She never knew that the wooden clogs she hated me wearing could be made light as a feather thanks to high-tech materials, or that pooper-scooper laws had made the streets of New York relatively safe for pedestrians. She would have been astounded to see that our rent-controlled, roach-infested apartment, in a building where the elevator was always broken and the heat never seemed to come on, was worth more than a half-million dollars as a co-op. Our Spanish-speaking neighbors were long ago replaced by successive waves of gay men, artists, and investment bankers.

But there is one change in Manhattan that I know she would have loved, and that is the flowers. Twenty-four-hour fruit-and-vegetable stands, mostly run by Korean immigrants, have sprouted on every other street corner in New York in the years since my mother died, and all of them cover their storefronts with flowers—dozens and dozens of bouquets, from plain old carnations to exotic orchids, bright pink tulips on the bleakest February days, walls of mums in autumn in every shade of orange, and buckets of sunflowers that make broiling summers in the city feel like Provence. Perhaps amid the gladiolas and the dahlias, the tiger lilies and the daisies, my mother would have found a little bit of Maine, and perhaps that would have brought her some small comfort.

Today there are articles in the paper about depression all the time, and everybody knows what bipolar disorder is. In my generation, new mothers chat openly about postpartum blues, and the alphabet soup of mental illness has become part of our Woody Allen–like obsession with ourselves. A neurotic colleague is said to be "very OCD" (obsessive-compulsive disorder). A lingering sadness over a death in the family is "PTSD" (post-traumatic stress disorder). If you prefer summer to winter, it's chalked up to SAD (seasonal affective disorder). And getting drunk or smoking pot, that's just "self-medication" for people who aren't self-aware enough to get professional help, i.e., a Prozac prescription.

But nobody talked about things like that when my mother was sick. As long as she wasn't imagining that the CIA had put electrodes in her dog, we all pretended that what was wrong with her was something she could just shake off. Even after we had a name for it (manic depression), and even after she had shock treatments, we shared an unspoken belief that she could get out of bed and clean the house—if she really wanted to.

Now, of course, I think about it differently. The question I ask myself now is not why didn't she get out of bed, but why was she there in the first place? If she'd had that little house by the side of the road she always wanted, and if she'd married a different sort of man, would she have ended up the way she did? Or was her childhood so awful that she was doomed?

I even asked a psychologist, someone I went to high school with, for her take on all of this. Sarah (not the same girl who'd lived upstairs from me) pointed out that my mother's condition was not the normal type of depression people get when they have a lousy life.

"If your mother's life had been easy in adulthood, my guess is she would probably have had a tough time anyway, but perhaps not quite as tough, or not quite as soon," she said. "My best guess is that she had a built-in predisposition for depression or bipolar disorder that was bound to come out in some way, depending on the conditions of her life."

Given that my grandmother was famous for threatening to set her hair on fire and jump out the window, that built-in predisposition seems likely. (As my Aunt Achsah had put it so succinctly, "Any crazy streak we have, we come by natural.")

Sarah also observed that abandonment had been a terrible theme running through my mother's life, and perhaps that had helped trigger her illness. She was abandoned as a child by her mother, who died, and her father, who neglected her. She then, in turn, abandoned her younger siblings, escaping to live with the Connicks, ending up in reform school, and feeling so guilty about it that she sent care packages to her sisters for the rest of her life. She was abandoned in marriage by a husband who preferred his girlfriends, his drinking buddies, and his war stories to sitting at home with her. And finally, she was abandoned by her children, who grew up and moved out, my sister marrying at age eighteen and me going to college at age sixteen—both of us leaving home as soon as we could. And all of this was exacerbated by stresses over money, a troublesome teenage daughter, the birth of an unplanned baby, and generous quantities of liquor, caffeine, and alcohol.

"My guess is that with medication, your mother probably could have gotten up out of bed more and changed her clothes," Sarah said, "but she probably would have found life difficult to face."

In some ways, that was the awful bottom line. Even if she had gotten help, there was little in life for her to enjoy. Sarah didn't know my mother, but hearing those words, I felt as if she had.

12

HOUSE BY THE SIDE
OF THE ROAD

Our house in Maine.

I guess I was about thirteen or fourteen when my mother told me about her mother. It happened as she sat in the big armchair where she sat if she wasn't lying down, wearily reading the paper and sipping a wineglass filled with sherry, an old salt-and-pepper shawl wrapped around her shoulders. The room had grown dark that winter afternoon except for the pool of light from a reading lamp by her side.

I can't be sure what got her going that day, but maybe it was the sight of snow falling heavily outside, coating the grimy windows of our apartment and the black iron fire escape with a dusty layer of white.

And I don't know why I had wandered out of my bedroom and into the living room where she was; I was a sullen teenager, and she was the crazy mother with whom I barely exchanged a few words each day.

I don't even remember if she first said something about the weather outside or if the remark came out of the blue. But when she said, slowly and deliberately, looking off into space, "It was snowing," I knew for certain that she was not referring to the here and now, but to some other time and place that no longer existed. It was as if she had gone into a trance and traveled back through the years, and I was right there with her. I can't recall if I remained standing or sat down, if I was on the rug or in a chair; I only know that I stopped in my tracks and waited for the rest of the story to come.

"The snow was piling up outside the door, and my father couldn't start his truck. He tried, and he tried, and he tried, but it wouldn't start."

I imagined the sound of an engine coughing and sputtering to a stop, a man banging the steering wheel in frustration, a houseful of children listening and waiting.

"Finally he came back inside and told me I had to go get the doctor. I was the oldest and it was up to me. He wanted to stay with my mother to try to help her, but I had to go get the doctor."

I knew that my grandmother had died in childbirth, and many times I had imagined the weeping and horror and numbness of my mother and her four little sisters and their father, sitting with the dead body and a screaming newborn boy in a shack in rural Maine on a winter's day in 1933. But I had never heard this particular story, that my mother, then eleven years old, had been sent to fetch a doctor.

"So I started walking through the snow to the doctor's house," she continued, enunciating each word carefully. "I went across a field, but I didn't know how deep the snow was. And then I lost my shoe. I tried to find it, but it was buried. I looked for it, but it was gone. I kept digging in the snow, but it wasn't anywhere."

She started to cry and I waited for the rest of the story. Did she find the shoe or continue on without it? Did she ever get the doctor or did her mother die without him? After a few minutes I realized she was done; that was it. The rest would go unsaid.

"It wasn't your fault," I finally said, unsure whether it was better to say nothing.

"Yes it was," she sobbed, and I went back into my room. We never discussed her mother's death again. I felt like I had known the story all my life, and yet it seems so dreamlike the way I remember it that sometimes I wonder if the conversation even really happened.

Nancy heard it the same way I did, after she ran away from home, when our mother tried to guilt-trip her by telling her the story of her life. Our aunts Achsah, Deen, and Peanut were too young to have their own memories of what happened that day, but I wondered if maybe Aunt Lee could help, since she was the oldest next to my mother. Maybe she knew whether my mother was right to blame herself, or whether it was something crazy she'd dreamed up. So when I went down to visit her, I told her the story and asked if she knew anything about it. When I got to the part about my mother losing her shoe in the snow, Lee knitted her brow and interrupted me. "Oh!" she said. "See, that part I don't remember."

But as I continued on with the story as I'd heard it, she grew resolute that the story wasn't quite right, the way you do when you reach back into your memory and pull something out that you're not sure of at first, but that seems more certain the more you think about it.

"I'll tell you," she said, after hearing my version, "I always thought they sent Perley to get the doctor. I don't think your mother was the one."

I suppose I shouldn't have been surprised when my Aunt Lee mentioned Perley, but I was. Perley was a name I'd heard a few times, but he was someone I hadn't really thought about much; he didn't quite seem real to me. He was actually my uncle, my mother's half-brother, but my mother had never, ever mentioned him, not even once. I only knew about him because after my mother died, my Aunt Achsah told my sister and me that they'd had an older half-brother named Perley. It turned out he was Lizzie Noyes's son from her first marriage, before she married our grandfather. She'd only been fifteen when she married Perley's father, and the marriage didn't last. She'd gone back to live with her parents and grandparents after divorcing, and she met Bill Farrell a few years later.

After Lizzie Noyes died, Perley disappeared. Aunt Achsah said her father hated him and kicked him out; he was a teenager at the time. Many years later, as middle-aged adults, Perley and Achsah resumed contact, and they called or saw each other once every few years after that. One summer Achsah took my sister to meet Perley, in a small town in Maine, and during their visit, he unearthed a photo album with a few old black-and-white pictures of the family, including one of Lizzie Noyes. It's one of those early twentieth-century formal portraits, the type of studio picture that even working-class families lined up for in their fanciest clothes. In it, Lizzie gazes at the camera, a plump matron with spectacles, her dark, glistening hair neatly pinned into a roll, and a carefully ironed crease visible on the sleeve of her lace-collared dress.

Copies of the photo were sent to each of my mother's sisters. Deen keeps hers up on the wall by her bed; she said she had no recollection of what her mother looked like until she saw that picture. For Lee, it is a replacement for the pictures that were lost in the fire, pictures that she still regrets not having rescued.

But there's another photo from Perley's collection that captivates me, one that shows him in his mother's lap, all dressed up in a sailor suit, a beautiful, smiling boy. There is no photo like this of Lizzie with any of the children she had by Bill Farrell; perhaps he thought a portrait like that was a waste of money. Or perhaps Lizzie had no time to sit for a picture once her other babies started arriving. Either way, I some-times feel like I could stare at the photo of Lizzie and Perley all day; to me it is another mystery from my mother's life to be endlessly con-templated. For most of my childhood, I thought my mother had four sisters. Eventually I learned the story of Frankie, the baby brother who was run over by a car. Later still, I found out the secret of Bill Jr., the retarded brother. And then after my mother died, I learned there was a third brother, Perley. With each revelation, the family stories had to be edited and rethought; every picture I had imagined of my mother and her siblings at play or in mourning had to be reconfigured to add in these three boys, one at a time, to the five girls I'd always known about.

On the one hand, it was understandable; Frankie died as a little boy,

Bill was in an institution, Perley had had no contact with his sisters since 1933. But on the other hand, there was something surreal about it all. Most children know from a young age how many siblings their parents have. I knew from the time I was very small that my father had five brothers and sisters who were alive and six who had died. But it seemed as if my mother's family was actually comprised of endless numbers of missing siblings, and their existence could only be revealed by random events, like answering the phone when we shouldn't, or asking an innocent question, the way fake bookshelves move aside when leaned on accidentally in old horror movies.

Hearing about Perley the first time from Aunt Achsah was just a little too much for me; I put it out of my mind for the most part until Aunt Lee mentioned him again as we talked that day about who was sent to fetch the doctor. And then I began to focus on the fact that I had an uncle I had never met, living somewhere in Maine, who might have some of the answers I was looking for.

Aunt Lee encouraged me to seek him out. "Anne was eleven years old when our mother died," she said. "She'd just had her birthday. December fourth, wasn't it? I was nine and a half. But Perley was fifteen or sixteen. It stands to reason that they would have sent him for the doctor."

"But what about the shoe in the snow? You think she was blaming herself for something that didn't happen?" I asked.

She leaned over and patted me on the shoulder. "I think Anne imagined this," she said softly. "I honestly don't think it's true. I think it's made up. Or something in her mind that she thought was true. I don't mean that Anne was a liar. I think she was sick and I think she must have thought it happened. Honest to God, Bethy, I'm not saying this to be mean, but I think your mother imagined it. She might have thought she was to blame, but it was nobody's fault."

Then she brightened and smiled. "I tell you what," she said. "When you go up to Maine this summer, go see Perley. He's still living, I think. Of course he will know if he ran for the doctor or not. Ask him if Anne was sent. He'll know."

It was a good idea, and I resolved to do just that.

. . .

We go to Maine each summer, just like we did when I was a kid, only now that my parents are gone, it's my sister and me, our kids, and my husband. I found Perley's address in the phone book while I was there, and wrote him a letter. It seemed too weird to call him out of the blue and say, "Hi, I'm the daughter of your half-sister Anne, whose name used to be Lena, whom you last saw in 1933 and who died twenty years ago." It made more sense to explain it in a note.

He called me a few days after I sent it. "Well, come on over!" he said in a tone of voice that suggested he'd been expecting me for seventy years and what the heck took me so long.

I went with my sister and found him sitting on a chair in his yard in the shade of a big old tree. He was eighty-three, wearing a T-shirt and pants with suspenders, and he seemed happy to see us. He'd worked most of his life in a sawmill that burned down after he retired, and he raised three sons with his late wife Hattie in the house where he still lives.

"I have a good time here," he said, "but wintertimes is kinda hard." Summer and fall are the best seasons, he added, because that's when the country fairs are held. He likes the "pulls," competitions where horses and tractors drag heavy loads across a track, and he likes to eat the spicy sausages, hot dogs, and hamburgers sold at the concession stands. He's had surgery a few times and is now fighting cancer, but he seemed chipper about his chances. "I been to the pearly gates twice and I ain't gone in yet," he said with a smile. "It's a long walk up there and they closed the door on me."

His grandchildren stop by often to help out and run errands; the wife of one grandson drove up before we left to check on him. My sister and I told him about our children and he shook his head, saying he was glad he wasn't a parent of a young child today.

"They ain't your kids no more," he said. "You can't lick 'em and you can't make 'em mind. That's the way I see it." I agreed with him that it was hard, but I said that life in the old days seemed harder to me.

And that led us to the reason we had come. What did he remember about my mother, and his mother, and my grandfather? We reminded him that our mother had been Lena, but that later she changed her name to Anne. He seemed to search his mind for a picture or a memory to conjure up the image of this sister from long ago, but nothing quite registered.

"I don't remember too many of the kids because I got out so young," he said. "My mother had so many kids, so many times. The girls, she had 'em one after the other, one about every year, year and a half."

But he remembered Bill Farrell well. "He wasn't no angel," Perley said. "After my mother died, I got away from him quick as I could. He drank quite a lot, and he threatened to throw her out the window two or three times. I'd have killed him if I was big enough. He'd give us hell. He was hard on us when he was drinking. Our mother was hard, but she weren't that hard."

Perley said that when they lived in Athens, he spent as much time as he could with his mother's parents at their farm nearby. "If I didn't like what Bill and my mother were having for supper, I'd go back to grammy and grampy's," he said, then grinned like an eight-year-old boy who knows he's been fresh and is sort of proud of it. "Maybe that's why Bill never liked me."

He paused, then continued. "Bill used to give his money to the priest, then he'd come home and the kids would starve to death," he said. "Lena can tell you more about that." Gently, I explained that Lena was our mother; she had passed away, but she was the one we had come about. He thought about this for a moment, but said nothing.

I started prompting him, asking him about this story and that. He remembered a pet dog my Aunt Lee had mentioned, and the goat my mother told us had pulled them around on a little sled. He even remembered the Gypsies my mother was so afraid of, the Gypsies my sister and I had doubted even existed. "The Gypsies tried to bust the safe open in the store in town in Athens," Perley explained. "It blowed up the store and started a fire." My sister and I looked at each other and smiled. No wonder our mother had been afraid of them.

He remembered the house at the Morey Farm, too, the nicest place they ever lived. Perley said he was hired out there as a field hand and that Bill Farrell took all his pay. So when the other hired boys went to get ice cream, Perley had no money to join them. The boss asked why not, and he explained that his stepfather kept whatever he earned. From then on, the boss put a little money aside so Perley could join the other kids after a hot day of haying in the sun for an ice cream in town.

He worked on other farms other times of the year, too, and was often kept out of school to do it. "I didn't go through grade school as much as I'd have liked," he said. "I'd go for a day, and then I'd be kept out three or four days to work."

I asked about the fire that broke out in the house in Athens, the first place Bill and Lizzie had lived, and if he remembered the story Lee told me about their father pulling them away from the fire on a sled.

His face lit up with recognition. "The hired man got me out of the house," he said.

"What do you mean?" I asked.

"Well, I was home with the girls, and Bill Farrell put them on the sled and started down the road," he explained. "But he didn't bother with me. He closed the bedroom door on me and put a trunk up against the door so I couldn't get out. He hated my guts."

My sister and I looked at each other. It was horrible, but completely believable, that Bill would have tried to kill Perley like that. Achsah had told us that Bill hated Perley so much he used to beat him all the time. "That's awful," I said. "It's just incredible. So how did you get out?"

"He had a hired man to help him cut wood, and the hired man saw that Bill had taken the girls and gone down the road with them," Perley continued. "So the hired man came and busted in the house and cut me out. I was about ten years old. Then he wrapped me in a blanket and took me to a neighbor's house. I didn't have boots on and I chilled my feet." He sighed and added: "Oh well!"

It hadn't occurred to me until then that when Lee told the story, as her father had told it to her, the rescue included her and the other sisters who were born, but not Perley. She was too little to remember it herself, and Bill Farrell never told her where Perley was that day. Now I knew why.

Then I asked him about the day their mother went into labor with

Frankie. "She pounded on the floor from upstairs for everybody because she couldn't get up," he recalled. "I told Bill. The ambulance came and took her and she died in the hospital. When Bill came back from the hospital, they said she was dead. That's the way it was. They'd told her not to have any more children."

"But who got the ambulance?" I asked.

"It weren't me," he said readily. "I don't remember who in hell it was."

I told him the story my mother told me, about how she had been sent to get the doctor.

"I got no recollection of that," he said. "I can't remember nothin' about that."

After a moment he added, "We didn't have a funeral. Someone just came in the house and said a few words. Laid out in the bedroom she was. But I had trouble with Bill over that, too. Bill was going to put her somewhere else, and I said, 'No, you ain't either!' I put her up in Athens where my grandfather had a plot."

Aunt Achsah had told us that her father threw Perley out after their mother died, but he told it a little differently. "Bill was going to hold me right there," he said. "I was home about three days after she died when Bill come out with papers for me to sign. He had it all written out. But he kicked me out because I wouldn't sign the papers."

What did the papers say? Perley wasn't all that clear, but he was certain that if he signed them, he could expect years of going out to work without getting to keep his pay. Whatever those papers said, he knew he was better off on his own than signing his soul away to a stepfather who hated him, with his mother dead.

The school janitor took Perley in the night Bill Farrell kicked him out. The next day, Perley went to stay with his mother's brother Lee, who made his living cutting and hauling trees. The work didn't suit Perley, so a short time later he went to live with his mother's sister Alice. He got a job at a sawmill not long after, and worked there for most of his life.

Bill ran into Perley a few years after Lizzie died and tried to talk him into coming to live with him and the rest of the family in Harmony, one of the places they lived after the house in Mechanic Falls burned down.

"He wanted me to come over there because I was working and I had a little money," Perley said.

Perley later found out that the day after he ran into Bill Farrell, the state came and took Bill's kids, and that Bill had disappeared, only to be thrown in jail when they finally caught up with him. I don't know why Bill tried to get Perley to be there the day state authorities were coming to get the kids, but I assume he was hoping it might change the outcome—that Perley would either provide the money to keep Bill out of jail, or maybe even get taken away himself if Bill wasn't on the premises and the authorities were unsure of who was responsible for the kids.

I asked Perley if in all the years since they'd lived together, he'd ever heard from my mother, from Lena.

"Not yet," he said. "And that's about all I can tell you."

My sister and I smiled wanly at each other. There was no point in reminding him that Lena was dead.

I have worked as a journalist for many years, and you learn very fast in the news business that the best stories consist of a straightforward narrative. When reporters say, half-joking, but also half-serious, "Don't let the facts get in the way of a good story," they mean that you have to discard extraneous or contradictory information; you have to pare down the mess that is reality into a tale of good guys and bad guys, right and wrong; and you have to find anecdotes and facts that confirm and illuminate what you believe to be the essential truth. If five people tell you the victim worked nights as a waitress and one person tells you the victim worked days as a secretary, you keep the part of the story that explains why the victim was coming home so late at night. Most likely, the story about the victim being a secretary isn't a lie, exactly; but the person who told it was probably mistaken, misinformed, or using outdated information. Or maybe the victim was a secretary moonlighting as a waitress; in any case, you need the victim working nights to make your story work, so that's the part you choose to keep.

But what part do you keep when the story is about your mother, and what part do you throw away? What part is true, what part is a lie, and what part is merely a conclusion that you have wrongly made? How do you judge other people's memories when you don't even trust your own? And how do you create one straightforward narrative when there are so many small stories to tell?

Maybe my mother did go for the doctor that morning as her mother was dying. And then again maybe she didn't. I had evidence to support both versions, but I also didn't have enough proof to be certain of either. What Aunt Lee said was so logical; why would they have sent Lena to get help? And yet it seemed that Perley had not gone in her place—at least, not that he recalled.

But could my mother have made up such an involved story out of whole cloth? I learned from my husband, who is a criminal defense attorney, that lawyers always look for telling details when they are trying to determine someone's veracity—the kind of detail that's neither so far-fetched that it strains credulity, nor so common that it's obvious. The sign of someone telling the truth is in a story that you couldn't make up if you tried. It seemed to me that a girl losing her shoe in a blizzard was just that sort of story, and at the end of the day, I do believe it happened.

Obviously my mother was not to blame for the fact that Lizzie Noyes died; the hospital and the fire station and the doctor and maybe even Bill Farrell will share the blame for eternity for that. But was my mother justified in dreaming that maybe, if she'd gotten help in time, she might have saved the day? It was so tempting to imagine that if Lizzie had lived, Bill Farrell would have kept his nose to the grindstone and everyone would have lived happily ever after. No fire, no flood, no people from the state taking the kids away to live with strangers. No reform school, no working as a maid, and maybe even no running away to New York. One young girl running through the snow had the potential to change the destiny of everyone in her entire family, but she squandered her power when she lost that shoe. A chain of "if onlys" had started breaking when Lizzie was sent home from the hospital (if only she'd stayed there to deliver the baby . . .), and Lena had to believe that "if only" she had gotten help in time, all of the hardships that followed might have been avoided. No wonder it weighed her down for the rest of her life, combined with enormous guilt over having failed to step into Lizzie's place. No reasonable person would expect an eleven-year-old to become mother to four little sisters and two little brothers. But I think she felt she should have, and that's why later, she tried to make it up to all of them with her letters and her gifts and her boxes of clothes.

But I'll never know any of this for sure. And by the time I talked to Perley, I had come to accept that. I was looking for a crystal-clear picture when I set out to find Annie Farrell, but I ended up with a strange and beautiful collage.

After my mother died, my sister asked Aunt Achsah, who was then selling real estate part-time, to keep her eye out for an inexpensive house on a piece of waterfront property. She found one not too long after in a place called Morrill Pond, which by New York standards would qualify as a lake. But in Maine, at a mile long by a half-mile wide, it barely registers on the map. It's smack in the center of the state, in a rural county where the biggest sources of jobs are a tanning factory in one direction and a paper mill in the other. It's about as far as you can get from the boutiques of Blue Hill, the tourist crowds of Bar Harbor, the Bushes of Kennebunkport, and the summer camps full of rich kids, but it's just a few miles from Athens, where our mother was born, and a short ride to Howland, where she is buried.

I recently decided that the purpose of adulthood is to let go of all the things from your childhood that were awful and recreate all the things that were wonderful. Maine was the best thing about my childhood, and so my sister and I have been taking our vacations there now for twenty years, bringing our children there each summer just as we were brought to Maine by our mother. There is nowhere on earth that I would rather be on a beautiful summer day than on our little pond. This *is* my forest primeval, a physical place of murmuring pines, but also a place that exists in my mind as much as it does in the real world, a place that brings me back to the happiest times of my childhood. It wraps me up in memories, and leaves me rocking on a porch sucking peppermint sticks, while my mother finds mint leaves by the shore and my father *put-puts* home in his little blue boat with the outboard motor, a silhouette against the sunset with a cigarette in his mouth and a string of bass, chained through the gills, dragging in the wake.

"It is strange how much you can remember about places like that once you allow your mind to return into the grooves that lead back," E. B. White wrote in an account of his own childhood vacations in Maine, *Once More to the Lake*. "You remember one thing, and that suddenly reminds you of another."

And so it is with me. The more I think about how much my summers in Maine today remind me of my summers in Maine as a child, the more real my memories become. Some evenings on Morrill Pond, there is an old man in a small blue boat, out fishing around sunset, and in the glare of the long rays of light flattening out across the water as the sun begins to drop behind the trees, he reminds me of my dad. Sometimes my sister and I will say to each other, joking, "Look, there's Daddy," but sometimes I am so truly transported that I have to stop myself from calling out to him. I know he's always gone before the darkness comes, but I must remind myself he's not coming home to me.

On Morrill Pond, if we want fresh vegetables, we go up the road to see our farmer friends, who homeschool their children and grow organic produce and walk us through their fields with a knife and a paper bag, picking out for us whatever looks good and ripe. If we want conversation, we go next door to visit a couple of women who have become surrogate grandmothers to our children, treating them to chips and cookies, showing them how to make quilts and birdhouses, and rescuing us from the various predicaments we find ourselves in as inept city folk trying to live the country life. There is always a motorboat or a lawn mower that won't start, troublesome insect bites, or a fishing rod that won't reel in properly, and our neighbors have always been generous with their advice and assistance.

Just as I did, my kids catch frogs and snakes and fish and chase hummingbirds and butterflies; they stop in their tracks when they hear loons calling their throaty trills, and they collect rocks and shells and wildflowers. They swing in the hammock until they are dizzy and swim in the water until they are shivering, and at dusk we build campfires by the shore, roast marshmallows, and sing songs. When the sunset dies away, we see the steady glow of Venus, then the moonrise and the Milky Way and even shooting stars. We spend day after day doing nothing, and I remind myself that it's okay for a kid to be bored sometimes. They know this is something special, something magic, something that will always be inside them no matter how much the rest of their life is shaped by the city. And I have to admit, as crazy as it sounds, I do fantasize every now and then about how easy it would be to hide here with my blond, blue-eyed boys, should we ever have to run from the terrorists or anybody else who might come looking for us on the streets of New York.

Back home in the city, when my older son can't fall asleep, we have a little ritual. "Mommy," he says, "what should I think about?" And I always tell him to think of Maine, and the canoe gliding through the water, to imagine the sky so blue, and the lake so blue, and the trees so green, and the world so quiet you can hear the wind. It's our very own *Goodnight Moon*, and he always falls asleep in no time. The Maine in our minds is the safest place we know, a place that holds us, and wraps us, and rocks us, like the waves that lap the water, like a sunny spot on a cold day, like the campfire flames that light up the evening, like the hammock in the trees and the arms of a mother who always reaches out to catch you as you're falling, falling, falling in your dreams, through the fire and the dark, into sleep.

In 1890, Fannie Pearson Hardy, a well-known nature writer of her day, wrote of her retreat to the Maine woods, "We ran away this fall. In fleeing the telegraph, the post-office, the doorbells and all our many masters, we experienced a sweet guilty satisfaction." Maine's tourists in the twenty-first century—those, like us, who dare to let go of their cell phones, e-mails, video games, cable TV, pagers, beepers, and Palm Pilots—would say the same thing. In Maine, you can still have a mountaintop or a cove in a lake or a trail in the woods all to yourself. It's still the Northeast's last frontier, and we know we are not alone in viewing Maine as a refuge from everything in America that drives us crazy and all the stress that we think we can't live without.

And yet in my family, we also know we're kidding ourselves if we think Maine is immune to the problems of postmodern life. Maybe it's because my mother's family is from Maine, or maybe it's because we have never taken our vacations in expensive hotels in Ogunquit or on the ski slopes of Sugarloaf. Whatever it is, I know full well that there is another Maine most tourists never see—a Maine of trailer homes and small-time dope dealers, pregnant teenagers and smart high school grads who don't see the point of college. That Maine is not all that different from the Maine my mother left, a place where poor kids talked for years about the people from away who drove up in a fancy car.

The cemetery where my mother is buried is not far from the small town in Northern Maine where my Aunt Peanut has lived for more than forty years. When I was small, my mother took us to see Peanut every year, and now that I am grown, I bring my children to see her. I think about how our lives are always doubling back, my children's childhoods connected to mine, my childhood connected to my mother's. We stop at the gravesite on the way, and as we pull up to Peanut's house on Main Street, we pass the diner where we have been having lunch for years. My sister is with me, and while she and I and Aunt Peanut sit and chat, my husband takes the kids to play on the tire swings at a playground behind the local school.

Peanut's nickname still fits; she is still small and skinny, and she is also funny and quick. She never speaks sentimentally about all the awful things that have happened to her, and she readily shares her opinions in colorful language, calling an overweight woman whom she dislikes "Piggethy" and her ex-husband "Hitler." I ask her what she remembers about my mother, and she tells me about the letters, birthday cards, and Christmas gifts, and how my mother encouraged her to begin writing her father, even though she could barely remember him.

"And after I was married she sent me two dollars," she recalls. "Well, two dollars then was like twenty dollars now. And she would always send me boxes of clothes, and she'd bring boxes of clothes when she came to visit me. If it hadn't been for her, I never could have clothed those kids."

She says it with no self-pity or regret; that's just how it was. When her kids were little, she installed her own plumbing, using the older ones to help her dig up the yard with a pick and shovel. She's still quite good at fixing and building things, but she shrugs it off. "It just comes natural," she says.

Even though Peanut is old enough to retire, she is still hard at work. In the years since her kids grew up and left home, she's run a pointer saw and made dowels in a factory, fired the boiler in a power plant, and cared for elderly people so disabled they could not feed themselves. Her latest job requires her to wake up a few hours after midnight for the predawn shift at a local filling station.

She is not on speaking terms with all of her kids. One of them made the newspaper as a teenager for shooting Hitler in the leg as he beat Peanut up, and Peanut knows that this particular child—who, in the family tradition, legally changed her name to Anne—feels she could have done more to protect them all from Hitler. "But at the time I felt that I did what I could," she says.

Peanut also tells us that when she was a teenager, she lived for a short time with her sister Lee and Lee's first husband. "He raped me repeatedly," she adds, matter-of-factly, without any prompting from me.

I know this story; it's been told to me in hushed tones before. And I know that Lee didn't realize what had happened until years after and that she still feels anguish about what happened to Peanut. I also know that it takes a lot of courage for Peanut to tell me about it now without a trace of emotion. I stop myself from getting up to give her a hug; I don't want to take away her dignity by feeling sorry for her.

But I also need to ask my aunt, ever so gently, the question that has always been on my mind.

"Why," I say softly, "didn't you tell anyone?"

"I didn't have any words in my vocabulary to explain anything like that," she says readily, as if she answered this question in her own mind a long time ago. "I knew it was wrong, but I didn't have any words for it."

"You've had such a hard life," my sister murmurs.

"I did," she agrees, "but somehow I just managed to grin and bear it." We are quiet for a few minutes. It would be easy to view Peanut as some sort of a victim if you didn't know how strong she was; she is a survivor, and I admire that. She could curl up in a ball and wallow in self-pity, but instead she gets up before dawn every morning, heads out to make her living, and talks openly about the many troubles this life has visited upon her.

I can't help but think that maybe if my mother had been as forthright about the things that haunted her, she might not have ended up the way she did. After all, she's the only one of the five sisters whose stories I never got to hear firsthand; nearly everything I know about her life— the deprivations of her childhood, the fire and the flood, reform school, working as a maid, her father's neglect and possible abuse, her love for Ruel, my father's betrayals and everything else—I know because some-one else told me.

Finally I ask Peanut the other question that's on my mind. "Didn't you ever feel resentful that my mother was living in New York and seemed to have such an easy life? She didn't have to work, she only had two kids . . ."

"It never crossed my mind to be resentful of her," she says without hesitation, adding that she was surprised when my mother died so sud-denly. "I didn't realize she was sick," she explains. "But Achsah did say toward the end that she didn't write much anymore."

One bright morning we drive from Morrill Pond to Athens. The country road is lined with small farms on one side and you can see blue patches of a lake on the other through the trees; I imagine it is not that different from what it might have looked like when my mother was a little girl growing up here. We park at the general store and go in to buy night crawlers so the kids can go fishing later. Near the register I see something I haven't had since I was a child: a bright orange package containing Clark's Teaberry gum. It smells like cinnamon, and inside the sticks of gum are a dusty pink. It's sweet and spicy, like mulled cider, and it leaves my mouth tingling. There's a drawing of a five-leafed plant on the wrapper, and when I get back to the pond, I look to see if anything like that is growing by the shore, where I remember my mother finding teaberry leaves for me when I was a child, so long ago. But nothing looks right or smells right or tastes right, and there is no one else to ask.

In the days and weeks that followed my mother's death, I kept seeing people who looked like her, all over Manhattan. She was on the subway with me, sitting too far away in a crowded car for me to get a good look, or crossing the street just before the light changed, leaving me on the curb. She was three steps ahead on an escalator, disappearing behind the closing doors of an elevator, or whirling through a revolving door and vanishing into the crowds as I tried to catch up. I told everyone it was just as well she had died, because her life was so miserable, but there I was, stalking strangers, playing tag with a ghost. Sometimes I would get near enough to the person I was tracking to make sure it wasn't her. There was never recognition in their eyes—only curiosity and fear. It made me feel crazy, and ashamed.

Then I saw her—really saw her—in a dream. She was sitting in a rocking chair on the porch of a wood-frame house, the kind of house you draw in second grade, with a triangle roof on a square box, circles of smoke coming out of the rectangle chimney into a clear blue sky with one puffy white cloud. There was a garden of orange daylilies on one side of the porch, and an empty country road winding into the distance on the other—a little gray ribbon of a road surrounded by dark-green woods, just like the view that I remembered waking up to as a child arriving in Maine at the start of our annual vacations.

I was just walking by when I suddenly came upon her there. I stopped, incredulous, hyperventilating, tears in my throat. I felt utterly betrayed that she had been hiding here, in the middle of nowhere. Didn't she know how many people I had stopped on the streets of New York, searching for the face that matched hers? But I couldn't say any of those things to her. I couldn't even go up the steps to touch her. I was frozen in place, panicked and stuck.

"What are you *doing* here?" I finally sputtered angrily, almost shouting. "You're supposed to be dead!"

She smiled placidly. She didn't seem at all surprised to see me, or in any hurry to answer me. She had a cigarette in her hand, and the smoke drifted up to shroud her face in curls of blue as I waited for her to speak.

"I didn't die," she said simply, after a moment. "I just ran away. Can't you see?"

I looked again and I realized.

She was in Maine. This was her house, by the side of the road. It was the house she never had. It was her dream.

Then I woke up. It was my dream, not hers. And she was gone.

Notes and Sources

Quotes and anecdotes from my relatives and friends of the family came from interviews I conducted by mail, e-mail, telephone, and in person in 2000, 2001, and 2002, as well as from a videotape of eulogies delivered at my father's funeral in 1993.

Quotes and facts from letters, diaries, birth certificates, U.S. Army records, and other primary documents come from my personal collection of family-related material.

Sources for quotes from old newspaper articles, radio and TV interviews, and other nonbook archived material such as Census data are cited in the text.

Sources for other factual and anecdotal material, as well as sources for further reading on various subjects, are as follows.

CHAPTER 2, CHRISTMAS

For background on the causes and frequency of maternal mortality in the 1930s, I used Irvine Loudon's *Death in Childbirth* (Oxford University Press, 1992).

For facts and anecdotes about Roosevelt's election and the impact of the Great Depression on New England, I drew from Ronald Edsforth's *The New Deal: America's Response to the Great Depression* (Blackwell Publishers, 2000), and from Ronald Barlow's *The Vanishing American Outhouse* (Windmill Publishing, 1989).

For the anecdote about Neal Dow and Prohibition, I drew from Charles E. Clark's *Maine: A Bicentennial History* (W.W. Norton & Co., 1977).

For background on how French Canadians living in Maine and their descendants differed from the descendants of early English settlers, I relied both on Clark's *Maine: A Bicentennial History,* and on Gerard J. Brault's *The French-Canadian Heritage in New England* (University Press of New England, 1986).

Information about the South Portland Reformatory for Boys is from the school's 1900 Annual Report, archived in the New York Public Library. For background about the social movement that led to the institutionalization of poor children in such reformatories, I relied on Stephanie Coontz's *The Way We Never Were* (Basic Books, 1992).

For the description of Lewiston in the 1920s, I drew on two Internet sources, the *Walking Tour of Lewiston* from www.androscoggincounty.com, the Androscoggin County Chamber of Commerce Web site, and the *Environmental History of the Androscoggin River* from www.bates.edu, Bates College's Web site. For background on the lives of French-Canadian factory workers, I drew on Brault's *The French-Canadian Heritage in New England,* cited above in the earlier source notes for this chapter.

I received information about the anonymous hobo ballad "Only A Bum" from Fran DeLorenzo, who recently recorded the song, and Ralph Butts, who responded to my query on www.mudcat.org, a Web site that is a treasure trove for people who love old and obscure songs. With their help, I found "Only A Bum" printed in its entirety in George Milburn's *Hobo's Hornbook* (Ives Washburn Publishers, 1930).

CHAPTER 4, NEW SHOES

For the description of town farms, I relied on an Internet source, *Historical Survey of Methods of Poor Relief in Maine,* from www.poorhousestory.com.

Information about the laws that permitted the state of Maine to remove children from their home, incarcerate their parents for failure to pay for their support, and place older children in reformatories came from the state's Public Laws of 1933, Section 204, Chapter 1 ("Complaint in Cases of Neglect to Children"), and amendments passed in 1937. The law books are located in the Maine State Archives in Augusta.

Information about the Hallowell State School for Girls, also known as the Stevens Institute or the Industrial School for Girls, came from the school's 1945 Annual Report, which is archived in the New York Public Library, and from an Internet source about the school's founder, John L. Stevens, *Some Vienna & Mt. Vernon, Maine, Notables,* from www.rootsweb.com.

For background on why girls who had broken no laws were committed to such institutions, I relied on Coontz's *The Way We Never Were,* cited in the sources for Chapter 2.

Information about the Conys came from Judge Cony's obituary in the Jan. 2, 1945 edition of the *Kennebec Journal,* and from entries about his ancestors,

Daniel and Samuel Cony, in edited excerpts from Appleton's 1886 Encyclopedia, which appear in *Virtual American Biographies*, part of the www.famousamericans.net Web site.

To get a feeling for what New York City was like in the late 1940s, I read E. B. White's classic essay, *Here Is New York*.

CHAPTER 7, ANCESTORS

For facts, theories, and anecdotes about the history of prefamine Irish immigration to the United States and Canada, and conditions in Ireland in the late eighteenth century, I drew extensively from chapters one and eleven of Cecil Woodham-Smith's *The Great Hunger* (Harper & Row, 1962).

For background on early Irish immigrants in New Brunswick, I used the Saint John *Times Globe's Out of Ireland* series, June 9 to July 25, 1997; *The Irish Story*, from new-brunswick.net; *The Catholic Encyclopedia* entry on Saint John from its 1910 edition, which is archived at newadvent.org; and Joseph A. King's *Genealogy, History and Irish Immigration,* an essay published in *The Canadian Journal of Irish Studies,* June, 1984, Vol. X, No. 1.

For background on the history of Maine, its settlement, population patterns, and economic development (including the history of the lumber, shipbuilding, and fishing industries; and the impact of the Civil War, the opening of land in the West, and the California gold rush), I relied on the following sources:

Brault's *The French-Canadian Heritage in New England* (cited in sources for Chapter 2)

Bill Bryson's *A Walk in the Woods* (Broadway Books, 1998)

Charles C. Calhoun's *Maine* (Fodor's Travel Publications, 2000)

The Catholic Encyclopedia entry on Maine from its 1910 edition, which is archived at newadvent.org

Census data for the state of Maine

Clark's *Maine: A Bicentennial History* (cited in sources for Chapter 2)

The Davistown Museum's Information File on *Lumbering in Maine*, available at www.davistownmuseum.org

Clarence Day's *Aroostook: The First Sixty Years*, which is archived at www.nmdc.org

The Federal Writers' Project of the Works Progress Administration's *Maine: A Guide Down East* (Riverside Press, 1937)

Lloyd Irland's "Maine Forests: A Century of Change, 1900–2000," an essay published in *Maine Policy Review,* Winter 2000

Henry David Thoreau's *The Maine Woods* (Ticknor and Fields, 1864)

For the history of Van Buren and the Farrells, I drew from the following sources:

Susan Bouchard's *A Jewel in the Crown of Maine* (Keepsake Enterprises, 1998)

John Deane and Edward Kavanaugh's *Survey of the Madawaska Settlement, July–August 1831, History of Madawaska Territory,* and *Native Peoples in Madawaska,* all available at www.upperstjohn.com/aroostook

Do You Bear the Name of Dube? unsigned article from www.parsonstech.com/genealogy

Family stories related via e-mail by Susan Bouchard, Len Gravel, Doris Lapointe, Joyce Miller, and Matt Watson

Family trees available at www.ancestry.com

Genealogical and Family History of the State of Maine, Vol. IV (Lewis Historical Publishing Co., 1909), available at the Maine State Archives in Augusta

Martine A. Pelletier and Monica Dionne Ferretti's *Van Buren History* (St. John Valley Publishing Co., 1979)

St. Bruno's parish records, available at the Maine State Archives in Augusta

For background on the deportation of the Acadians by the British, I relied on *Van Buren History,* cited above; Edward Everett Hale's introduction and notes to Henry Wadsworth Longfellow's *Evangeline,* in the 1897 University Publishing Co. edition; and information presented at the Grand-Pré National Historic Site in Nova Scotia, Canada, the presumed site of the Acadian deportation.

For background on Native Americans in Maine and Canada, I relied on Census data, the www.penobscotnation.org Web site, Jill Duval's *The Penobscot* (Children's Press, 1993), and Mary Olga McKenna's *Micmac by Choice* (Formac Publishing Co., 1990).

CHAPTER 9, NUTS

For the facts and details of D-Day and the invasion of Normandy, Operation Market Garden in Holland, the Battle of the Bulge in Belgium, and the history of the 101st Airborne Division, I relied extensively on the following sources:

Col. Robert E. Jones, Col. Ted A. Crozier, and Maj. Ivan G. Worrell's *101st Airborne Division Screaming Eagles* (Turner Publishing, 1995)

Leonard Rapport and Arthur Northwood Jr.'s *Rendezvous with Destiny: A History of the 101st Airborne Division* (101st Airborne Division Association, 1948)

The Epic of the 101st Airborne: A Pictorial Record of a Great Fighting Team (101st Airborne Division's Public Relations Office, 1945)

I also gathered some details and historical context for understanding the battles from the following Internet sources:

The Paratrooper Experience, from *The American Experience: D-Day*, available at www.pbs.org

The 101st Airborne Division (Screaming Eagles), from www.normandyallies. org

Mark Fielder's *The Battle of Arnhem (Operation Market Garden)*, from www.bbc.co.uk/history/war

101st Airborne Division History Page, from www.campbell.army.mil

CHAPTER 10, KHAKIS

For definitions of Yiddish words, I relied on Leo Rosten's *The Joys of Yiddish* (Pocket Books, 1968).

CHAPTER 11, MAD HOUSEWIFE

The Fannie Pearson Hardy quote comes from her book *Tales of the Maine Woods*, which was first published in 1891 and reprinted in 1999 by the Maine Folklife Center.

In addition to all of the works mentioned above, there are several works of literature about Maine, by writers from Maine, that helped inspire me to write this book and that will captivate anyone who loves Maine. They include Sarah Orne Jewett's *The Country of the Pointed Firs*, Louise Dickinson Rich's *We Took to the Woods*, E. B. White's *Once More to the Lake*, and the poems of Edna St. Vincent Millay and Edwin Arlington Robinson.

I was also inspired to write this book in part by reading the memoirs other people had written about their mothers, including Jacki Lyden's *Daughter of the Queen of Sheba*, James McBride's *The Color of Water*, and Nuala O'Faolain's *Are You Somebody?* I found myself picking all three books up over and over again while writing this one.

Acknowledgments

I am profoundly grateful to the many people who opened their homes and hearts to me during the writing of this book, sharing memories, secrets, facts, stories, letters, opinions, and documents.

My biggest debt is to my mother's four sisters, Lee, Achsah, Nadeen, and Peanut. They sat for hours and hours of tape-recorded interviews, and answered endless questions by phone, mail, and e-mail for a year and a half. They conjured up for me in vivid detail their childhood in rural Maine during the Depression, and they helped me make sense of my mother's life twenty years after she died. It is only through their eyes that I was able to see. A similar thanks is due to my mother's half-brother, Perley.

Aunt Achsah died shortly after the manuscript for this book was completed. Despite her weak state in the weeks before she passed away, she insisted on reading the four hundred typewritten pages to make sure I'd gotten everything right. God bless her, she found several errors, which I corrected, grateful for her incredible memory and attention to detail.

I am the type of person who throws everything away, but thank goodness most people are not like me. A family friend, Ruth Clark, and my aunt Achsah gave me their collections of letters from my mother, enabling me to tell part of her story in her own words. My cousins Gilbert and Sharon were incredibly generous with genealogical material that they collected, including family trees, documents, anecdotes, and information on the mysterious Lena Michaud, our great-grandmother. The research they did pointed me in the right direction when I began my own hunt.

Sue Bouchard, who lives in the Farrell-Michaud House in Van Buren,

Maine, provided meringue pie and encouragement and, most important of all, a copy of her own wonderful book on the house she lives in, *A Jewel in the Crown of Maine*. She helped me find facts, stories, and Matt Watson, who turned out to be my distant cousin. E-mails with Matt led me to several other distant cousins, including Len Gravel, Joyce Miller, and Doris Lapointe, all of us descended from a single ancestor, the Irish immigrant Michael Farrell. Through this network of Farrell descendants I gained access to a treasure trove of family stories that have been handed down for two hundred years, providing much of the rich material in Chapter 7. Thanks to all of you for your willingness to share with me the information that you have, in some cases, spent years painstakingly collecting.

My first readers provided invaluable feedback and help in editing. They were, of course, my husband, chief cheerleader-in-residence; my lifelong friend, Linda Lombardi, who is never afraid to tell me I'm wrong; and my sister, Nancy, who helped me fact check my own early memories and in turn shared hers.

Cousins from my father's side of the family, especially Joyce Freedman, helped me with anecdotes and facts for the chapters on him.

Richard Pyle, who has covered wars around the world for the Associated Press, gave me confidence that my chapter on World War II made sense. Robert Shaffer, a history professor at Shippensburg University, helped me improve the sections of the book that look beyond my family to the times in which they lived. Jacqueline Barsh Sigman helped me understand the plight of World War II wives. Dr. Sarah Rattray, a psychologist, helped me understand the relationship between genes and environment in depression, and provided an incredibly insightful analysis of my mother's state of mind.

The miracle of the Internet enabled me to track down everything from my fifteenth-century ancestors (let's hear it for Ancestry.com, my favorite Web site!) to a recipe for Lazy Man's Bread to the text of the poem "The House by the Side of the Road." But it was in the old-fashioned paper collections at the New York Public Library, the National Archives' Manhattan office, and the Maine State Archives that I found the most intriguing nuggets of information. I am grateful to all the archivists, anonymous government employees, and hardworking librarians who have preserved and made accessible records of births, deaths, marriages, crimes, immigration, maternal mortality, wealth, juvenile detention, and the many other arcane facts I sought to check. I also made extensive use of the book collections of both the New York Public Library and the Brooklyn Public Library, devouring everything I could find about Maine, from histories and travel guides to the writings of E. B. White and John Irving.

Finally, this book would not have been written without the support of my agent, Jane Dystel, and my publisher, St. Martin's Press, and my editors there, Thomas Dunne and Sean Desmond. Thank you for taking a chance on a memoir about an unknown person by an obscure writer.